Affect, Animals, and Autists

# Affect, Animals, and Autists

## FEELING AROUND THE
## EDGES OF THE HUMAN
## IN PERFORMANCE

## Marla Carlson

University of Michigan Press
Ann Arbor

Published in the United States of America by the
University of Michigan Press
Manufactured in the United States of America
♾ Printed on acid-free paper

2021   2020   2019   2018        4   3   2   1

A CIP catalog record for this book is available from the British Library.
Library of Congress Cataloging-in-Publication data has been applied for.

ISBN: 978-0-472-07382-5 (Hardcover : alk paper)
ISBN: 978-0-472-05382-7 (Paper : alk paper)
ISBN: 978-0-472-12393-3 (ebook)

*Cover description for accessibility:* The cover features a close-up of the
character Christopher John Francis Boone from a theater production of
*The Curious Incident of the Dog in the Night Time.* The stage is dark and projected
onto it is the outline of a large dog. Inside this shape a young man dressed in
jeans and a T-shirt lies on his side with closed eyes with one of his palms pressed
against the outline. The book's title is at the top of the cover, and the subtitle is
split into two lines that curve above and below the figure of the boy. The
author's name, Marla Carlson, appears across the bottom.

# Contents

# Preface and Acknowledgments

## DEDICATIONS

This book began on a flight from Seattle to Chicago for the 2006 conference of the American Society for Theatre Research, when I was seated next to Stalking Cat on his way to the Midwest FurFest in nearby Schaumburg. Cat was so visually striking that, upon first glimpsing him from the other end of the plane, I was surprised that the airline had allowed him to fly wearing what I mistakenly took to be a mask. He had tiger stripes tattooed over his face, pointed ears, cheeks and forehead reshaped by silicone implants, and a feline mouth shaped by moving the nasal septum, cleaving the upper lip, and replacing his teeth with catlike dentures. His arm and leg tattoos had a fish-scale pattern—connected to feline food rather than appearance, and his claws were purple. His companion had brought along a pouch of tuna for his in-flight snack. I might not have engaged with him if the flight attendant hadn't broken the ice—I have the received notion that it's rude to comment upon another person's appearance, a rudeness compounded if that person is a stranger. But he was happy to talk, and the conversation got me thinking about how people feel about animals and about each other, about forms of sociality channeled through those feelings, and about the ways that performance intensifies and circulates these affective investments.

Beginning in earliest childhood, Cat experienced a spiritual connection to all feline species and particularly to tigers. He said that his thirty-year modification project of tattoos, implants, and surgical alterations intended to bring him as close as possible to physical identity with his totem animal, the tiger, simply used technology to accomplish a sort of transformation long-practiced among his Huron and Lakota ancestors. Also known as Cat Man, Tiger Man, or simply Cat, he grew up with the name Dennis Avner in Oscoda, Michigan, a small town on Lake Huron a couple hours north of Flint. He served in the Navy as a sonar technician and worked as a computer technician in the San Diego area after his discharge in 1980. He began the transformation project that he had long imagined with the tattoos, because they were easiest to arrange, and added the surgeries gradually. Steve Haworth of Phoenix, who describes himself as a "body modification and human evolution artist," did most of them.[1]

Twenty years after beginning these modifications on his own, Stalking Cat went to a furry event at a science-fiction convention. He says that when he walked into that room in 2000, he felt comfortable with other people for the first time. Furries are people who enjoy anthropomorphic art and fiction, even taking on animal identities themselves; some are involved in role-playing games; many use online avatars to perform in virtual space and then sometimes perform in actual space by donning ears, tails, or complete fur suits at fan conventions. Furry fandom provided Cat with community, friendship, and material support. When we met, he was living on Whidbey Island with a couple that he had gotten to know through informal fur-friendly gatherings of science-fiction fans in Southern California. In 2005, the couple relocated due to employment in the aeronautics industry, and Cat moved north with them, doing some work on their house and looking for computer-related work in the Seattle area.

This chance encounter came to mind during a conference the following spring when Anthony Kubiak discussed the recent creation of a chimeric human-cat protein intended to block allergic reactions (in humans).[2] This potentially beneficial hybrid resembles a particular instance of "aparallel evolution" that Gilles Deleuze and Félix Guattari describe in A Thousand Plateaus: a type-C virus links the baboon to the cat by carrying along genetic information from one species when it attaches to another. The process alters the DNA of all three—cat, baboon, and virus.[3] The anthropocentric focus of transspecies genetic experiments distinguishes them from Deleuzo-Guattarian philosophy, to be sure. Yet these material linkages made me curious about others forged through interspecies affect rather than DNA, and I set out to map the vectors of desire connecting Stalking Cat with other human and nonhuman creatures. I wondered whether most furries were socially awkward men employed in technology—in other words, to what extent the furry stereotype coincides with the Asperger syndrome stereotype and how these stereotypes might map to reality. The limited ethnographic research that I conducted did not support this hypothesis but led me in other directions. Kubiak (in conversation) wondered about a link between Asperger syndrome, animals, and shamanism—and Cat self-identified as a shaman, a claim that I neither support nor contest.[4] The spiritual side of this construct did not grab me in the same way as it has interested Kubiak; instead, Cat's intentional self-positioning on the borderline between human and nonhuman struck me as significant for the present understanding of what it is to be human, particularly in combination with the borderline position created by what I have come to think of as neurodiversity.

So I interviewed Stalking Cat in April 2007 on Whidbey Island and stayed for the first hour or so of the household's monthly fur-friendly party, observing their role-playing game based on the anthropomorphic novel-in-progress that another member of the household was writing. Cat later told me that he was asked to move out that summer, when expenses and dynamics became unworkable. He never did find work in Seattle. A friend from furry fandom gave him a place to live in Tonopah, Nevada, and a job in housing renovation. That friend moved on, and the work dried up. Through all of this, Stalking Cat struggled to maintain his permanent feline performance as a profession. When we met, he was working on a deal to market a Stalking Cat action figure that failed to materialize. He hoped for a talk show that didn't work out. Fees for public appearances at venues such as Ripley's Believe It or Not and at wildlife sanctuaries provided crucial though not dependable income. When we last spoke, in 2009, Cat was seeking clients as a home health aide, and the small consultation fee I was able to provide enabled him to fix his truck but not to leave Tonopah. In 2011, when I was finishing the article that formed the seed for this book,[5] his agent informed me that Cat was on the road, busy with public appearances, but never finding quite enough work. I could no longer reach him, and his brother let me know through Facebook that Cat couldn't afford Internet access at home and used the prepaid cellphone a friend had given him primarily for work-related text messaging. And then in the middle of the night on 5 November 2012, I learned that Cat was dead, apparently a suicide by shotgun in the garage of the house from which he was being evicted. Whereas progressive people with money have been crucial to the flourishing of the artists that this book analyzes, Cat's furry network didn't have the same resources (and perhaps not the inclination)—he looked for ways to monetize his uniqueness, and the attempts did not meet with sufficient success to sustain his life (let alone enable flourishing).

This book is for Cat but not about him. His difficulties and his death soured my enthusiasm for performance ethnography focused on furry fandom, at least for the time being, and this project turned more solidly back to my primary research expertise in theater, dance, and performance art. I never wanted to diagnose Stalking Cat or simply treat him as a cultural symptom. I tried to write about him with respect, taking him at his word and exploring the locations to which he gave me access—an exploration that led me to this book.

This book is also for but not about my son, Eli Dardis, who has read this preface and given his explicit approval for my discussion of his early childhood experience. When he was four years old in August 1994, just before I began my doctoral studies, I took Eli to watch an open rehearsal for *Mirage*, a work in progress by choreographer Ann Carlson in the Brooklyn Bridge Anchorage. The eight vaulted chambers of the Anchorage lie underneath the Brooklyn end of the bridge. The arched ceilings are nearly fifty feet high, framed by piers that support the bridge, with brick and stone walls. The bridge's engineer, John Roebling, envisioned this space as a commercial arcade or vault for the national treasury, but instead it housed an open-air farmers' market and a children's playground before being walled off from the street in the 1930s as a Works Progress Administration project and used for municipal storage. Outside, the Anchorage is surrounded by bridge and expressway access ramps, noise, garbage, and the view of Manhattan from Brooklyn Heights. Inside, it is dark, cool, and quiet. Visitors liken it to a cathedral, a monastery, or catacombs.[6] In the central chamber Todd Gilens had created a movable grove of trees: five-foot branches stuck in green-burlap-wrapped cement bases. Four big flower pots stood near doorways in the side walls. Opposite the entrance was a low platform. High above it, a bright green catwalk supported a small stage, backed by a painting of white clouds in blue sky. Eli and I first wandered into a chamber on the left, where costumes waited: papier mâché exoskeletons bearing bobbling antennae and translucent silvery globes to transform children into aliens, along with blobby gold shapes to make them into gold nuggets. Pat Oleszko's gigantic balloon figures occupied another chamber on the right. A reclining clown nearly filled one end, leaving room for a bucket of plaster and rolls of gauze that visitors were using to cast impressions of body parts. Another clown and a dancer towered over pens and paper, with which we were invited to draw our dreams, and pans of tempera paint for making handprints in old books.

Back in the central chamber, a lone woman fiddled with balky sound equipment, but it looked like we missed the rehearsal. She finally began to dance, though, her movement pulling her off center in falls and jerks, and Eli followed her. He climbed into a flower pot when she did, drooped, wilted, and sent up shoots. During breaks, he rearranged trees. As we got ready to leave that Wednesday, another woman who had been making sure that both Eli and the trees remained undamaged invited him to return for a children's rehearsal. I was surprised. He was enthusiastic, so we did return the following Saturday. I was skeptical about Eli's participation. When he was three, his daycare program had expressed concern about his reluctance to join in group activities and called us in for a meeting. To our dismay, roughly a dozen representatives of the child development center that housed the daycare presented their observations of Eli and grilled us about his behavior and ours. They recommended testing. The pediatric neurologist who we eventually consulted talked about different cognitive styles that tend to run in families, said she could have predicted what Eli would be like after meeting the two of us and hearing about our families, and said that there was no entirely appropriate diagnosis but that PDD-NOS (Pervasive Development Disorder–Not Otherwise Specified) was the closest and would get him the services that he needed. We agreed to pragmatic language therapy. Eli excelled at this sort of one-on-one exchange with adults, but nothing changed in daycare. We argued about medicalization and categorization. Our experience was much like that of other autism families, but we had no idea and no support. This was one year prior to Asperger syndrome's debut in DSM-IV. We used that diagnostic term strategically later to communicate with teachers in his Brooklyn public schools, but the category doesn't clearly locate my son.

Some categories fit better and some worse, and none is entirely adequate, but they all exert a pull or torque that does, in fact, change the contours of one's lived experience. Donna Haraway observes that "we live in a world where people are made to live several non-isomorphic categories simultaneously, all of which 'torque' them"; in other words, "people have to live in relation to several simultaneously obligatory systems of standardization that they can't fit, but must live with."[7] I introduce these concepts here as critical to my reflection upon this experience and as fundamental to this inquiry, but they were certainly not available to me at the time.

Eli did participate in the activities at the Anchorage, but rarely with the other children. They were older—ranging from six to twelve—and more cooperative. When they put on green burlap booties to sneak around, holding sprays of sumac in front of their faces, he explored the alien costumes.

While they moved the grove of trees from the left chamber into the central area, he joined in briefly but then discovered the video equipment as the other children hid behind, lay down with, and skipped over the trees. By the time Mary Ellen Strom began videotaping the children's improvised dances, Eli was playing on the forty-foot stairway above them. They paraded as gold nuggets and aliens while he knocked trees over domino fashion. I tried to stay calm and not to interfere unless danger threatened. I had a hard day. I thought our presence was a disaster, but Eli was invited to be a part of *Mirage*. He had no reservations: he wanted to be there, so over the next few weeks I gratefully, albeit gradually, relinquished the project of controlling my child and watched sections of *Mirage* develop. On this very personal level, the event had a tremendous redemptive power at a time when I was under pressure *to* control him. My small child was accepted and valued, and this was *his* project.

Eli almost always chose to dance with Olga Tragant, "Wall Flower," in the flower pots during these rehearsals, and he also began to imitate the bird-like movement of Andrea Mills, "Aquila." Carlson eventually decided to put a jester hat on him and allow him to do whatever he wanted to do, whenever he wanted to do it. But until he got used to the different atmosphere of performance, he disappeared, initially spending nearly all his time on the carousel and swings near the entrance or outside playing in the magenta-dyed gravel. The audience density and the sound volume were overwhelming. And he asked me why Mills wouldn't talk to him anymore: he was comfortable with this woman wearing feather pasties and G-string, Lucite and glitter platform sandals, and one large wing, but not with her performance demeanor that excluded him. After we talked about the concept of staying in character, he did feel free to approach her. Other people tended to maintain their distance from the nearly naked woman, watching from the doorway as she lurked in a chamber that opened out near the cotton candy station, bathed in eerie blue light. She hid, she preened with nervous, fast, bird flutters. She simultaneously concealed and displayed herself. During one performance, as she lay face down in the central chamber, felled by a simulated gunshot, Eli sat on a golden pillow a few feet from her head, watching her and eating cotton candy. Another time, he walked up and bounced a superball near her head. As a proper Jester, he undercut the seriousness of the moment. He continues to undercut mine and to teach me that I do not know.

## RESEARCH SUPPORT AND PROTOCOLS

A Faculty Research Grant from the University of Georgia Research Foundation funded a preliminary study in 2009. After approval by the Institutional Review Board, I interviewed a dozen participants at Furry Weekend Atlanta. My field research protocol accommodated confidentiality or an alternative consent form for performers with a recognizable public persona. Both the interviews and my participant observation aimed to provide a more serious and nuanced picture of furry fandom, which had been sensationalized and trivialized in the media. Subsequent research received support from a University of Georgia Provost Summer Research Grant in 2013 and a 2015–16 research fellowship provided by the Willson Center for the Humanities and Arts at UGA. With Institutional Review Board approval, I interviewed a small number of the creative personnel involved in the public performances that this study analyzes. Confidentiality was neither possible nor desirable for these artists, and the interviews ultimately enriched my understanding but in only a very few instances do I rely upon the information they provided. I thank Christopher Knowles and Sylvia Netzer, Barbara Knowles, Lauren DiGiulio, Frank Hentschker, Kit (Cation) Schneider, Deke Weaver, Paula Josa-Jones, Jennifer Monson, and Ann Carlson for their time and generous conversation in person, by phone, and through e-mail. Thanks also to Emily Bates of Gavin Brown Enterprise, Laura Colby of Elsie Management, Ken Cerniglia of Disney Theatricals. New York Public Library (NYPL) resources have been critical, including the video documentation held by the Theatre on Film and Tape archive (TOFT) and the Billy Rose Theatre Collection, both at the Library for the Performing Arts, and a 2016 residency in the Allen Room in the Schwarzman Building facilitated both research and writing. The Willson Center for the Humanities and Arts provided funds to support image costs.

Many other scholars contributed to the development of this work. I particularly benefited from exchanges with members of the American Society for Theatre Research working sessions on Empathy (2008), Biopolitics (2012), Animals Perform I and II (2014–15), and Transspecies Performance (2016); the International Federation for Theatre Research working groups on Feminist Research (2013) and Disability and Performance (2016); and audiences for ASTR plenary presentations in 2007 and 2013, panels at IFTR in 2012 and the Association for the Study of the Arts of the Present in 2015, and the Theatre Symposium of the Southeastern Theatre Conference in 2013 and 2015. I cannot overestimate the importance of conversations with Jennifer Parker-Starbuck, Kim Marra, and Kirsty Johnston both within some of these conference settings and outside them. I am forever grateful to LeAnn Fields and Jenny Geyer at the University of Michigan Press, as well as the two anonymous readers whose suggestions improved the book so much. The doctoral students in my 2013 seminar helped me to think through theoretical approaches to affect, emotion, and cognition. Sara Warner was tremendously helpful as I was organizing that seminar, and the help that I get from Rhonda Blair and Stan Garner stretches before, through, and beyond this project. As always, Tony Dardis has contributed both intellectual and personal support.

As a fairly neurotypical human animal, I write from a position of relative privilege as an ally of nonhuman animals and people with divergent cognitive styles. I speak only for myself and from my own perspective, but my research strives to understand the full complexity of my experience's articulation with that of other beings.

# CHAPTER I

# *Locating the Human in Performance*

*Affect, Animals, and Autists* analyzes the ways in which theater and related performing arts both reflect and contribute to a redefinition of the category *human* that is more inclusive of human difference and less hierarchical in relation to other species. Case studies include spectacular puppets playing animals; actual animals present on stage in theater, performance art, and dance; representations of autism in theater; collaborations between autistic and neurotypical theater makers; and performances that challenge these distinctions. My argument builds upon the premises that categories serve hierarchies and thus organize oppression; rational argument only goes so far to create change, because these categories affect us subliminally; affect theory makes their various pulls visible to consciousness, a necessary step in countering their torque; theater and related forms of performance constitute exemplary affect workshops; and because language is our primary tool of categorization, looking at those oppressed due to a perceived lack of language offers a special window into its operations.

## TERMINOLOGY

I pause here to define a few terms with which some readers may not be familiar: Rosemarie Garland-Thomson coined the term *normate* to designate "the social figure through which people can represent themselves as definitive human beings."[1] Matching the norms renders further descriptors optional; for example, I need not refer to myself as a two-legged or a verbal human. Nor do I in most situations mark myself as *neurotypical* in order to designate normate cognition. Writing about autisms requires me to do so, though, in order to position myself as an ally not a self-advocate (and certainly not an expert). To avoid reifying a diagnostic category undergoing continual revision, I purposely use the term *autist* rather than "autistic person" or "person with autism," thus marking the designation as a historical situation rather than a given fact, "a performative accomplishment compelled by social sanction and taboo," to borrow Judith Butler's definition of gender identity.[2] Although current clinical terminology groups various conditions as autism spectrum disorders, I prefer not to use this phrase because spectrum suggests a gradation, like the color spectrum, inadequate to the diversity of characteristics currently grouped by the label autism. I align myself with the neurodiversity movement in recognizing the tremendous neurological variation among humans and even within any given individual.[3] Finally, I will often but not always refer to nonhuman animals simply as *animals*.

## LANGUAGE AND CATEGORIES

I recognize the danger in focusing on animals and autists to map current shifts in the boundaries of the human, because human oppression so often operates by animalizing particular sorts of people. These two categories reach around the edges of the human to touch one another in an especially productive way, though, because classification as autist or as animal entails communication that differs from normate human language use. I propose not that they are equivalent but that examining the common grounds for exclusion can aid efforts at ending oppression. Unexamined assumptions about the hierarchical superiority of the properly human—whatever that may be—have sometimes brought advocacy for nonhuman animals and for disabled humans into conflict. Noting that philosopher Martha Nussbaum conceives of a functional threshold below which life is not fully human, for example, Tobin Siebers summarizes the notorious debate between philosopher and animal rights activist Peter Singer, who asserted that people with severe disability do not qualify as human and recommended euthanasia, and disability rights activist Harriet McBryde Johnson, who prefered to remain alive and asserted her full humanity. Siebers points out that the trope of disabled inferiority underpins other forms of oppression—the supposed inferiority of women and persons of color was premised upon their physical or mental deficiency, or both.[4] "Disability is the other other that helps make otherness imaginable," Siebers writes.[5] I would note, then, that mental disability constitutes the other-other other when invoking normate cognition to support claims for full humanity irrespective of physical differences. The trope of animal inferiority reciprocally grounds the oppression of persons perceived to be mentally deficient, a denigration that would lose power if humans did not consider themselves superior to all other beings. This presumed superiority enables humans to rationalize eating nonhuman animals, using them as a labor force, manipulating their reproduction, and precipitating their extinction. Sunaura Taylor argues that "questions about normalcy and nature, value and efficiency, interdependence and vulnerability, as well as more specific concerns about rights and autonomy" are crucial to both disability studies and animal ethics because "limited interpretations of what is natural and normal leads to the continued oppression of both disabled people and animals."[6] Yet when Taylor speaks about this shared oppression, people often respond: "You don't have to compare yourself to an animal."[7]

An important humanist tradition interprets the ability to describe and reflect upon one's sensations as evidence that human thoughts and feelings operate at a higher level than those of other animals. To give only the most prominent example, René Descartes makes this argument in his *Discourse on the Method*.[8] The same tradition has relegated humans with atypical communication styles to the periphery of the human realm, considered them feral, neglected and warehoused them. Wild children figured in myths of humans raised by animals, most commonly wolves (as in the case of Romulus and Remus) or bears. Factual accounts of such children begin in the seventeenth century, a time when philosophers such as Descartes, Thomas Hobbes, and John Locke were articulating modern conceptions of human nature and the state of nature. Giorgio Agamben notes that Carl Linnaeus, who in the 1730s recognized the similarity of apes and humans and classified all of them as "Anthropomorpha" or "manlike," registered as a variant *Homo ferus* to account for the *enfants sauvages* who appeared at that time. He recorded "five appearances in less than fifteen years." Agamben concludes, "At the time when the sciences of man begin to delineate the contours of his *facies*, the *enfants sauvages*, who appear more and more often on the edges of the villages of Europe, are the messengers of man's inhumanity, the witnesses to his fragile identity and his lack of a face of his own."[9] Up through the end of the eighteenth century, as Adriana Benzaquén observes, such accounts stress that the children were isolated from human civilization, either abandoned by or stolen away from their parents, and nurtured instead by nonhuman animals.

Supposedly feral children such as Peter, who appeared in Hamlin in 1724; Marie-Angélique "Memmie" le Blanc in Champagne, 1731; Victor in Aveyron, 1797; and Kaspar Hauser in Nuremberg, 1828, all became popular curiosities, visited and observed by those with the means to do so. Starting in the early nineteenth century, a conception of norms for human development became more important to these narratives, introducing wild children who had been confined, mistreated, and abused by humans. Other animals faded from the stories.[10] None of these purportedly wild children spoke human language when they first encountered civilization. Some of them remained mute but grew to understand what was said to them, some learned to speak, and others even to read and write. They exhibited various hypersensitivities and insensibilities that in some cases abated. Their socially unacceptable behaviors were to some degree tamed by their (presumed) benefactors.

Looking past the Romantic idealization that characterizes these historical accounts, Roy Richard Grinker suggests that these children may have been abandoned by their parents because of characteristics now classified as autistic.[11] Their purported wildness aside, some of these children would have been considered idiots at the time and others, imbeciles. Shifts in diagnostic terminology both reflect and shape conceptions of difference. Patrick McDonagh notes the uncertainty whether "someone called a 'fool' in the sixteenth century would, if transported through time, be called 'simple' in the eighteenth century, an 'imbecile' in the 1890s, or 'moderately or mildly retarded' in the 1960s; nor do we know if someone called an 'idiot' in 1760 would still be one in 1860."[12] The terminology shifts, but the practice of exclusionary classification remains. Many of the white middle-class parents who brought their children to Leo Kanner's office in the early twentieth century challenged the diagnosis of their child as feebleminded—this was the social context within which he defined autism in 1943, based on observation of just eleven children.[13] Karen Sirota observes that he depicted them as wild, closed off, and "all but impervious to culture."[14] Parents used animal imagery in describing their children to Kanner; for example, Charles entered a group of children "just like a foal who'd been let out of an enclosure," and Elaine's "animal wildness" disappeared as she grew older.[15] John Duffy and Rebecca Dorner note that Kanner's initial article provided "a template for decades of subsequent autism research" including the common use of animal metaphors "to describe the inner mental states of the putatively mindblind."[16] I both critique this theoretical paradigm in chapter 3 and discuss the history of autism at greater length there and in chapter 5. The need to do so exists in some tension with my understanding of disability, as Siebers puts it, "as a minority identity that must be addressed not as personal misfortune or individual defect but as the product of a disabling social and built environment."[17]

Some autists have seemed to share a special affinity with nonhuman animals, alternatively viewed in a positive light as shamanic or negatively as subhuman. Some autistic life writing—or *autie-ethnography*, a term introduced by Irene Rose[18]—articulates an enhanced understanding of other species. Temple Grandin has popularized the notion that autism can produce a special understanding of animal consciousness and contribute to enhanced interspecies communication. She believes that animals think in pictures, as she herself does, and she attributes her ability to design more humane animal-handling equipment to the fact that she notices the things that they notice, details that neurotypicals overlook.[19] Dawn Prince says that the comfort she found in being with gorillas enabled her to learn from her interactions with them how to interact with other humans. Her extended visits to the zoo led to employment and an assignment to observe the gorillas; like Grandin, she would notice things that other humans would not.[20] Both of these women have earned doctoral degrees related to their work with other species—Grandin in animal science and Prince in anthropology. Olga Solomon points out that "what is at stake in [their] accounts of human–animal relationships . . . appears to go beyond concerns for animal welfare; their own wellbeing is intrinsically connected to the wellbeing of the animals."[21] As Taylor argues, though, slaughter by humans—no matter how humane—hardly counts as well-being.[22]

Autists and animals also connect therapeutically, with most of the discourse on this topic coming from neurotypicals. Journalist Rupert Isaacson took his son Rowan to Mongolia in search of a shamanic cure, having been surprised when contact with horses not only ended a tantrum but enabled the boy, who had retreated into silence, to speak again. As the documentary *The Horse Boy* shows, the Mongolian horses did not have the same effect on Rowan as the horses at home did, and the efficacy of the two shamanic ceremonies remains entirely uncertain even to the parents.[23] Connecting stories of children raised by wolves to the potential for canine facilitation of human interaction, Solomon notes that dogs have been used therapeutically for roughly fifty years.[24] They perform social actions that are "highly anticipatory, unhurried, structurally simple and easy to interpret," thus creating a well-organized background for interaction that helps children to easily anticipate the next move. As she puts it, "the dogs reside not only in [the] 'here and now' but also in a 'here and now' that happens over and over, allowing the children to practice being intentional, intersubjective agents."[25]

In addition to questioning this focus on neurodivergence as impairment, my inquiry participates in an ongoing posthumanist reevaluation of the humanist tradition, displacing the human from the center of the ethical universe. Cary Wolfe proposes an ethics based on "a *compassion* that is rooted in our vulnerability and passivity," arguing that "the ethical force of our relation to the disabled and to nonhuman others is precisely that it foregrounds the necessity of thinking ethics *outside* a model of reciprocity between 'moral agents.' . . . The ethical act might instead be construed as one that is freely extended without hope of reciprocation by the other."[26] Such an ethics entails recognizing and appreciating the feelings of nonhuman animals and the complex systems of communication that other species share. To mention just a few recent examples of the growing body of research in this area: Nathan Lents argues in *Not So Different* that human and nonhuman animals share a common behavioral scaffolding that "is tweaked in unique ways across species and even among individuals within a species"; Debra Herrmann studied "fifteen species of birds and over 300 individuals native to 6 different continents . . . over a period of 30 years" in order to illuminate with *Avian Cognition* both "*who* birds are" and "*why* they engage in certain behaviors"; and Michael Garstang's *Elephant Sense and Sensibility* presents evidence that elephant behaviors, including their adaptation to an increasingly inhospitable lifeworld, "draw upon advanced mental processes."[27] As evidence of animals' capacity to learn human languages as well as their own, Donna Haraway and Cary Wolfe both discuss the border collie reported to recognize more than 200 words and, more significantly, to very quickly recognize that an unknown word refers to a new unknown object and then remember that word weeks later.[28] Research with African gray parrots and primates is too well known to require elaboration here, although Koko the gorilla will make several appearances.

Dawn Prince, who always "had the gift of language" but used it in ways that led her "further from meaningful communication with human beings," says that she also "talked to animals in that language of silence" when she was young. Some years after she emerged from a period of homelessness and human isolation, Dr. Prince met the bonobo Kanzi, who used a symbol board to communicate with humans. She "fell into the gorilla language," playing and dancing with him until he suddenly grabbed the board and began pointing first at a symbol and then at her, while making a hand gesture. The human researcher who had introduced them figured out that Kanzi was pointing at the symbol for gorilla and using American Sign Language to form a question. He was asking Prince whether she was a gorilla. "What was amazing, though, is that he didn't know American Sign Language: he had seen a video of the gorilla Koko using it and must have not only remembered the signed words, but, not having known other gorillas, assumed that all gorillas understood sign language."[29] Appealing though I find this story, the research is not without controversy. Erica Fudge, for example, traces the history of overinterpretation and unconscious signaling, beginning with Clever Hans the calculating horse and extending through research with Koko, Kanzi, and other primates. She says: "I want to believe that Koko has an interior life; unfortunately I believe that if she does have one she might not choose to live in the compound in San Francisco. That's the danger. If we could hear them speak, we might not want to hear what they say.[30]

Humans continue to interpret the ability to communicate using human language as evidence of thought and thus of mind, inner life, or whatever concept indicates a value equivalent to the human. Thus the fact that some autists do not communicate verbally led historically to uncertainty about whether the nonverbal person thought, felt, or had value.[31] Alternative communications systems have by now established that many humans who do not speak do indeed think. Autists, therapists, teachers, and families communicate using diagrams or other pictures, objects, systems of sign language, touch, or facilitated communication. Writing may be possible even if speech is not; Soma Mukhopadhyay, for example, invented the Rapid Prompting Method to teach her son Tito how to communicate. Although he still does not speak, he writes independently. His and other autie-ethnographies convey a vivid sense of cognitive styles and struggles to communicate.[32] Some autists describe thinking in pictures or in movement and sound rather than in words. Some experience synesthesia that contributes to math-savant abilities or, conversely, exacerbates a math incapacity but enhances linguistic ability. The variation among their self-descriptions of cognition belies any simple stereotype of autism.[33] Even these first-person accounts generate controversy, though, as some researchers dismiss the authors' capacity to know their own mental states.[34] And the controversy concerning facilitated communication resembles that about sign-language research with primates, only the stakes are perceived as higher. Critics argue that the facilitator, who maintains some degree of physical contact that enables the autist to type, actually produces the communication's content in Ouija-board fashion. Autism self-advocates such as DJ Savarese and Sue Rubin, in contrast, insist that their words are their own. Rubin learned to type with a facilitator but no longer requires assistance. Savarese's degree of independence is more variable.[35]

## PERFORMANCE AND THE AFFECTSPHERE

Although this book does not directly enter these debates, their intensity grounds the movement of human affect through the network of performances that I analyze here, all of which negotiate the blurry boundaries of the (post)human. Advocating equally for nonhuman animals and for disabled humans, my research specifically seeks to understand the formation, reinforcement, and transformation of norms. *Affect, Animals, and Autists* analyzes dramatic and postdramatic theater, performance art, and dance as affect ateliers. Theater traffics not only in the identifiable emotions that actors display on stage and spectators recognize, perhaps finding their own emotions evoked, but also in more inchoate circulations of affect. The commercial imperative to produce uplift does not necessarily mean that audiences require a happy ending. They may equally well be drawn to the intensification of affect and intellectual engagement that live performance can offer, leaving the theater enlivened by solving a puzzle of meaning, by an affirmation of political agency, by righteous outrage. In each case, meaning is embodied and braided together with feeling. Audiences come to the theater specifically for this embodied encounter, to share its intensity, which makes the theater an especially useful venue for analyzing the contemporary affectsphere; that is, the public sphere created not through discourse but through feeling, what Lauren Berlant calls a "shared nervous system."[36]

Whether colloquial or philosophical, ethical considerations often stress the importance of developing empathy in spite of differences, and theatrical performances offer excellent practice. Yet both theater and empathy itself can just as effectively shore up conceptual boundaries and solidify power hierarchies, and empathy takes on additional significance when autisms are construed as empathy deficits, as I will discuss in chapter 3. Analytic philosophy generally positions empathy as a supremely human capacity; for example, Peter Goldie defines empathy strictly in terms of consciously "*imagining the experience of a narrative* from that other person's point of view." For

Goldie, empathy requires a *"characterization"* of the person imagined, impossible without to some considerable degree understanding that person's psychology and situation, and also requires adopting a central viewpoint as opposed to imagining the experience from a distance.[37] Nussbaum further stipulates that empathy need not involve feeling; for her, neither judgment nor shared affect is essential to the conscious imaginative effort of empathy.[38] These definitions imply that neurotypical humans cannot empathize with either nonhuman animals or nonverbal autists, because they cannot imagine experience without language—indeed, they construe imagination as operating by means of language. In contrast to empathy, Goldie says that "emotional contagion . . . typically does not even involve awareness of what the other's emotion is about" and is thus "neither necessary nor sufficient for understanding emotions in others."[39] Contagion corresponds more closely to what neurobiology would classify as automatic empathy, distinct from the perspective-taking of cognitive empathy.[40] This conception of empathy is compatible with research on cognition and behavior that seeks to bridge the divide between humans and other animals.[41] The terminology varies from one discipline to another, even one author to another within the same discipline, but the discourse aims to explain something about how we know what others think and feel including how their thoughts and feelings affect us.[42] For my purposes, empathy proves too capacious and variable a term to specify much about this knowing and sharing.

Affect offers to literary theory, aesthetics, and performance theory a conceptual framework within which to take both embodiment and felt experience into account. Some of the motivation for current interest in affect comes from political manipulation of constituencies through emotional appeal, through the affecting sound bite or photo opportunity, rather than through reason. That political realities lend an urgency to affect analysis is not particularly novel: Plato's *Republic* objected to poets for their ability to sway opinion; Aristotle offered his *Rhetoric* as a toolkit for more effective manipulation. Some performance scholars have cautioned that affect theory might tend to bypass cognition and abandon the analysis of rational discourse.[43] But if we adopt a more inclusive conception of cognition as both embodied by the individual and embedded in the social, and furthermore include affective phenomena as part of cognition even if not always rational and conscious, the apparent opposition between cognition and affect dissolves into a more complex relation better suited for the boundary-blurring project at hand.[44] This book does not ignore the importance of decoding the various messages that performances may communicate to their audiences, and thus the case studies analyze the ways in which affect interacts with the narrative structures, symbolic and semiotic economies, and polemics of the performances at issue here.

## FEELING, AFFECT, AND EMOTION

In conversation, most English speakers use the terms *feeling, affect,* and *emotion* as synonyms, and the critical literature with which I engage uses them in various ways. I consider feeling, affect, and emotion to be different dimensions of experience that we cannot fully separate from one another, none of them fully bounded by the individual human body. I have chosen a set of definitions to facilitate conceptual clarity, distinguishing the individual experience of sensation (feeling) from what circulates between individuals and their environment including but not limited to other individuals (affect), and both of these from that which is conceptualized, named, performed, and thus interpreted by others (emotion). These definitions suit performance analysis and may not always correspond exactly to the ways in which another discipline uses a particular term.

I begin with the most bounded of these three terms and define *feeling* as an interpreted sensation. In his persuasive and thorough treatment of feelings and their place in performance, Martin Welton builds upon Teresa Brennan's definition of feelings as "sensations that have found the right match in words,"[45] but he drops the linguistic requirement. Welton stipulates that sensations register sensory and proprioceptive stimuli, and feelings interpret these sensations—but interpretation can occur at many levels.[46] This broadening makes it possible to refer, for example, to an uneasy feeling that one can't quite put into words. Most nonhuman animals and some nonverbal autists lack words but assuredly have feelings, and verbal humans experience inchoate as well as expressible feelings. Although feelings might be easily conceptualized as internal phenomena, they arise in response to stimuli that may be external to the body. Even postural proprioception registers the body's shifting equilibrium in space. I may discuss *feeling an emotion* or *feeling an intensification of affect,* but I will avoid referring to the subjective experience of an emotion as "a feeling."

Brennan carefully distinguishes feelings from affects, but she does not differentiate between affect and emotion. This is fairly common, even among psychologists or philosophers who take pains to distinguish emotions from other sorts of affective states such as mood.[47] Because philosopher Gilles Deleuze provides a framework for analyzing under the rubric *affect* the heightened sense of immersion in the present moment that witnesses to performance often share, I will take care in laying out its conceptual basis and will return to it in my concluding chapter. But the earlier chapters rely upon an understanding of the affect system as delineated by psychologist Silvan Tomkins.

Tomkins begins with the axiom that a motivational system must ensure survival (the animal does what it *must* do) and also ensure some sort of striving/improvement (the animal does what it *can* do). Freudian psychology identifies a set of biological drives as the motive force determining human behavior and psychology, but Tomkins finds this conceptual scheme inadequate and outlines a related but separate system of affects. The difference between these two systems is not that one is higher or more important, but rather that affects are more general and drives are more specific.[48] The affects are quite flexible with respect to stimulus and satisfaction, whereas determinate biological drives (for oxygen, food, water, and sex) can only be suppressed or redirected.[49] Tomkins delineates nine "categorical" or "discrete" affects that overlap but do not entirely coincide with the fifteen basic emotion families as Paul Ekman has come to define them:

| Categorical Affects (Tomkins) | Basic Emotions (Ekman) |
|---|---|
| | contentment |
| | satisfaction |
| interest–excitement | excitement |
| | amusement |
| | relief |
| enjoyment–joy | |
| | pride in achievement |
| | sensory pleasure |
| surprise–startle | |
| distress–anguish | sadness/distress |
| fear–terror | fear |
| | embarrassment |
| shame–humiliation | shame |
| | guilt |
| contempt | contempt |
| disgust | disgust |
| anger–rage | anger |

Ekman acknowledges a great variety of other affective phenomena but refuses them the label *emotion*, considering them instead to be cognitive states (interest); emotional plots (romantic and parental love, hate, grief, and jealousy); moods (saturated with emotions but lasting longer and having a wider variety of causes); and affective personality traits (hostility).[50]

For Ekman, an emotion must have a uniform cause and matching physiological expression across humans and, quite likely, other primates: "Because emotions can occur with a very rapid onset, through automatic appraisal, with little awareness, and with involuntary changes in expression and physiology, we often experience emotions as happening to us. Emotions are unbidden, not chosen by us."[51] Much emotion research has depended upon self-reported description of emotional experience, usually via questionnaire and thus relying upon the memory of feeling an emotion, although more recent research also uses neuroimaging techniques to study patterns of activation. Ekman focuses primarily upon the facial expression of emotions, going so far as to develop a Facial Action Coding System used in ongoing research. The system uses photos of actors (popularly referred to as "Ekman Faces"); Tomkins and Carroll Izard advised him on posing them to facilitate cross-cultural research on emotion recognition.[52] Ekman argues that "evolution gives us universal expressions, which tell others some important information about us, but exactly what an expression tells us is not the same in every culture" due to differences "in the words for emotions, in what is learned about the events which call forth an emotion, in display rules, in attitudes about emotions, and [he expects] in meta-emotion philosophies."[53] This research assumes that all faces and bodies worth considering are capable of expressing these basic emotions, and chapter 5 engages with ways in which disability studies must challenge this assumption.

Tomkins theorizes affect as a motivational system; Ekman studies emotion as an expressed content. Whereas Ekman offers useful tools for analyzing the normate actor's performance of emotion, Tomkins offers a rich and robust framework for understanding the ways in which performances elicit their audiences' specific affective engagements. Yet neither Tomkins's nine categorical affects nor Ekman's fifteen basic emotion families map precisely to the affective transactions that I analyze here. I find *shame* and *disgust* playing important roles, as they do; however, in addition to *interest*, these performances frequently elicit the related but intensified responses *wonder* and *awe*. They also engage forms of *tenderness* and create *anxiety* with respect to compulsory happiness. Affect plays an important role in aesthetic judgment, without necessarily becoming conscious, and I will in some cases draw upon discussion of the associated aesthetic categories; hence, discussions of the sublime illuminate the workings of awe, the cute aids in understanding tenderness, the zany clarifies particular anxieties, and the merely interesting offers insight into interest and boredom. My thinking owes a particular debt to Sianne Ngai, but my inquiry centers on audience affect rather than the categories of aesthetic judgment.[54] I neither present nor adhere to a comprehensive taxonomy of affect, but chapters 2 through 5 of *Affect, Animals, and Autists* analyze the ways in which specific performances elicit categorical affects to manipulate their audiences, whether to affirm, expand, or obliterate the boundaries of the human.

My concluding chapter examines affect that exceeds subjectively felt emotional categories, instead circulating as relational intensity. As Brian Massumi explains for his translation of *A Thousand Plateaus*, Gilles Deleuze and Félix Guattari use the term *sentiment* to denote the personal feeling of affective energies. They take their definition of *affect* and *affection* from Spinoza:

> L'affect (Spinoza's *affectus*) is an ability to affect and be affected. It is a prepersonal intensity corresponding to the passage from one experiential state of the body to another and implying an augmentation or diminution in that body's capacity to act. L'affection (Spinoza's *affectio*) is each such state considered as an encounter between the affected body and a second, affecting, body (with body taken in its broadest possible sense to include "mental" or ideal bodies).[55]

In order to know anything at all about a body of any sort, Deleuze and Guattari say, one must learn "what it can do, in other words, what its affects are, how they can or cannot enter into composition with other affects, with the affects of another body, either to destroy that body or to be destroyed by it, either to exchange actions and passions with it or to join with it in composing a more powerful body."[56]

As Patricia Clough explains, affect thus comprises an autonomic substrate of conscious experience, a morass of bodily responses from which consciousness extracts those components that can be narrated as perceived emotional experience. Conscious experience reciprocally affects the bodily substrate—Clough refers to a "reflux back from conscious experience" that is "registered as affect" when it reactivates autonomic responses that conserve but do not effectuate "past action and contexts."[57] Elizabeth Grosz values this conceptual framework as a way to think of the body "as neither a locus for a consciousness nor an organically determined entity" but rather as something to be "understood more in terms of what it can do, the things it can perform, the linkages it establishes, the transformations and becomings it undergoes, and the machinic connections it forms with other bodies."[58] Like an echo, affect resonates between the body's sensory surfaces and the experiential body emerges, moment by moment.[59]

This book's case studies analyze both the performative manipulation of categorical affects in Tomkins's sense and what Massumi calls "intensity"; that is, the affect that always escapes capture by consciousness. The sense of vitality that emerges from one's background awareness of this continuous escape can send desire along unexpected vectors and stimulate new directions for conscious thought.[60] Deleuze and Guattari provide in *Anti-Oedipus* a model of desire as motivation, which can stem from a drive (thus, sexual desire) or a categorical affect (shame, for example). They argue that "desiring-machines" link together in binary series, forming lines or vectors that extend "in every direction." Each "machine is always coupled with another" in such a way that the first produces a flow that is interrupted or drained by the second, the second by a third, and so on ad infinitum.[61] The Deleuzo-Guattarian conception of affect presents an embodied subject coextensive with the environment rather than being contained by bodily boundaries, both spatially and temporally fluid. James Thompson stresses the relational aspect of affect as an embodied response or attachment to an object, whether that be tangible (a person, a thing, an event) or intangible (an idea or memory).[62] As Brennan argues, the transmissibility of affect "undermines the dichotomy between the individual and the environment and the related opposition between the biological and the social."[63] This strand of affect theory offers ways to talk about culture and its participants as coemergent and positions the aesthetic encounter as a potential "shock to thought"—an encounter that impels the audience to produce meaning through the attempt to understand feelings that exceed familiar emotional categories rather than (or in addition to) decoding a meaning that the performance has conveyed.[64]

Understanding affect as an experienced bodily capacity makes it possible to account for affective experience without requiring a precise emotional label. For Massumi, "emotion is qualified intensity, the conventional, consensual point of insertion of intensity into semantically and semiotically formed progressions, into narrativizable action-reaction circuits, into function and meaning. It is intensity owned and recognized."[65] Maintaining a clear distinction between affect and emotion with respect to subjectivity, Laura Cull defines emotion as an owned, fixed experience belonging to an individual subject and affect as "a particular kind of 'encounter' between bodies." She thus argues that the agreement or disagreement of bodies that we contact causes our affect to increase or decrease: "Joy is not an emotion, it is an increase of my power to act and an extension of *what I can do*." Sadness would be the inverse, experienced when we encounter disagreement or a dampening force.[66]

Some scholars seek to reconcile Tomkins and Deleuze. Anna Gibbs, for example, notes that both authors understand affect to be "intricately involved in the human autonomic system and engaging an energetic dimension that impels or inhibits the body's capacities for action," but Tomkins "enables the specification of the energetic dimension of affect in very precise ways."[67] To my mind, Lauren Berlant suggests a useful way of maneuvering in between affective intensity and personalized emotion, observing the "distinction between a structure of affect and what we call that affect when we encounter it." What one feels is not quite the same as what one is perceived to be performing. "What looks like a shamed response in one decade, may look angry in another one. One can experience the world not being there for one because of one's singularity or because one's singularity includes *the kind of thing* one appears to be to others. One might experience that as shame, but also many emotions at once."[68] In spite of affect's multiplicity, emotional performances that do not conform to expected, readable codes can entail penalties. In the flux of affective experience, misrecognition does important work; for example, explanations for an affective intensity that produces tears generally try to capture the feeling with a label such as sadness or joy, but the affect often escapes the bounds of this terminology.[69]

## MAPPING THE CHAPTERS

Without explicitly reconciling the various approaches to affect theory or advocating for one over another, I consider them complementary. *Affect, Animals, and Autists* begins by analyzing specific structures of affect with the vocabulary of emotions and in the end adopts a Deleuzian analytical framework. I select these approaches as most appropriate to the performances that I seek to understand. The first two chapters begin in the commercial sphere with tremendously successful young-adult novel adaptations that ostensibly concern animals (for chapter 2) or autists (for chapter 3). London's National Theatre produced both of these works—*War Horse* and *The Curious Incident of the Dog in the Night-Time*—during Nicholas Hytner's tenure as artistic director. Programming during this period made evident the National's abiding concern with what it means to be human. Joe Kelleher notes, for example, that Alan Bennett's *The History Boys* (2004) offers "lessons . . . about how to recognize a 'human,' . . . especially when such a creature appears in an *over*-familiar guise, as a teacher for example."[70] In Nick Dear's adaptation of *Frankenstein*, directed by Danny Boyle for the 2011 season, the audience watches the Monster hatch from an egg; learn to walk, talk, and read; and finally bring his creator Victor to admit that he viewed his creature as an equation or theorem. As the Monster notes, Victor didn't anticipate that he would have feelings.[71] The National has explored the boundaries of the human with consummate theatrical verve, simultaneously blurring the significance of its "national" designation and the distinction between commercial and subsidized arts.

Comparing *War Horse* with another puppet spectacular, Disney's *The Lion King*, and a previous National as-horse drama, *Equus*, clarifies both its skillful manipulation of awe and tenderness and the veiling of supporting technologies that are essential to its affect production. Chapter 2 demonstrates that these plays ultimately foster a nostalgic affection for bygone ways of life and naturalize the species hierarchy that brings about the vanishing of these animals from the Anthropocene present. In contrast, Deke Weaver's fragmented and multilayered presentation of an *Unreliable Bestiary* unsettles rather than reassures its audiences, fostering affective engagement with human responsibility. Chapter 3 compares *Curious Incident* with Mike Leigh's *Two Thousand Years* (which also premiered at the National) and Annie Baker's *Body Awareness*. All three position a son who fits the profile for Asperger syndrome as disruption to a family's happiness. I engage with the history of this diagnostic category and the deployment of gendered stock characters within autism rhetoric outside of as well as within the theater. *Curious Incident's* staging at some times startles, at others delights, adds shared distress and reassuring tenderness to the anxiety and amusement that all three plots share, but its investment in the neoliberal family both limits its capacity to torque existing structures and ensures its commercial success. In contrast with these three Asperger-family dramas, Deanna Jent's *Falling* refuses cruel optimism with respect to the profoundly autistic character at its center. This realist drama engages fear and fosters potentially productive anger with social structures unable to accommodate neurodiversity. The chapter ends with two postrealist family deconstructions, Pig Iron Theatre's *Chekhov Lizardbrain* and Elevator Repair Service's *The Sound and the Fury (April Seventh, 1928)*, both of which zanily bring autism tropes together with modernist literary masterpieces.

Moving on to performances that incorporate animals rather than simulating them, chapter 4 begins with a common relation in dramatic theater between animal death and moral disgust. After briefly discussing the use of dead animals followed by live ones in *Curious Incident* and Martin McDonagh's *The Lieutenant of Inishmore*, I spend more time considering the reverse trajectory from alive to dead in Edward Albee's *The Goat, or Who is Sylvia?* and Sam Shepard's *Curse of the Starving Class*. I then turn to art performances for which Otto Muehl and Hermann Nitsch had living animals killed in the audience's presence, producing an intensification of affect closely related to disgust. Next, this chapter examines performative encounters between humans and pigs—Carsten Höller and Rosemarie Trockel's *A House for Pigs and People*, Kira O'Reilly's *inthewrongplaceness* and *Falling Asleep with a Pig*, and Miru Kim's *The Pig That Therefore I Am*—that purposely dwell in the zone of indistinction where species blur, moving through and dissipating disgust to engage their viewers' interest as they trouble the separation of humanity from a shared animality. The chapter concludes with Ann Carlson's *Animals* series and Paula Josa-Jones's *Ride* and *All the Pretty Horses*, dances born of affective bonds in which nonhuman animals are present as themselves and as part of culture rather than functioning metaphorically. Carlson's *Doggie Hamlet* provides surprising evidence of pastoral multispecies performance's disruptive power.

Chapter 5 maps the affective linkages between audiences and performances that include persons perceived to be autistic, tracing vectors of wonder and shame. Focusing my analysis most closely upon Christopher Knowles's collaboration with Robert Wilson on *A Letter for Queen Victoria* and the further elaboration of this work's entr'actes in the improvisations of *DiaLog/Network*, I then map its development into Knowles's solo performance *The Sundance Kid is Beautiful*. I trouble the use of the category autistic as appropriate to Knowles, to Wilson, or to their postdramatic performances that challenge the audience's capacity to become interested and instead produce wonder. Knowles's work reveals the affective crux common when performers are perceived to have intellectual disabilities; that is, audiences express anxiety about the performers' agency and comprehension. Arguing that a complex relation to shame underpins their ethical concern, I go on to discuss performances that include self-identified autists as well as other cognitively diverse performers. In particular, Back to Back Theatre's *Ganesh Versus the Third Reich* explicitly confronts its audience's shame and employs some affective strategies similar to those I identify for *Queen Victoria*. The chapter finishes with a consideration of autistic actors in mainstream theater and recent theatrical performances of autistic self-advocacy including Cian Binchy's *The Misfit Analysis*, Company AT's *History of Autism*, and Tectonic Theater Project's *Uncommon Sense*.

Finally, my theoretical framework shifts from Tomkins to Deleuze and Guattari for chapter 6 in order to consider affect as a relational intensity rather than in terms of subjectivized affective flows (or emotions), as in the previous chapters. I begin with portions of Paula Josa-Jones's solo project *Of This Body* to introduce aims, methodologies, and a conceptual framework and then remap some earlier examples within this framework. At the heart of this chapter, choreographer Jennifer Monson's *Bird Brain Navigational Dance Project* and *Live Dancing Archive* reveal an ethical potential of affective attunement that depends crucially upon the practices engaged as well as the paradigms structuring those practices. The chapter ends with general conclusions.

The temporal and geographical limits of this study derive in part from my location in the United States. Most of the performances that I discuss have been created since the turn of the twenty-first century and use English when spoken language is involved. I have seen most of them, either live or through performance video. I know the pig performances (Höller and Trockel, O'Reilly, and Kim) only through photo documentation and written accounts; *Curse of the Starving Class* only through the script and critical literature. A few earlier works, ranging from the 1960s to the end of the 1980s, demand inclusion for their performative innovations that still appear radical today and also enrich the contextual analysis of related work. Those that were created elsewhere have affected U.S. audiences directly through international tours (*Ganesh Versus the Third Reich*); productions on Broadway (*War Horse, Curious Incident, Equus*) or Off-Broadway (*Two Thousand Years, The Lieutenant of Inishmore*); or a mix of media, scholarship, and arts tourism (Muehl, Nitsch, Höller and Trockel, O'Reilly). Some of the work arose within a therapeutic context and continues to derive support from agencies (*Ganesh*), but its aims and reach have expanded beyond that context.[72] The recent growth of autism-friendly/relaxed performances on Broadway and beyond remains beyond the scope of this study. Likewise, I do not address the interesting topic of animal audiences.[73] This being qualitative rather than quantitative research, I theorize the audience through my own response, supplemented by the written response of others, particularly when I have not experienced the work live and in person.

This book is neither proscriptive nor prescriptive. I do not condemn any of the performances that I analyze here, although I disapprove of the animal killing. I do not presume to tell any of the artists that they should have created different artworks. My analysis proceeds in a direction at times tangential to their accomplishments; indeed, I criticize at length works that I have heartily enjoyed and thoroughly respect. My aim here is rather to help those of us in the audience understand more fully the foundations for and implications of our affections.

# CHAPTER 2

# *Performing as Animals*

As they prepared to step down after ten years' leadership of London's National Theatre, director Nicholas Hytner and executive director Nick Starr noted that their international hit *War Horse* "started as an experiment in the National Theatre Studio—literally, actors with cardboard boxes on their heads. [They] spent about £50,000 on its development, and about £500,000 putting it on. In the last four years it has made the NT £11 million. Without it, the artistic programme of the NT would look entirely different."[1] Tom Morris initiated the project, which he codirected with Marianne Elliott, as a vehicle for collaboration with the South African founders of Handspring Puppet Company, Adrian Kohler and Basil Jones. After an extensive series of workshops, this stage adaptation of Michael Morpurgo's young-adult novel *War Horse* (1982) filled the slot in the National Theatre's 2007 season that had traditionally entertained families with a Christmas pantomime.[2] *War Horse* then followed its West End transfer with a Tony-winning Broadway production and tours of North America, Holland, the United Kingdom and Ireland, Berlin, and South Africa. Jones says that Handspring did its best to offer "a real horse on stage, . . . a horse that is disinterested in what the humans are saying around him" and that remains "slightly unpredictable," and he attributes the tremendous audience appeal of the horse puppets in general and of the equine protagonist Joey in particular to the production's studied avoidance of anthropomorphism. He notes a contemporary "holism" in the human relationship to the rest of the world and a hunger for representations of "our day-to-day relationship with animals" on stage.[3] If Jones is correct, then the National Theatre made more than eleven million pounds because audiences wish to engage both thoughtfully and affectively with the lives of nonhuman animals.

This chapter argues that the National's *War Horse* in fact doubly subverts this wish, a subversion that contributes materially to the production's success: first, the dramatic narrative reinforces a comfortable anthropocentric viewing position as its morally differentiated human characters offer up a lesson in stewardship over other species; second, this affective engagement with nonhuman animals serves primarily to focus human social concerns and celebrate human achievement. Reading *War Horse* (2007) against its genre predecessor *The Lion King* (1997) throws this strategy into clear focus: their animal-centered narratives make the work of theater artists previously relegated to the avant-garde accessible for a popular audience, and the innovative puppetry makes a sentimental story more palatable for a sophisticated audience.[4] The end of the chapter offers as a counterexample the ongoing series of performances that Deke Weaver, the creator, calls an *Unreliable Bestiary*, focusing particularly upon *ELEPHANT* (2010) both because it makes use of an immense puppet and because human relations with this species offer parallels to those with the horses and African species of the two commercial puppet spectaculars analyzed here.[5] The *Unreliable Bestiary* does away with a feature that I consider crucial to the tremendous success of *The Lion King* and *War Horse*; that is, a clear and unified storyline with a climactic plot structure that resolves in a feeling of uplift—an augmentation of affect that remains available precisely because the plays repress uncomfortable problems resulting from human species dominance. The public discourse surrounding these shows' spectacular puppetry also contributes to this diversionary strategy: in a parallel sleight of technology, both *War Horse* and *The Lion King* draw attention to the productions' archaic stage machinery (including but not limited to certain features of the puppetry), directing attention away from the sophisticated technology at work so effectively in the background. Even as these two shows channel human affect through nonhuman species by visibly animating their inanimate puppets, I propose that they generate a highly positive emotional engagement with human technical expertise, masking it with the nostalgic appeal of animal life. Audiences thus marvel at the very latest in puppet technology even as they are led to think of this stage technology as hundreds of years old, and they revel in their experience of humane concern for the harshly treated horses that one show's puppets embody and for the endangered natural "kingdom" that the others represent.

Interpreting the dramatic storylines and the marketing materials for these shows can reveal a great deal about the social anxieties lurking beneath their surfaces, and this is where the chapter begins—first with *The Lion King* and then *War Horse*. Yet in order to fully account for the success of these puppet spectaculars and to understand the cultural work that they perform also requires an analysis of the ways in which they mobilize audience affect. Thus, my close reading of these two productions' staging, and in particular their opening scenes, demonstrates their skillful manipulation of aesthetic categories: even as they use multiple channels (visual spectacle, music, narrative) to amplify each discrete affective engagement, they keep moving back and forth between the sublime and the cute, alternately triggering awe and tenderness (or *aww*). Yet the narrative conservatism and nostalgia of the commercial blockbuster foreclose any challenge to familiar structures of feeling—precisely the sort of challenge that *ELEPHANT* presents.

## FROM ANTHROPOMORPHISM TO COMPANION SPECIES

*The Lion King* resembles children's books by authors such Beatrix Potter as well as *Cats* (1981), the unlikely megamusical that Andrew Lloyd Webber based on T.S. Eliot's *Old Possum's Book of Practical Cats* (1939). Potter introduced the model that Disney's cartoon films and other entertainment commodities expand, with her illustrations for the tales of *Peter Rabbit* and other small animals providing both visual appeal and merchandising opportunities. The stories themselves offer lessons in proper behavior along with enticing examples of rebellion. The anthropomorphized animals, wearing clothing and drinking tea, engage in species-appropriate adventures: Peter (1902) raids Mr. McGregor's garden, and the fastidious housekeeper Mrs. Tittlemouse (1910) busily fends off the various insects that invade the tunnels that she lives in, finally helped out by a wet and messy frog who eats some and drives the others off.[6] One might debate whether the typically highbrow T.S. Eliot raised the profile of anthropomorphic literature or lowered his own by writing cat poems for children. Like Potter and Disney, though, he uses the animals to offer models of human behavior: the good and the bad, the sane and the mad, as he categorizes "types of mind" in "The Ad-dressing of Cats."[7] In all of these works, the mixing of species characteristics facilitates a mixing of whimsy with seriousness that enhances cross-generational appeal.

Eliot's poems map each individual cat to a set of human characteristics. Andrew Lloyd Webber further mapped each human type to a musical style, and director Trevor Nunn worked closely with choreographer Gillian Lynne to translate the musical settings of the poems into physical theater, what Vagelis Siropoulos describes as "a corporeal spectacle, in which characters are reduced to their bodily attitudes and their essence is communicated basically through movement."[8] Not incidentally, *Cats* established the model for the internationally franchised megamusical. As Jessica Sternfeld points out, the megamusical has a big plot, big music, big spectacle, and big emotions. An intensive marketing campaign including an immediately recognizable logo, a catchy theme song, memorable slogan, and merchandise related to the production all help to appeal directly to audiences, decreasing its dependence upon critics. De-emphasizing dialogue in favor of visual and aural elements increases appeal across language barriers, and the successful megamusical also avoids location- and time-specific plot developments in favor of "universal" issues,[9] something that anthropomorphism also facilitates. Alan Filewod notes that *Cats* began the progressive transformation of "Broadway" from a specific location into a delocalized "moment of reception" that can be experienced anywhere and everywhere, even while continuing to depend upon the stamp of approval that box-office success in an actual Broadway theater bestows.[10] He argues that "*The Lion King* restages the vocabularies of avant-garde and of community-based popular theater aesthetics as a performance of the transnational culture promised by global economic movements towards free trade, opened borders, and the subordination of nations as markets."[11] That the characters are ostensibly animals not only makes them cute but also helps to naturalize the conflicts, simplifying human relations and problems by placing them within a culture that masquerades as nature.

*The Lion King* draws from *Hamlet* its central drama of a usurping uncle, whom the rightful king's only son must kill; removes some of the problematic human elements, such as Hamlet's seeming jealousy about his mother's carnal relations with the usurper; and provides a happy ending rather than a tragic heap of bodies. The story also explores coming of age within a framework of seeming ecological concern as, before his death by usurper-arranged stampede, Lion King Mufasa teaches Lion Prince Simba about "the circle of life": grass dies as antelopes transform it into flesh, antelopes die when lions need to eat them, and lion flesh eventually decays to feed the grass. Director and designer Julie Taymor identifies this circle as her theatrical adaptation's central "ideograph"; that is, "an essence, an abstraction" that takes a complex idea and "boil[s] it right down to the most essential two, three brush strokes."[12] She began her puppet design for *The Lion King* with the Gazelle Wheel, a concrete representation of the circle-of-life ideograph. A single performer carries and turns this wheel, which holds multiple small gazelle figures, and Taymor explains that "the Gazelle Wheel represents the entire concept.... With one person moving across the stage you get eight or nine gazelles that leap. Which is a miniature, too. So you get the long-shot and the close-up."[13]

Yet Mufasa's lesson restricts the circle of life's cooperative geometry to its diachronic dimension; synchronically, the play maintains a strict food-chain hierarchy with the lion at its pinnacle. And this schema differentiates between acceptable interspecies alliances and others that cause problems: on the positive side, Zasu the bird serves as the lion king's major domo with a slapstick amiability, and Rafiki the baboon witchdoctor occupies the border between animal and human worlds as she interprets for the human audience—at times in an African language. In contrast, the evil (lion) uncle Scar forms an alliance with hyenas that draws its moral compass from melodramatic depictions of miscegenation, a somewhat uncomfortable but obvious fit with the American ethnic stereotypes used for the hyenas' characterizations. Because Scar rules without a proper respect for his own species and its place in the circle of life, and he depends upon the support of creatures that eat carrion rather than killing herbivores and thinning their herds, this period of misrule destroys the pridelands: the water dries up, and the herds move on. Skeletal gazelles cross the stage on their wheel, ribs prominent. This ecological model, familiar from the arguments of humans who hunt for sport, supports the narrative's concern for complex ecosystems while keeping everyone in his or her place.

Simba's transgression of species boundaries follows a different pattern but equally supports the hierarchy: The young lion does not spend his neo-Shakespearean sojourn in the green world either alone or accompanied by a lion buddy, killing the antelope that he needs to stay alive—the behavior that his father's life-cycle lesson would seem to recommend. Instead, he joins forces with meerkat Timon and warthog Pumbaa, learns their anthem "Hakuna Matata" (no worries), and subsists on grubs. The seemingly harmless camaraderie of this adorable trio appeals strongly to young children, but Simba's (passive) absence is what enables Scar to (actively) damage the circle of life. Only when the legitimate lion heir finally takes up his proper place in the food chain does balance return, with plump gazelles leaping once again.

*The Lion King* wraps its reinforcement of species hierarchy within a narrative of heterosexual romance and reproduction. With Mufasa trampled to death and Simba off eating grubs, single-adult Scar makes a play for feisty young lioness Nala, Simba's childhood friend and betrothed. As the equivalent of Ophelia rather than Gertrude, Nala provides a less Oedipally inflected target for Scar's and Simba's rival affections and also a more effectual female figure than what Shakespeare offers. Nala flees Scar's advances and happens upon the grub-eating trio, then actively draws Simba back to the pride. This empowered ingenue soon disappears into a more stereotypically maternal role, and the play ends as it began, with a royal lion couple displaying a new princely cub on Pride Rock. Taymor describes *The Lion King* as

> theatre operating in its original sense, which is about family and society. It's doing exactly what theatre was born for—to reaffirm where we are as human beings in our environment. It's precisely to reestablish your connection with your family, to know what your hierarchy is. And to watch families come and go through that with their children is a very moving experience for me.[14]

This understanding of theater as unproblematically positioned within a long historical tradition that supports both the heterosexual nuclear family and a hierarchical social structure as the natural order of things fits comfortably within the Disney Corporation's traditions.[15] Slick containment of any controversial material makes it possible for this production to please everyone. The thematic reiteration of the circle of life appeases environmentalists, for example, but the restoration of hierarchy and the heterosexual nuclear family reassures conservatives. What's not to like? A lot, perhaps, but different portions of the audience are likely to be dissatisfied with different parts of the play, ensuring enjoyment by the very broadest public.

Although they may appeal to a wide age range, anthropomorphic children's books and cartoons typically accommodate a younger reader or viewer than do stories featuring more species-realistic nonhuman animals. In most juvenile and young adult literature centering on relationships between humans and companion species, treatment of animals indexes morality; thus, owners who love and value the stories' animals provide positive models for behavior toward other humans as well, whereas those who devalue, abuse, and neglect the animals exhibit multiple character flaws. Anna Sewell's *Black Beauty* (1877), for example, traces the life of its eponymous horse through a succession of owners, from kind to cruel. The author explicitly wished to encourage humane treatment of horses at a time when they were still central to agriculture and transportation, specifically highlighting the cruelty of the checkrein used to hold a horse's head fashionably but painfully high.

Following in this tradition, *War Horse* traces the adventures of a horse subject to human companions who love him, contrasting with others who behave without regard for animals' suffering. The story begins with Devonshire farmer Ted Narracott spending the mortgage money on a colt. His son Albert bonds with the horse and gives him the name Joey. When the farmer accepts a wager that the horse will pull a plow, even though he's a hunter (half thoroughbred and half draft) bred for riding and unsuited to the work expected of a farm horse, Albert gets Joey to accept a collar and do what the bet requires of him.[16] This domestic prelude introduces characters and establishes affective links to Albert and Joey as well as setting up the moral economy to be further developed in the play's wartime narrative: Albert succeeds through love and respect for the horse; his father, a failure who drinks too much, hits the horse when he can't make it do what he wants; his uncle, an economic success but a moral failure, treats both humans and horse with cruel disregard. Albert's mother embodies solid working-class British practical sense and loving support for the boy, but she participates in the story only reactively—the production gives no appreciable stage time to domestic tensions within the nuclear Narracott family, unlike Steven Spielberg's 2011 film version.[17]

The family drama fades further into the background after the First World War breaks out and Albert's father sells the horse to the British army. Shipped to France, Joey moves through relationships with a further succession of humans, many of whom—like Albert—love him wholesomely as an equine companion: first the British Major Nicholls, who rides him into battle; then the French girl Emilie, who finds him loose in the countryside and hides him from the armies for a time; and finally the German Hauptmann (Captain) Friedrich Muller, who saves both Joey's life and his own by assuming the identity of a dead veterinary officer. The things that tame Joey are the things that later save his life; that is, the bridle and the collar. The initial misuse as a plow horse on the farm enables him to accept a collar from Muller and pull artillery rather than being shot. Other humans use Joey without loving him; thus, continuing the pattern set by the Narracotts, Offizier-Stellvertreter (Acting Officer) Karl "viciously strikes Joey, just as Ted did" (66.) Yet Joey's most formidable antagonists are the inhuman but manmade machines of war: the machine guns that kill Nicholls and many of the other soldiers and horses during their very first battle, a tank that Joey faces helplessly alone, and the barbed wire that entangles him when he flees to No Man's Land. The work of pulling heavy artillery wears his companion horse Topthorn to death, just as it did the pair that he and Joey replaced. This equine buddy relationship develops at the start of Joey's wartime adventures and parallels the friendship between Albert—who soon enough enlists in order to search for his horse—and another soldier. The play's emotionally gratifying but somewhat preposterous ending reunites Albert and Joey just in time to save the horse's life and the young man's spirit.

Morpurgo wrote his novel in Joey's voice in order to present the devastation wrought by the Great War from a nonpartisan perspective as far as the human participants were concerned, but the stage adaptation offers a nonspeaking horse. The production team decided that this would create a greater investment in the horse, because spectators would fill in his thoughts; however, it also encourages a particular sort of focus on Albert. The drama presents this boy's desire for his horse with a notable exclusivity and purity. The show remains entirely free of sexual complications, both belying the oft-repeated notion that it represents a significant maturation for British children's theater and also highlighting by its absence the extent to which dramatic narrative relies upon sexual desire as a plot engine.[18] Comparison to an earlier horsey hit at the National helps to clarify this show's redirection of desire.

Like *War Horse*, Peter Shaffer's *Equus* (1973) premiered in London and moved to Broadway, enjoying tremendous box office success and quickly spawning a film adaptation in which actual horses substitute for the theatrical versions. Both plays feature coming-of-age stories in which the young man's object of desire is not human but horse. *Equus* contains this desire within the blatantly Oedipal framework of its psychotherapeutic detective story as it uncovers the cause for teenager Alan Strang's blinding of six horses.[19] In spite of their boy-meets-horse stories, neither drama centers on its boy. *Equus* follows the psychiatrist as he unravels the mystery of Alan. An unseen wife and a friendly female magistrate wrap Martin Dysart within a superficially heterosexual economy as a screen for his desire flowing toward a "primitive" exaltation, which he imagines as frolicking with centaurs on a Grecian beach. The psychiatrist's own repression blocks this flow.[20]

The horses *as horses* remain entirely incidental to *Equus*; in contrast, *War Horse* traces out the flows of Joey's desire even though he does not speak. The play begins with the ensemble trapping the colt inside a corral, blocking his desire to run free. Albert uses oats to direct Joey's desires toward himself, and Joey subsequently transfers this desire to please a human companion to a series of other humans, until he finally reconnects with Albert. His equine friendship with Topthorn simply exists while they happen to be alive and together—the play presents some competitive sparring when they first meet, and Joey somewhat miraculously induces Topthorn to copy him in accepting a harness, but no horse-horse desire powers the narrative (although the stage directions for Nick Stafford's script describe a more pervasive intraequine sociality than what came across to me in two viewings of the New York production). The play presents entirely in terms of relationships with humans what we might otherwise identify as Joey's abiding, consistent desire to avoid being hurt. The plot's focus on human desire (boy loves horse and so forth) thus screens out the basic problematic of the horse-protagonist's always-thwarted desire for freedom. Underneath its explicit outrage at the misuse of horses (and humans) in war, *War Horse* suggests that our power over horses is ethically acceptable because they love us and, furthermore, they're better off under our loving control than they would otherwise be. Although the narrative of *War Horse* takes horses seriously in a way that *Equus* does not, the two plays' protagonists (Joey and Dysart) both remain trapped in a remarkably similar predicament, expelled from a longed-for Paradise in which they could have run free and wild, their penned-in affect channeled toward a needy British man-child.

Furthermore, these plays' characters and narratives present class tensions that suggest a nostalgia not so much for a rigid class structure but for meaningful working relations, both inter- and intraspecies. In a historical analysis of equine imagery, Peter Hammond Schwartz traces out the significance of the mounted rider who transcends the limitations of his or her own human body, dominates a large and powerful animal, and also dominates pedestrian humans:

> The equestrian image . . . sustained the myth that such virtue [transcendence] belonged to a specific social class. The domination of the horse by its rider indicated in bald enough terms the proper domination by one social class over all others. The escape from the human body and the escape from the corrupt, alien body social meant very nearly the same thing. Both were identified with the mounted horse, spurred, curbed, and whipped into submission.[21]

The knight towered over the foot soldier, physically and metaphorically, and the ruler made a ceremonial royal entry on horseback to signify his authority over a city or other region. These sorts of images symbolically consolidated class structure in medieval and renaissance Europe, and *War Horse* reflects the breakdown of this structure that the First World War accelerated. Albert and his family are the wrong class to be riding horses. Indeed, Albert's triumph over his father comes not astride the horse but behind the plow that he has surprisingly induced the sporting horse to pull, a relation symbolizing species cooperation rather than domination. Thus the story needs the presumably upper-class Major Nicholls to ride Joey into battle, but he's blown off the horse's back the very first time they engage the enemy, a death that evokes the leveling of classes as well as of species: anyone can drive a tank or shoot a machine gun.

World War I marked the end for the war horse, made obsolete by the modern machinery of war, and the beginning of the end for agricultural horses, unmarked by *War Horse* except in their absence from the Devonshire farm that needs them. Working horses had been sufficiently important for Britain to import nearly 200,000 of them between 1873 and 1882, mostly from North America—more than double the figure from the previous decade—because British-bred horses were considered to be of poor quality with the exception of the sporting breeds (of which Joey would be an example). A number of official reports responded to the ongoing shortage of good working horses, and Britain instituted an official Horse Census in 1917, shortly before the need for them began to decline. By the time this census was discontinued in 1934, the number of horses had decreased from slightly more than two million to just over 1.2 million primarily because machines had replaced working horses.[22] As a result, the "Joey" kind of horse predominates these days in addition to being the "best" quality kind being bred in England at the time of his fictional birth. That he was forced to do both agricultural and military work for which he was ill-suited makes him a phantasmal epitome of the British horse. He's the sort of horse with which those who ride—and their numbers doubled between 1994 and 2008—can most easily form an emotional connection. By 2008, horse-related recreation in Britain had become a seven-billion-pound industry, nearly as much as the 7.2 billion pounds earned from farming in 2009.[23]

The horses of *Equus* typify British horses in the second half of the twentieth century, existing to serve human sport and fantasy. Equine labor has become affective: if *Equus* were written today, perhaps it would be a horse providing therapy to Alan Strang after he blinded six men. Hippotherapy got started in England in the 1980s, around the time that Morpurgo wrote *War Horse*. Tellingly, he and his wife own a therapeutic farm, where he took inspiration from watching a previously silent and angry boy pour out his thoughts to a horse. Even as *War Horse* explicitly deplores military carnage, human and equine both, I see an implicit nostalgia for the clear roles that war created for living beings. In other words, the play mourns the demise of human warfare insofar as wars of the past actively facilitated human agency and inventiveness, necessitating active engagements with one another whether friendly or hostile. Our contemporary service economy built around amusing the rich devalues the manual worker's skills, and these plays position horses as the victims of changing class structures. *Equus* catches them between the religious mother who comes from horsey gentility and the resentful Marxist father, conflating them with the son who—in a twist on the climax of *Oedipus Rex*—strikes out their eyes instead of his own. *War Horse* uses Joey as the "regular Joe" whose bravery and other moral virtues no longer empower him: What good is the horse's pure heart when he's facing down a tank?

With *War Horse* as with *Equus*, it is a human as-horse performance onto which the audience projects its notion of animality—that which is imagined as lost. The character Joey channels sad outrage at manmade war machines at the same time as the puppet Joey channels joyous wonder at manmade theatrical machines. As with *The Lion King*, the theatrical event reinforces but also mystifies *War Horse*'s affective investment in human technology by seeming to be about nature, for which the animal puppets stand in.

## AWE, AWW, AND SUBLIMATION

As theatrical events, *War Horse* and *The Lion King* center on the liveliness and beauty of their puppets. Nick Starr, executive director of the National Theatre, proposes that getting the spectators to invest emotionally in the cane and gauze of a puppet as if it were an actual horse is what enables them to extend themselves empathically into the play.[24] This invocation of empathy and emotion makes a point without being precise, encompassing more than the "imagining into" of conscious perspective taking. For Nussbaum and Goldie, as discussed in chapter 1, the attempt to imagine the First World War from the perspective of a horse could produce only an illusion of empathy, anthropomorphic in spite of the puppeteer's (or author's) best intentions. Handspring's Basil Jones perhaps comes closer to an expanded conception of empathy as *feeling into* when he refers to the puppet as an emotional prosthesis into which the puppeteer pours all of her or his emotion. He describes the puppet as "more you than you," and Adrian Kohler says that the underlying story for any puppet is the struggle to live. "Part of its charm" lies in attempting to be like the spectator.[25] In this formulation, both puppeteer and spectator project emotion onto the cane and gauze of the puppet, and the imaginative effort intensifies their sense of coauthoring. Jones says that the audience participates particularly in the development of Joey's character because the horse does not speak, although the disciplined work of the puppeteers limits the spectrum of emotion and meaning that the spectator can attribute to the puppet.[26] Like Starr, Jones and Kohler seem to describe a response that exceeds empathy as analytic philosophers define it, but they remain understandably vague about how emotions operate or what they are. My close reading of these two productions' opening scenes will offer a more precise and nuanced explanation of the ways in which they engage audience affect, how their narratives package this affective energy as owned and nameable emotions, and the ends that the engagement and containment serve.

*The Lion King* begins with a parade of animals that enter through the audience space and make their way to the stage, culminating in their homage to the newly born princeling cub, Simba. Taymor literally surrounds the audience with this opening spectacle in order to create "this incredible sense of the space," which she believes can transform a theater into "a sacred space."[27] Adults often report crying near the end of the parade when the giraffes enter, and Taymor attributes this response to the simultaneous visibility of animal puppet and human puppeteer: "The fact that as a spectator you're very aware of the human being with the things strapped on, and you see the straps linking the actor to the stilts, that there's no attempt to mask the stilts and make them animal-like shapes—*that's* why people cry."[28] This opening is, quite literally, awesome, a contemporary colloquial replacement for the aesthetic category "sublime." Dacher Keltner and Jonathan Haidt find general agreement across disciplines "that awe involves being in the presence of something powerful, along with associated feelings of submission. Awe also involves a difficulty in comprehension, along with associated feelings of confusion, surprise, and wonder."[29] Keltner and Haidt rely primarily upon the proposition that Irish philosopher Edmund Burke articulated in 1757;

that is, the sublime combines a perception of power with obscurity. Tracing the concept from Longinus's *On the Sublime* in the first century through its development by Joseph Addison, Edmund Burke, and other eighteenth-century philosophers, Emily Brady delineates the two aspects that Immanuel Kant categorized as the "mathematical" and the "dynamic" sublime: the first category comprises objects or other phenomena too vast to be seen all at once or too numerous to count, such as mountains, the sea, and the stars; the second, forces strong enough to destroy us, such as violent storms, raging torrents, or rampaging elephants.[30] Brady argues that art can *depict* but cannot *be* sublime and offers persuasive analyses of painting, sculpture, and film. She exempts architecture and land art from this limitation due to their scale and their engagement with the natural sublime, and she sees a kinship between the sublime and tragedy's arousal of empathetic fear to produce pleasure.[31] Brady does not, however, consider the multisensory immersion that theater provides.

The size and scale of *The Lion King's* opening parade contribute to the power required to render this moment sublime, as does the audience's presumed imaginative transport to the high veldt among creatures large enough to crush them underfoot. Keltner and Haidt's taxonomy would suggest that the creative team's immense accomplishment in designing and bodying forth this spectacle more accurately elicits "admiration," a state in the "awe family" that does not require the same perception of vastness.[32] I would argue, though, that exposing the mechanics enhances the enormity of the spectacle and at the same time, somewhat paradoxically, produces the requisite "challenge to or negation of mental structures when they fail to make sense of an experience of something vast."[33] For the theater audience, a more complete illusion activates a persistent (even if subliminal) search for signs of the artifice responsible for the illusion, whereas purposeful exposure can relax the spectator's vigilance. As Taymor explains, "when you get rid of the masking, then even though the mechanics are apparent, the whole effect is more magical. And this is where theater has a power over film and television. This is absolutely where its magic works. It's not because it's an illusion and we don't know how it's done. It's because we know *exactly* how it's done."[34]

Maurya Wickstrom notes that widely quoted statements such as these serve to differentiate Taymor's staging from "its highly commodified film parent."[35] Her cogent analysis of *The Lion King* as "magical capitalism" in action goes on to quote Taymor from the show's program: "Hidden special effects can lack humanity, but when the human spirit visibly animates an object, we experience a special, almost life-giving connection."[36] Taymor brought to this project not only her considerable skill as a director but also "a rhetoric that attempts to distance the show from the world of the market and of the commodity and surrounds it, instead, in a discourse of 'the human spirit.'"[37] By focusing "entirely on the elation of the spectacle," as Filewod points out, critical reception has tended to legitimize not only the "real and invented interculturalism" of *The Lion King*, but also its "ideology of transnational economics." Thus the giraffes produce an overflow of affect, expressed in widespread crying, which seemingly restores for the audience "a sense of community." Yet Filewod identifies this shared affect as "an effect produced by illusion" and argues that "the more Taymor's *mise-en-scène* exposes the machinations and labors of spectacle, the firmer the illusion that these support."[38] Filewod and Wickstrom adeptly uncover the labors of capital behind the spectacle. But the show also masks its nonpuppet theatrical technology, which in turn veils its multichannel manipulation of audience affect. The show's opening musical number offers one easily delineated example.

*The Lion King* produces tears not through puppetry alone. Even as these magnificent creatures with their visible human operators surround the spectators spatially, the music surrounds them aurally. At first, this is the a capella call and response in Zulu of "Nants' Ingonyama" (Here Comes a Lion) between baboon/shaman Rafiki on stage and rams with curly horns in the audience space, backed by the chorus. The program credits South African composer Lebo M (Morake) with both the chant and the choral arrangement employing a chord progression "sung in close harmony" that Rebecca Coyle and Jon Fitzgerald note is standard for Zulu choral music, familiar to EuroAmerican audiences from its popularization by Paul Simon and Ladysmith Black Mambazo. The vocal timbre and call-response structure also characterize gospel music.[39] First one singer answers Rafiki's summons from the aisle of the main floor seating, then another from the balcony, and then another, more and more animal puppets moving through the audience to the stage. And just as the choral music reaches harmonic resolution and the chant ends, the orchestra—as scored by German composer Hans Zimmer—finally comes in underneath the vocals. Right at the moment of this satisfying upswell of sound, the giraffes cross the stage, bringing spectators to tears. I've argued for awe, but at this point affect briefly overflows any clear emotional category, soon to be contained once again.

Zimmer's orchestral underscoring also creates a bridge to "Circle of Life," which Coyle and Fitzgerald identify as a "typical Elton John-style 'big ballad' number."[40] This familiar musical style guides the audience's heightened affect into familiar emotional channels as the royal lions raise up the baby Simba to be adored by the animal kingdom onstage and the audience, off. The Simba puppet exemplifies "cuteness," which Sianne Ngai defines as "an aesthetic response to the diminutive, the weak, and the subordinate."[41] Cute things tend to be small and rounded or somewhat formless, often squishy, and we refer to them in softened voices with "soft" terms. *The Lion King* begins with awe and brings us to *aww* during its opening song, an affective trajectory supported by the music as well as the spectacular cutification. The opposite of the sublime, the cute seems to want us (our protection, our rescue, our nurturing), and this encourages us to want it—the cute is the perfect commodity. Ngai identifies "cutification" as the epitome of aesthetic objectification: "The more objectified the object, or the more visibly shaped by the affective demands and/or projections of the subject, the cuter."[42] Cute is a feminized category, and the *OED*'s arbiters of English usage held the term itself in mild contempt when they first noted its emergence in nineteenth-century U.S. English. The cute object evokes tenderness, seeming to ask: Are you my mommy?[43]

Tenderness is an "affect" in the sense that the cute object *affects* one in such a way as to produce it. Sara Ahmed offers an example from John Locke: grapes might affect some people in a positive manner; however, these affects are idiosyncratic and, moreover, changeable—the grapes that now affect me with pleasure might at some other point affect me differently due to a change in my physiology, my psychology, or the grapes. The affect can thus also be described in terms of my changeable evaluation of the object.[44] In spite of this contingency, though, affects become standardized and particularly so with relation to cultural artifacts. Ahmed develops a persuasive analysis of the "happy family" to which I will return in chapter 3, just glancing for now at her explanation of the way in which alignment of affects becomes a mechanism of social control: "When happy objects are passed around, it is not necessarily the feeling that passes" but, rather, an orientation to the object as holding the promise of happiness.[45] To translate her formulation into the terms of my discussion, as cute objects circulate, a tender orientation toward these commodities passes around. We might note that, historically, Disney entertainments showed their audiences very few mothers, leaving a convenient gap to be filled by the so-called maternal tenderness of the spectator, whatever the gender. As *The Lion King*'s story commences, the awe-related but rather inchoate affect that flows into tears as the music swells and the giraffes cross the stage gets sucked up into a tender regard for the play's protagonist.

Moving in the other direction, from *aww* to awe, *War Horse* uses cute puppets and a tranquil domestic landscape to draw in its audience. Puppet birds on long poles fly above the openness of the nearly bare stage against a sky with fluffy clouds. The space feels expansive but unthreatening, an impression that the lighting, the sound design, and the ensemble's folk-like songs all enhance.[46] The "Devonshire Carol," for example, begins by invoking "The lambkin in the manger / the light upon the lea." The first two stanzas end with a thrice-repeated "Peace walks upon this blessèd land" and finally "Goodwill upon all earth."[47] Composer Adrian Sutton calls these songs, upon which he collaborated with Songmaker John Tams, "the spirit of the village."[48] The foal puppet grazing within this scene may be not cute in the rounded and squishy way, but his stiff legs give him an endearingly awkward gait, and he has shiny eyes and expressively mobile ears. When the ensemble turn what had seemed to be rudimentary farm implements into a corral to trap him, the puppet's ears and his full-body behaviors register panic, wariness, and then what looks like growing affection as the boy Albert gains his trust with a bucket of oats. The actor playing Albert provides a channel for audience affect—like the boy, I responded to Joey's distress with my own distressed tenderness. I wanted the horse to run free and to be with his mother; failing that, I wanted to take her place in providing comfort. This response to the distress of the cute entity primes the spectator for sympathetic outrage later on in the show, when the adult Joey undergoes much more extreme ordeals. What Ahmed calls its "stickiness" keeps the affect available for replay in a different register.[49]

The taming accomplished and the protective affection of boy and spectator secured, the play makes a narrative jump, and I gave my first gasp of awe as suddenly the full-grown Joey puppet rushed toward the audience out of the fog upstage, slightly larger than life and with fully jointed legs. The cute persists alongside the awesome, though, in the endearing goose puppet always present for scenes at the Devonshire farm. Soliciting attention, following the humans around, the goose occupies the slightly distasteful edge of cute, glimpsed when Rose Narracott sprinkles feed for the goose but then slams the farmhouse door in its face. The squishy deformability of the cute object that solicits our tenderness hovers on the edge of eliciting disgust, an affect that easily tags along just underneath tenderness itself.[50] But affect is slippery as well as sticky, so an indulgent but demeaning contempt at-

Figure 1. *War Horse* puppets face to face at the New London Theatre. Photo © Brinkhoff/Mögenburg.

taches to the cute goose and frees our tender concern for the now-awesome horse from the taint of feminization, thus reassuring us that the tenderness is strong, pure, and good rather than abject and needy. Figure 1 shows the horse and the goose face to face. One puppeteer can be seen inside the chest, just behind the horse's front legs; another, outside, guides the head down toward the goose and controls its expressive ears. Costumed as a groom, he easily fits into the human surroundings. The goose's wings are folded in, the strings that control them extending outside the frame parallel to the rod connecting to the tail and pushing it toward the horse, its legs encompassed within a wheel.

Because Handspring, like Taymor, leaves the puppets' mechanics visible, spectators remain aware that humans have created these horses and give them life, from moment to moment, with great care taken for behavioral verisimilitude. New puppeteers first learn, as a team of three, to make a puppet breathe and then practice the movement and behavior of horses, so that they can behave in "unpredictable" horsey ways. They visit stables, watch DVDs, study horse gaits and horse psychology. Jones calls it "a total immersion":

Together with the rehearsals the puppeteers have two months of training before they see their first audience. Over scores of performances, the puppeteers become shamans of the horse. Their intuition as to what their fellow puppeteers are about to do becomes finely tuned. This triple performance is a pretty special event to watch on stage.[51]

*War Horse* engages its spectators in multiple levels of perception simultaneously: One sees the horses and follows the story, but one also watches—perhaps with less conscious awareness—the finely tuned physical performance of three puppeteers responding to one another as they animate the horse. Consider the team who first brought Joey's friend Topthorn to the stage in New York: Ariel Heller told the *Wall Street Journal* that "the audience tends to see the thought of the horse through the head." He was responsible for manipulating the horse's ears to "tell the emotional story," at the same time focusing on the horse's eyes and "imagining what the horse is seeing." Joby Earle, the heart (that is, chest and two front legs), functioned as a "middle man . . . throw[ing] impulses back and forth" as well as being "the main controller of the breath of the horse." The hind, Enrico Wey, described his job as "reading what Ariel and Joby are feeling, as well as pushing back and taking stock of the full stage picture" because "a lot of the angle work is based on where the hind is placed."[52]

Although Jones describes the horses as "real" rather than anthropomorphic, and the creators and performers go to great lengths to mimic horses with an impressive accuracy, I would suggest that the excitement that this spectacle generates for a spectator has as much to do with humans as with horses. I propose that *War Horse* channels our affection for the equine species but masks the degree to which that affection remains self-involved: the play's story does concern actual rather than metaphorical or anthropomorphic horses, but the theatrical experience centers on audiences' fascination with human engineering and cooperative effort, evident not only within the teams of puppeteers but also among the creative team as a whole. Scenic designer Rae Smith, for example, relies upon some theatrical technology from the nineteenth century as the stage floor's turntable rotates to create a greater sense of movement when Joey is forced to pull first a plow and then some heavy artillery. Less expected, the turntable later rises up to create the trenches below it—for me, the most awe-inspiring effect in the show. Figure 2 shows Joey entangled in barbed wire at the front of the raised turntable, his outside puppeteer kneeling to bring his head to the lip of the platform.

Figure 2. *War Horse*, directed by Marianne Elliott and Tom Morris; book by Michael Morpurgo; play by Nick Stafford; designed by Rae Smith; puppets by Handspring Puppet Company. Production at the New London Theatre, London, 2008. Photo © Simon Annand/ArenaPAL; www.arenapal.com www.arenapal.com.

Skeletal horse legs seem to be dripping from wheels in the illuminated area underneath, and soldiers can be seen on either side, one of them using a periscope to view the horse above him. Smoke billows from the back of the stage, and a projected image of fencing illuminated against a darkened sky hovers over the scene.

Smith used graphic art techniques even more antiquated than the turntable technology to create her own version of the sketchbook kept by Major Nicholls, the soldier who takes Joey into war: she drew by hand with pencil the English and French scenery as well as the horses, the style progressing from a bucolic realism for the countryside in 1911 Devon to a "dark grainy foreboding" for the waves of the crossing to Calais. The medium changes from pencil to charcoal erased in "sweeping strokes" to create the battlefield's explosions. As the war shatters Nicholls's world, the drawings fragment into cubist planes and slashes of rain, and the battle scenery takes its style from Vorticism, a British avant-garde movement contemporary with World War

I.[53] The sketches complete, Smith tore out a strip of paper, mirroring Albert's action in the drama: he receives the sketchbook after Nicholls's death and tears out a drawing of Joey to take along as he goes off in search of his horse. Smith suspended an enlarged version of this strip above the stage floor as a projection surface, about halfway up in the vertical space. During the opening scenes, filmic clouds turn it into the sky against which we see bird puppets in flight, and at times it presents line drawings of scenic elements such as trees and fences. At key moments, though, animated drawings of horses duplicate in miniature the action on stage, echoing and augmenting it—in fact, the projections are generally moving at least slightly. The company 59 Productions transformed Smith's drawings into digital animation that retains its hand-drawn look and modestly takes a supporting role rather than calling attention to itself.[54] All of *War Horse*'s visual elements have a look in keeping with the puppetry—what Jones refers to as "up-to-the-minute eighteenth century technology," sharing a nostalgic appeal that upstages the production's up-to-the-minute twenty-first-century technology.

Much of *The Lion King*'s "magical" staging also remains mechanically simple—as Filewod notes, using a number of effects developed by Nicola Sabbatini in the early seventeenth century such as the turning cylinders of the wildebeest stampede that tramples the elder Lion King Mufasa to death.[55] These commercial successes follow the pattern of their genre predecessors in effacing their technological sophistication. As Siropoulos points out, *Cats* resembled midcentury "poor" theater in its emphasis on the performers' physicality but depended for its impact upon a "groundbreaking and most powerful use of automated lighting" by David Hersey and Andrew Lloyd Webber's equally "groundbreaking" sound design, created in collaboration with Abe Jacob and Martin Levan.[56] And Walter Kerr wrote in 1975 that the avant-garde only seemed to be dead: Peter Brook had returned to Shakespeare, but his work and Jerzy Grotowski's influence lived on in *Equus*, on Broadway.[57] That play lived on in regional, college, and community theaters before resurfacing as a star vehicle for Daniel Radcliffe in a 2007 revival, bigger, glossier, and more expensive-looking: the poor theater become rich and then much richer still. *War Horse* carries this trend quite a lot further—the documentary *Making War Horse* quite amusingly includes brief footage of an early workshop with actors wearing *Equus* hooves, and Marianne Elliott actually refers to it as "poor theater" due to the puppetry's visible mechanics.

Disney and the National Theatre built *The Lion King* and *War Horse*, respectively, upon a solid foundation of avant-garde theatrical experiment. Kohler and Jones brought roughly twenty-five years of concerted technical development to their horses, raising the puppetry significantly above the level achieved by the daemons for the National's earlier production of *His Dark Materials*. Handspring Puppet Company, which they formed in 1981 with two fellow art-school graduates, began with school performances and bus tours out of its Cape Town base, then teamed with theater companies from other African countries and with various South African directors.[58] Their collaborations with artist and director William Kentridge—from *Woyzeck on the Highveld* (1992) to *Confessions of Zeno* (2002) and multiple projects in between—toured internationally, as did *Tall Horse* (2004).[59] *War Horse* represented a departure not only in its handsome financial returns but also in their designing puppets with which they did not perform as puppeteers.[60]

Like Handspring, Taymor came to the commercial theater from an impressive avant-garde theatrical career. She studied at the Ecole Jacques Lecoq in the early 1970s, then at Oberlin College with Herbert Blau— source of the ideograph concept that has remained central to her creative system—after which she spent several years in Indonesia. In the early 1980s, Taymor began creating puppets and other visual elements for directors in New York and launched her illustrious career as director/designer with a 1984 production of Carlo Gozzi's *The King Stag*.[61] This work, much of it in collaboration with composer Elliot Goldenthal, enjoyed critical acclaim and drew the attention of the Disney Corporation, which brought to Taymor not only healthy financial compensation and savvy marketing but also the opportunity to develop her work more fully than had been possible for previous projects. Discussing the shortcomings of her first prototype puppets for *The Lion King* in 1996, for example, Taymor notes the tremendous advantage of access to this producer's deep pockets: "See, a good thing about Disney is that they have money to do the next workshop."[62]

Analyzing the marvelous puppetry of *The Lion King* alongside that of *War Horse* makes clear that the same mechanism is at work in both: audiences respond to the visible workmanship of these puppets in a manner not unlike the response one might have to artisanal cheese, craft beer, or hand-knit sweaters. In all of these cases, responding to the visible work makes it easy to overlook the invisible technologies that bring the worked-upon surface into view—such as the sophisticated lighting and sound systems in these theaters or the infrastructure that enables me to order handmade crafts on Etsy. As far as interspecies relations are concerned, foregrounding the human bodies that animate these highly inventive but seemingly simple puppets—which are of course not simple at all—easily becomes a celebration of "the human spirit" that masks a human disregard for the nonhuman creatures being crowded out of the world we live in. Just as their narrative structures do, the spectacular components of these hit shows reassure their human audiences that they can occupy an ethical position in the circle of life while remaining at the top of a comfortable species hierarchy.

## THE ELEPHANT IN THE UNRELIABLE BESTIARY

Deke Weaver's ongoing project *The Unreliable Bestiary* unsettles any such reassurance but does so in a strategically engaging and even ingratiating manner. Weaver describes this series of performances and documentary materials as "an ark of stories about animals, our relationships with them, and the worlds they inhabit."[63] Inspired by the medieval bestiary, "which gave every living thing a spiritual purpose," Weaver set about creating a performance "for every letter of the alphabet—the letter representing a particular animal or habitat. Or idea." He began with "charismatic megafauna":

> These are the animals that are the stars in our fairy tales, cartoons, zoos, and national parks. Usually big, usually mammals, usually part of a long history in our human imaginations. People tend to empathize more with these sorts of animals because we have a lot in common with these particular creatures—family life, play, fear, etc. Maybe more in common with these animals than what you might see (at first) with snakes and reptiles.[64]

*MONKEY* (2009), *ELEPHANT* (2010), and *WOLF* (2013) premiered near his home base in Champaign-Urbana, Illinois, and Weaver has subsequently toured the full pieces or solo adaptations of the material to other venues and made "interpretive documentation" available on DVD. Weaver assumes multiple personae in each piece, at some times the titular beast and at others human, telling stories, enacting them, and commenting on them. His collaborator Jennifer Allen choreographs and codirects as well as performing.

*ELEPHANT* bears a slight resemblance to *War Horse* and *The Lion King* in its use of an impressively large animal puppet, but the affective hooks that keep the audience engaged are quite different, and the narrative framing provokes unease rather than comfort. This framework holds two primary narratives: the story of a circus elephant named Hero killed by "bored Lutherans" to end its rampage during a South Dakota blizzard in 1916 and the story of Weaver's quest for up-close elephant interaction at a sanctuary in Thailand. The piece is structured like sedimentary rock, with four overlapping layers of Hero's story and multiple layers of Deke's so-called training as a mahout (elephant handler). As with a geological formation, this structure breaks and erodes, and the layers mix and blur at these points of fissure.

The performance recorded on DVD took place in the Stock Pavilion at the University of Illinois, accommodating a cast of fifty and audiences of roughly 200 people at each performance, with two ninety-foot screens for video projection. Weaver describes the unpretentious pavilion as "a cavernous arena chosen for its associations with 4-H Clubs, circuses, state fairs, and Roman amphitheatre battles." During a twenty-minute preshow period, the audience filters into one end of the pavilion, for the time being closed off from the rest of the space. One of the smaller screens in this area (roughly nine by six feet) shows video of activities at a "mammoth museum"; another, a background of leaves and branches over which information about elephants scrolls: that their footsteps make no sound, that they "communicate telepathically" and "sense the seismic reverberations of thunderstorms, hundreds of miles away," that four of them "hold up the earth while standing on a giant turtle," and that they're "cute and cuddly."[65] Each piece of information is presented as a question ("Is it true that . . ?") and simply affirmed ("Yes. It is true") regardless of the source's reliability: Pliny the Elder's description of a dragon drinking the elephant's cold blood to counteract the desert heat (164) is not differentiated from a classification of Asian elephant calls from the *Journal of the Acoustical Society of America* (166). Chris Peck's sound montage samples "elephant rumbles and trumpets, Thai pop music, cowboy music, chains, and the Thai Elephant Conservation Center" (164). Four dancers play on the pavilion's railings, "quietly singing elephant jump-rope songs and Thai nursery school elephant songs" (163). Noting that they wear gray jeans, Marissa Perel writes: "The clothing doesn't give anything away, but as they continue tilting their heads and necks, it becomes evident that they are in fact embodying baby elephants."[66] The stage direction supports this description and adds "part circus roustabouts, part teenage cool-kids, part five-year-olds" (163). Over the course of the show, these dancers perform as young elephants being trained for circus routines, guide the audience into a new seating configuration, and finally operate the elephant puppet.

As the show begins, Weaver impersonates the dead elephant Hero on a visit from the afterlife for a talk-show interview, wearing a set of biggish ears and a tiny trunk along with a suit patterned in pinstripes/elephant hide. Hero comes off as a fast-talking rambler, free associating from the nuanced differences between types of cheese to various words that designate kinds of snow, types of camels, and finally types of elephants. Then a video segment about money and elephant poaching gradually begins to connect intangible financial considerations to the tangible environment that elephants require and the ways that human development creates pressure on elephant populations. Hero gets to the point: "Language can change the landscape. A single word can completely alter a biosphere" (170). The word he analyzes is "cull," as in killing elephants to reduce the herd to a size that the landscape can accommodate. He describes the elephant as a big canary in the environmental coal mine and illustrates with the example of young bull elephants with post-traumatic stress disorder raping rhinos. But like the preshow text, Hero is unreliable—we don't know what *not* to believe as he shares information about elephant size and the amount an elephant eats and drinks, tells a story about an elephant killing a lion and another about an elephant keeper suffocated by dung from the elephant to whom he administered an enema. Finally the talk-show host (Gary Ambler) pushes a reluctant Hero to talk about his lonely, snowy death. A quick run-through of historical elephant deaths in the early twentieth-century United States takes the conversation back to the earlier presence of mammoths in North America and surprisingly characterizes the continent as an elephant graveyard, where Hero could pay tribute to his ancestors. Running through the snow in 1916, "maybe [he] was thinking, it's a good day to die" (174).

This opening segment establishes an unstable affect along with skepticism about the information on offer—in direct contrast to the commercial puppet spectacular, the awesome and the cute keep the audience off balance rather than drawing them in. Their banter amuses, but neither Hero nor the talk-show host seems particularly likeable. Their conversation does create an appetite to get closer to elephants, though—to get at the "truth." And as they talk about the deaths of Topsy (publicly electrocuted in Coney Island, 1903), Mary (hung in Tennessee, 1916), Jumbo (hit by a train, 1916), and Norma Jean (struck by lightning, 1916), the canvas panels that block off the main part of the pavilion slowly rise (173), and the performance shifts in such a way as to suggest that revelation might be imminent. Another twenty people run through the space at this point, rearranging hay bales to provide new audience seating in between video of the snow-covered prairie on the gigantic screens, all of this backed by drumming and enlivened by "circuslike colored spotlights" (174). Neither the script nor the DVD can quite capture the atmosphere, of course. Perel reports on the way that the space and the sound design affected her:

> It was enough just to be sitting in this place where livestock pass every-day [sic] to feel a mixture of awe and melancholia about animals and what we do with them. Peck's use of sound shaped this atmospheric quality. The almost imperceptible echoing of the sounds of chains crashing, waves lapping, snow falling, foot-falls on various grounds, and, of course, elephant cries and trumpets, created a resonance that brought the audience into the events of those distant places.[67]

Another audience member's detailed description includes the olfactory and tactile appeal of fresh hay: "u put your hands down and hay would stick to your palms; I just loved that part most."[68]

Spectators get a whimsical taste of elephant-ness as they join hands and pass, like circus elephants joined trunk to tail, into the pavilion to take seats on the hay bales. The four dancers serve them cups of water, both an act of communion and a reminder of resource scarcity in elephants' habitats. Perel notes: "This is a small gesture, but with stark lighting in the otherwise darkened pavilion and blue light from two massive screens on each side, the pouring of water became a haunting symbol of this basic elemental re-source." The audience's physical participation in this busy transition gives way to a contemplative mood as the sound quiets to "a low drone, spare bells" (174). This interlude epitomizes the piece's layering of affect: projected text presents the story of Hero's death for a second time, colored now by video that places the audience in Hero's position, surrounded by a snowy farm in the midst of prairie. Sandwiched in between the raw facts ("nine hours and three hundred bullets") and his likely thoughts ("Hero would have had memories of the warm jungle and a large family of mothers and aunts. What a strange thing to die alone, in a blizzard"), information about the role of spindle cells in elephant as well as human cognition supports the notion that a human audience can empathize with the elephant. This subdued pre-sentation leaves space for the spectators' as-elephant feelings instead of asking them to react to a filmed elephant or an as-elephant performance. The sound score and the relative darkness encourage a tight visual focus on a

Figure 3. Deke Weaver's *ELEPHANT* at the Stock Pavilion, University of Illinois, Urbana-Champaign, 2010. Photo by Valerie Oliveiro. Courtesy of Deke Weaver.

single action within this newly vast space: a papier-mâché white elephant, four feet high but looking small in the vast space, lowers from the ceiling. Figure 3 gives a sense of the scale, with the elephant figure descending over four people putting hay bales into place, dwarfed by huge screens on either side of the space that show from above a snow-covered patchwork of agricultural landscape, a line of spectators coming to their seats below each screen. When this interlude evaporates, a layer of melancholy sticks to the story fragments and the ideas.

The dancers, now sequin clad, parade the elephant out of the arena. Weaver enters in Mahout-Deke persona to tell the story of his experience at the Thai Elephant Conservation Center. In contrast to the snowy Great Plains, the video of elephants against forest greenery gives the impression at first of a situation more natural. But as Weaver's monologue and the supporting video develop, this impression gives way to a more complete picture of mahout-training tourism; in particular, making it clear that these conservation centers exist to provide employment for the mahouts who previously worked with their elephants in logging operations now outlawed in

Thailand. The message is pointed: the close and cooperative relationship between the mahout and his elephant, what Weaver got a taste of in Thailand and reports enjoying like a five-year-old, is built upon the violence of animal training and no more natural than the circus. As they move around the space, the baby-elephant dancers add another layer of reinforcement, first playing with soccer balls, then walking in formation with the balls between their feet as if shackled—they echo the shackled elephant feet on the video as well as the dejection of the elephant filmed from behind against a grassy background, top and bottom of his body outside the frame, repetitively lifting a section of chain with his trunk and dragging it across in front of him from left to right.

Just as the snow from Hero's earlier free association recurred in his snowy death, the camels return in the story of Semiramis, queen of Assyria, who displaced her husband as ruler and attempted to counter the war elephants of India: she had camels outfitted with ox hides sewn into elephant shapes and supported by scaffolding to create the illusion of a 20,000-elephant army—but the Indian elephants, trusting their mahouts, charged through the puppet army and destroyed it.[69] Deke, now just an elephant head, ears at his shoulders and a big rod-operated trunk attached to his waist, interrupts this story to explain that he learned about Hero from a friend who comes from the circus family that owned (and killed) the elephant. At this major point of fissure, the fragmented dramatic logic of the piece mixes together with the associative logic that operates across the several dramatic narratives. The narrative, in falling apart, pushes the spectators back from the spectacle, a disengagement not quite Brechtian, offering no particular clarity. Some of the questionable elephant truths from the preshow return in song: Peck accompanies himself on ukulele for an elephant-and-dragon tune. In the otherwise darkened space, animated versions of Eadweard Muybridge's locomotion studies cross the screens in procession—beginning with a mouse, ending with an elephant. The sound grows ominous with Peck and a small chorus singing the catalog of elephant sounds while the baby elephants dance and the video screens show extreme close-ups of elephant skin—some of it on living elephants; some, discrete bits of hide. The language and the images accumulate and prime the audience to seek meaning in the repetition.

Weaver returns now costumed as "Anastasia," wearing a curly gray wig and driving a mobility scooter. She tells for a third time the story of Hero's death, backed by video of Elkton, South Dakota, with a brief clip of the actual Anastasia holding up an overnight bag made from Hero's hide. This gives way to Gary Ambler reading a letter from the circus owner's son, who was present that day in 1916, telling the story for a fourth time with much greater detail, this time illustrated by Claymation on the big video screens. Ambler's voice is hushed, nearly a whisper, the affect dampened, and the crude animation somehow makes it easier to pay attention to the horrifying and dramatic details of the story. Xs inscribe the clay eyes when they are shot out, one after the other. One can feel the first-person narrator's fear during the chase after the rampaging elephant but also the elephant's rage, fear, and bewilderment. Then Mahout-Deke talks about riding his Thai elephant Jojo after the elephant had been injured by a substitute mahout during a rampage, and this narrative helps to answer questions the chorus has just posed, in song, about Hero's death—"Why did you go for the elephant? . . . Why did you chase that elephant, when he went stray? Why didn't you let that elephant just get away?"[70] There is no place for an elephant to go. Where could Hero "go" in South Dakota, in 1916, when he ran away? Where could Jojo live in Thailand, aside from the sanctuary? This is the question that War Horse avoids: Where could Joey run free yet not starve to death— the dilemma facing the remaining wild horses in North America? There seems to be no way out of our species intertwining, since humans have so thoroughly altered other species' habitats.

At last the elephant puppet (created by Andy Warfel) crosses the space as shown in figure 4, twelve feet high, a dancer under its framework at each leg and one in the middle, the mechanics visible as with Taymor's and Handspring's creations. The moment is perhaps awesome—one can only imagine the effect based on documentation. Matthew Green recounts a friend's response: "Her breath was literally taken away when, in a climactic moment, a huge elephant puppet, controlled from within by performers, appeared to the amazement of the assembled crowd. She looked across the table at me, her eyes still wide with wonder even after all this time."[71] Doing nothing beyond crossing the space, this puppet carries intact the echoes of Semiramis's puppet army, of Hero, of Jojo. This immense human-made idea of an elephant is the only elephant we can ever really know.

As Perel notes, we laugh at Weaver's stories: she likens his delivery at times to A Prairie Home Companion, his studied, folksy unpretentiousness part of the formula for success. Her appreciative description of the choreography—which is barely visible in the video documentation— suggests that the dancers as baby elephants offer up the cute for consump-

Figure 4. Elephant puppet designed by Andy Warfel in Deke Weaver's *ELEPHANT*, 2010. Photo by Valerie Oliveiro. Courtesy of Deke Weaver.

tion, and I'm reminded of the source for my own affective attachment to elephants ever since I was about six years old, when one was born in captivity for the first time at the Portland zoo. (He just recently passed away. RIP, Packy.) Baby elephants are round and adorable. They are far too large for "squishiness" at human hands, but elephant images certainly scale down effectively. I had a collection of little elephant figurines, cute without being squishy. Weaver's narrative of elephant training transfers any remnant of contempt from the deformable elephant image to ourselves as the collective agent of deformation. *ELEPHANT* leaves its audience with awe and with questions: How can we not only keep these—and other—creatures alive, but find a more ethical path forward in our interspecies relations?

*The Lion King* and *War Horse* stir up audience affect—both openly and subliminally—and skillfully direct it into familiar emotional frameworks, resolving in a reassuring uplift. One knows how one should feel when watching these shows, and their theatricality keeps the audience fascinated even when they might scorn the sentimentality. *The Unreliable Bestiary*, in contrast, poses an affective challenge for its audience. Some of the emotional packaging is familiar, and it's clear that Weaver wants his audience to care about species extinction, but he doesn't prescribe a clear trajectory for the caring. *ELEPHANT* offers no reassurance, only the hope that our affective engagement will make a difference. One audience member reported being "dragged through every alcove of human emotion and left the event a very different person than when I entered";[72] another more fully articulated the power of this affective engagement after seeing a solo version of *WOLF*:

> As a scientist and longtime leader in the conservation field I have had to keep a tight rein on my emotions. I frequently am called names and threatened but through it I have had to remain calm and reasoned. The wolf piece made me realize for that moment how much I have repressed and how angry I was about the ignorance and injustice I had seen associated with the wolf. The old and comfortable mask came down quickly afterwards but it was good for me to know that this other set of feelings was still there as well.[73]

As *WOLF* puts it, our experience of other species and our behavior toward them is mediated by stories—myths, folk and fairy tales, children's books, cartoons, adventure yarns, film and theater—and "we need better stories."[74] Weaver challenges his audience to imagine those stories.

# CHAPTER 3

# Performing as Autists

In 2012, the National Theatre commissioned an adaptation of Mark Haddon's 2003 novel *The Curious Incident of the Dog in the Night-Time*. The production sold out its initial run in the Cottesloe that summer and played to 40,000 additional viewers in cinemas through a live-performance simulcast. In March 2013 the show reopened for a commercial run in London's West End, winning Olivier awards for best new play, director, actor, actress in a supporting role, set design, lighting design, and sound design. The Broadway production that opened in October 2014 won Tony awards for best play, director, actor, scenic design, and lighting design. The protagonist of *Curious Incident* displays features that audiences associate with Asperger syndrome (AS), although he never uses this label but describes himself as having "behavioral problems." The plot gradually reveals that the dissolution of his parents' marriage set its events in motion, with clear indications that the challenge of raising an atypical child in turn contributed to the marriage's failure.

In its staging, *Curious Incident* inventively shares its protagonist's experience of the world. Yet I will argue that both its postrealist innovation and its about-ness are contained by the dramatic narrative that characterizes a genre I'm calling the autism family drama (AFD). As I see it, the play's success as well as its shortcomings are bound up with its investment in the family romance, and it structures this romance in particularly neoliberal terms: the parents function as technicians of their son's self-fulfillment, which ideally leads to independence and (at least the possibility of) economic advancement. The theatrical event elicits affective investment in the neoliberal happy family and cruel optimism with respect to the stated goals of its protagonist. Enjoying particular favor for its capacity to stir up affect, the family dominates drama—especially post-Ibsen domestic realism, often enough shoring up an idealized family with a plot that resolves domestic problems. Even plays that expose the family's dysfunctions, provide escape routes for its discontents, or reimagine its contours tend to maintain its status as "happy." As Sara Ahmed explains, this does not mean that the family "causes happiness" or even that it "affects us in a good way," but rather that "we share an orientation toward the family as being good, as being what promises happiness in return for loyalty."[1] Lauren Berlant calls this kind of attachment to something that we may not fully believe possible or that may not in fact be good for us *cruel optimism*.[2] This chapter analyzes three realist AFDs that adhere to cruel optimism with respect to the family even while attempting to torque its structures, one that explicitly refuses it, and two zany post-realist deconstructions of the family romance.

## THE CURIOUS INCIDENCE OF DRAMATIZED AUTISM

Interest in autism on stage owes a lot to two notions: first, that we're in the midst of an autism epidemic; second, that autism is an empathy deficit that results from faulty wiring rather than being a product of the environment. Depictions of autism in works of art and entertainment have grown more common with increasing frequency of diagnosis, but terminology has scarcely become more precise or agreed upon since Eugene Bleuler's first use of the term "autism" in 1908 to describe what he understood as an uncommunicative patient's schizophrenic withdrawal from reality into a private world.[3] The term came into wider use after Leo Kanner in the United States and Hans Asperger in Vienna, independently of one another, wrote about "autistic" behavior among children in the 1940s.[4] Kanner considered this relatively rare condition to be a form of childhood schizophrenia, and a narrow definition limited the diagnosis to approximately one child in two thousand. Diagnoses began to increase during the postwar years. In 1946, for example, the chief of psychiatry at Bellevue Hospital in New York, Loretta Bender, described one hundred children diagnosed as schizophrenic who manifested behaviors that would now be labeled autistic: echolalia, unresponsiveness, and the types of repetitive movement now commonly referred to as stimming. In 1954, she saw 850 such children, 250 of these cases new since 1951.[5] Bruno Bettelheim's *The Empty Fortress*, published in 1967, popularized a conception of autism as a psychological disorder caused by cold and intellectual parents—particularly mothers.[6] During this same period, theater and film channeled increasing concern about children outside the borders defined by human language and sociality toward historical accounts of feral children. Influential treatments by Peter Handke (*Kaspar*, 1967), François Truffaut (*The Wild Child*, 1970), and Werner Herzog (*The Enigma of Kaspar Hauser*, 1974) all explored social integration and manipulation by means of language but paid no particular attention to the contemporary existence of nonspeaking or atypically communicating children who occupied the shadows of representation, often shut away in mental institutions. Autism had not yet moved into the foreground of popular culture.

Research continued to expand and diagnoses to increase, and in 1980 the American Psychiatric Association for the first time included autistic disorder in the *Diagnostic and Statistical Manual of Mental Disorders, Third Edition* (DSM-III).[7] In England, Lorna Wing examined Hans Asperger's cases from 1944 alongside her own research and in 1981 proposed substituting the term "Asperger syndrome" for his "autistic psychopathy." She and Judith Gould went on to propose that autism comprises a spectrum characterized by a "triad of impairments": social, communicative, and imaginative. Wing contributed these influential ideas to DSM-III-R, published in 1987.[8] Temple Grandin's first account of her own autistic experience, *Emergence: Labeled Autistic*, had just been published in 1986, and the film *Rain Man* (1988) quickly became a touchstone for the popular conception of autism as characterized by a sweet simplemindedness and a particular savant skill—in the case of the film's protagonist, a freakish counting ability. DSM-IV (1994) changed the umbrella term to Autism Spectrum Disorder and expanded its criteria to include three separate diagnoses: autistic disorder, Asperger syndrome, and pervasive developmental disorder–not otherwise specified (PDD NOS).

As autism settled into place as a zeitgeist condition early in the twenty-first century, *The Curious Incident of the Dog in the Night-Time* replaced *Rain Man* as its cultural referent. This young-adult novel began to inform and even determine what many people understand autism to be: *Curious Incident* has been used as a classroom text for middle and high school as well as provided to policemen, nonspecialist teachers, and others who might need to deal with autistic individuals. By 2000 the incidence of autism spectrum disorder diagnoses in the United States had grown to one child in 110; by 2010, one in 68.[9] DSM-V (2013) omits the subcategory diagnoses introduced in 1994 and instead uses numbers to indicate the severity of the autism.[10]

Yet Asperger syndrome, its acronym AS, and the adjective or noun "Aspie" so thoroughly infiltrated the popular lexicon over the previous two decades that the subcategories persist unabated. Stuart Murray suggests that autism serves as the emblematic symptom for the postmodern condition, much as schizophrenia did for modernism, and Ian Hacking likens its literary function to nineteenth-century tuberculosis as "the pathology of the oughts."[11] Murray analyzes the literary genre that *Curious Incident* exemplifies, featuring a "sentimental savant" who enriches the human understanding and experience of the neurotypical characters and—more crucially—of readers or spectators.[12] This is an instance of what David Mitchell and Sharon Snyder delineate as the prosthetic function of disability common in narrative structures: stories center on a deviance that they identify, explain, and either purge or remedy and thus normalize.[13] The autism family drama substitutes autism for the secret that typically drives the plot in realist drama, where the interactions comprising the plot expose a past action that the protagonist has kept hidden, creating a dramatic conflict that comes to crisis and resolution. Like Nora's past forgery in Ibsen's *A Doll House*, for example, autism functions as a visible disruption of the kind of automatic and assumed empathy that makes social life run smoothly. The disruption facilitates dramatic engagement with a separate social issue—forgery was not Ibsen's central concern. Mitchell and Snyder observe that "within literary narratives, disability serves as an interruptive force that confronts cultural truisms."[14] Just as physically disabled characters within ableist narratives most often serve to illuminate the psychological and ethical sphere of normalcy, the autistic character typically reveals the shortcomings of the cognitive and social mainstream "rather than allowing for the presentation of autism within the terms of the autistic individual."[15]

Haddon's novel takes its reader through the thought processes of its first-person narrator as he solves a dog-murder mystery, passes his Maths A-Level exam, reunites with his mother, and begins to reconcile with his father.[16] Fifteen-year-old Christopher Boone displays a collection of sensory and cognitive difficulties: he cannot stand to be touched; he excels at math and accumulating facts, but people and their emotions confuse him; prior to the story's beginning, he has never independently left the block on which he lives. He must learn to ask for directions and to screen out the overwhelming sights and sounds first of the railway station in rural Swindon and then of Paddington Station and the London tube. Small-scale domestic tragedy—the dissolution of his parents' marriage—lurks in the background of the novel at the distance that this literary genre imagines it existing for the protagonist. Isolated and depressed, Judy has drifted into an affair with her neighbor and, two years before the story begins, gone off with him to live in London. Rather than attempting to explain the situation, Ed has told Christopher that she died. The novel purports to be Christopher's notebook, and its first portion gradually establishes these background details as he sets out to discover who killed the neighbor's dog, Wellington. When Ed confiscates the notebook in an effort to stop this investigation, Christopher's search for it uncovers a box of letters that Judy has sent him. This discovery leads, in turn, to Ed's confession that he killed Wellington, to Christopher's journey alone to find Judy in London, and to the end of her new relationship. Mark Osteen characterizes this as the "fairly typical path" for a bildungsroman, with the unique feature of assuming an autistic voice to trace its steps.[17] Even in adopting this voice, though, the novel depends upon the ability of its presumably neurotypical reader to fill out scenes beyond Christopher's matter-of-fact narration.

References to AS pervade analysis of the novel, although its fit with this diagnosis has been the subject of considerable critique.[18] Haddon says that he did next to no research on autism for fear that it would limit his creativity: "I know very little about the subject [autism]. I did no research for *Curious Incident* other than photographing the interiors of Swindon and Paddington stations, reading Oliver Sacks' essay about Temple Grandin and a handful of newspaper and magazine articles about, or by, people with Asperger's and autism." He further explains, "I deliberately didn't add to this list. Imagination always trumps research. I thought that if I could make Christopher real to me then he'd be real to readers. I gave him some rules to live by and some character traits and opinions, all of which I borrowed from people I know, none of whom would be labelled as having a disability. Judging by the reaction, it seems to have worked."[19] One might note that Bettelheim's imaginary construct, the refrigerator mother, also "worked" remarkably well for a previous generation.

Unlike Haddon, members of the creative team for the National Theatre's adaptation conducted preparatory research at four schools for students with autism. The brief documentary filmed as an introduction to the *NTLive* broadcast of the Cottesloe production shows actor Luke Treadaway participating in some of these visits,[20] and AS features prominently in publicity and program essays. To bring this world to theatrical life, director Marianne Elliott drew on some of the same strengths that she brought to *War Horse* as codirector; that is, inventive physical theater techniques take the place of autistic first-person narration just as spectacular puppetry replaced the horse's perspective in the earlier production. Even as the adaptation sincerely attempts to show the sensory overload that Christopher experiences and his ways of coping with this, the parents' embodied presence on stage and the use of realistic acting for central domestic scenes move the family drama to the foreground.[21]

The opening scene sets up the production's stylistic variety. A white grid projected on the dark stage is divided by both a diagonal X and a vertical cross, with a thicker band of light lining the upper V of the X. At the juncture of this V and the cross the word "now" appears. This grid establishes Christopher's mathematical mind, suggesting that he projects a set of coordinates onto the world in order to graph its occurrences and remove them from chaos. A percussive electronic sound score evokes data processing to reinforce this symbolism even as it builds anticipation. Actors enter quietly and seat themselves on white cubes at the perimeter. The volume increases, with even louder crashes interspersed. Then the lights go out, the sound continuing to intensify until a sudden flash of bright light illuminates the German shepherd lying on its side at the "now" position. The simple grid is still present, but the projected V and X are gone: the "now" that they marked has happened. This sensory flood of sounds and lights gives the audience a feeling of Christopher's experience even as the pool of light expands to reveal Christopher (Luke Treadaway) kneeling in front of the dog, staring at it, hands lightly clenched just above his thighs, vibrating slightly. He is clearly tense and upset. The audience has multiple, mutually reinforcing channels for understanding this character, many of which—such as this last—depend upon reading conventional postural cues of the type that (according to popular conceptions of AS) Christopher himself would be unable to interpret.

His teacher Siobhan (Niamh Cusack, seated on one of the cubes) now reads the opening of Christopher's book, which describes the tableau on stage. This device provides aural variety and introduces the production's strategy for presenting several time frames at once—the present interaction between student and teacher (Christopher has given Siobhan his book, and she reads it aloud in his presence); the past action described by the book (Christopher discovering Wellington); and the moments, past or present, that Treadaway and the ensemble act out. At the line "the dog was dead," Treadaway brings his fists between his thighs. He reaches out to touch the dog's side, near the pitchfork that seemingly skewers it to the floor. As the neighbor, Mrs. Shears (Sophie Duval), yells again to "get away from my dog," he finally reacts to her, rising to back away. He rubs the back of his head as Siobhan continues to read the introductory details of his book—his name and the proud fact that he knows capital cities and prime numbers—and then curls up with his head on the floor covered by his arms when Mrs. Shears yells at him again. He begins moaning, and a policeman replaces Mrs. Shears in the scene. Attempting to formulate answers to the police-man's questions, he rocks from side to side on his knees and twiddles the drawstring of his hoodie. Some questions cause him to change focus so that his gaze passes across the policeman but never rests there. The questions and answers accelerate and intensify, driving his head back down to the floor with more moaning. Getting no further response, the policeman grasps Christopher's arm, causing him to rise and hit at the man's back. As he is arrested for attacking a policeman, Treadaway looks at the floor and shakes his head rapidly at the question "do you understand?" Siobhan reads from his book, "I find people confusing." As she continues with a passage about ambiguous expressions, Treadaway uses chalk to draw a schematic face on the grid: he shows the audience an example of the diagrams that he matches to facial expressions in order to read explicitly what others have learned to accomplish as a background task (that is, an automatized behavior that does not require conscious attention). He does not use this sort of diagram at any point in the play, but showing and explaining a fairly well-known teaching tool reinforces the impression that an AS diagnosis is appropriate for Chris-topher and that an inability to interpret others' emotions characterizes AS.

Although the multimedia staging and narrative structure are postrealist from the start, Treadaway's acting stays within realist bounds for this open-ing setup of character and story. The other actors playing central characters (Ed, Judy, and Siobhan) maintain this style, but the staging becomes more inventive as Christopher embarks upon his adventure. Treadaway moves back and forth between modes, playing the interactions with his parents realistically so that we observe him "objectively"; that is, we see him from the outside within the dramatic world. As Ed explains how he happened to kill Wellington, for example, Treadaway sits on the floor, shirtless, twisting the fabric of his pants at the knee. His back is in a shallow C-curve, and we can see his breathing change as he listens, his gaze fixed in the mid-distance. He subtly contracts his body inward, bit by bit. When Ed moves closer and puts up a hand to touch fingertips, Treadaway refuses to reciprocate and keeps his hand near the opposite arm. The fingers remain curled in on themselves but agitate as if they fight uncurling and returning the touch. The moment could slide easily out of its abstract stage setting and into a realistically detailed film set without adjustment. These family scenes create a familiar spectator position: we watch the interaction from outside yet feel both with and for the characters and are left with the impression that Ed and Judy have done a pretty good job at the cost of admirable self-sacrifice. In the last lines of the play, Christopher speaks of his accomplishments: getting a Maths A-Level, going to London on his own, solving the puzzle of who killed Wellington, writing a book that's been turned into a play. He asks Siobhan three times: Does that mean I can do anything? She doesn't respond. He might be overly optimistic, but we can share his optimism with respect to some of his goals.

If Christopher actually were to accomplish everything that he plans— get his Further Maths A-Level, attend university, get a first-class honors degree, and become a scientist—he would become as strange to his working-class family as his presumed AS makes him. His father is a plumber, and his mother works as a secretary for a manufacturing firm. As James Berger notes, the novel marks her borderline secretarial skills with rampant spelling mistakes in her letters to Christopher. For Berger, the novel's Swindon exemplifies "a post-Thatcher England" that seems to lack both social and familial networks: "The small detached houses of Swindon are inhabited only by nuclear families, or fragments of them. This is a social world that, for reasons Haddon does not investigate, has been flattened, atomized, each household an isolated and fragile entity." Berger sees this as a picture of "pervasive social autism," implying no concrete relation to the psychiatric diagnosis but instead using the term to characterize contemporary social structures that leave people in autistic-like solitude, able to rely only upon themselves, unable to truly share or even to communicate effectively. He notes that the novel's "political points are not developed, and the extended metaphor of a social autism is offered but then withdrawn. The novel's focus returns, at last, to the family, to human emotion, and to difficulties in personal relationships that appear to go beyond or beneath any particular social structures."[22] Curious Incident presents Christopher navigating a world without any real dangers or disappointments. He interacts with benign (if somewhat obtuse) neighbors, a caring (if somewhat condescending) teacher, an ultimately flexible (if initially balky) school principal, and helpful policemen and strangers. The only fully negative character is his mother's lover, whom she immediately leaves when he has too many beers and grabs Christopher's arm. That this character is an attorney and thus a class or more above Ed and Judy goes unexplored. We don't know, in terms of plot, whether his parents will get back together romantically, but they're both present and actively involved in his life. Although this may seem admirable as far as actual parenting goes, I note that it restricts the scope of concern and responsibility to the nuclear family.

As a most subtle and effective ideological state apparatus, the family interpellates its members into appropriate roles that ensure the continuation of the family and of the state.[23] This family needs to be "happy" in the archaic sense of working well and remaining intact. Ahmed notes that happiness has been associated with emotion only since the eighteenth century. The *OED* defines happiness first as good fortune and second as the pleasurable state of mind that positive attainments bring about. In Middle English, the root "hap" referred to chance—a concept that persists in the form "happenstance" as well as in "happen"—but the possibility of mishap has disappeared from happiness just as bad fortune has been severed from the concept "fortunate."[24] The happy family enjoys a certain degree of flexibility with respect to gender, sexuality, and individual roles. But for this to be a family rather than simply a marriage, there must be children, whether born or adopted into the family. Primary responsibility for these children rests with the parents, and the state enforces, supports, and supplements the exercise of parental duty. The liberal state removed children from the modern home to benefit from free public education and, during much of the twentieth century, also removed persons categorized as insane or mentally deficient from the home to institutional settings. Under the most generous interpretation, both of these removals offered nurturance in excess of what the family could provide even as they freed the parents to function as economic agents. Here again, the family structure remained flexible: both partners might exchange labor for money, or one partner might provide support for the other's career. The liberal family advanced as an economic and social unit, and the liberal state offered various forms of remediation to minimize the family's chances of failure.

Gil Eyal and his coauthors argue that the postwar baby boom brought "a sea change in the perception and government of childhood, in the roles and responsibilities of parents (especially of mothers), and in the position of medicine vis-à-vis both children and parents."[25] The role of experts began to shift away from taking over the care of children unlikely to be "healthy or normal" and toward identifying such children.[26] Contemporary neoliberalism leaves the postmodern family with a responsibility to cultivate the happiness of each family member, construing this as an emotional state rather than a contingent evaluation.[27] Wendy Brown points out the neoliberal imperative to be "entrepreneurial actors in every sphere of life," with failure attributed to mismanagement and "moral lapses" redefined as "mistakes in judgment."[28] Parents must facilitate the growth of their children, so that they reach their maximum potential. This means not only shopping for the best educational setting but also effectively assessing what that might be for each particular child. In the case of a child who falls outside behavioral norms, this management responsibility extends to finding the right diagnosis and treatment regime as well as securing the appropriate education. The possibilities include public schools with additional services, private or therapeutic schools, and homeschooling, but largely exclude institutionalization. One would be hard pressed to regret the passing of unhappy institutionalization, but Osteen observes that "parents of autistic children constantly feel guilty and inadequate; if they don't try every possible therapy, diet or medication, they may believe they haven't done enough for their child."[29]

The happiness of an object such as the family connects to but does not fully coincide with the emotion, happiness: the pleasure that the "happy object" creates overflows the object's boundaries to invest the time and place of the happy (pleasurable) encounter; likewise, an object can become happy (lovely) if presented by someone whom the recipient loves. Ahmed describes the feeling of happiness as both contagious and fragile, wont to dissipate or become anxious at the moment when it becomes conscious.[30] As an affect—that is, a relational property both slippery and sticky—happiness circulates between people. As Catherine Chaput explains, affect continues to accumulate in a reciprocal reinforcement of neoliberal imperatives:

> Economic and rhetorical circulatory processes work in tandem to sustain the vitality of late capitalism in much the same way that the muscular and skeletal systems work together to animate human motion. Circulating material values, which form the backbone of capitalist production, are attached to the affective energies circulating through communicative exchanges, providing connective tissue and giving motion to the economy's skeletal framework.[31]

The autist impedes the circulation of affect and also threatens the family's success. If the autistic child cannot grow up to *enjoy* an independent and fulfilling life, the parents have failed in their duties. This threat forms the core of the autism family drama, which circulates anxiety as its primary affect.

*Curious Incident* remains fully invested in the happy family—not surprising for a production successfully targeted to family audiences. Yet the show appeals to these audiences because it so creatively and convincingly presents a version of Aspie experience that conforms to certain popular paradigms of autism, in particular the stereotypical association between AS, enhanced mathematical abilities, and impaired empathy.

## TORQUING STOCK CHARACTERS AND TIRED PARADIGMS

Art tends to use familiar paradigms because they catch the imagination of artists and, just as important, audiences easily recognize them. Each successful fleshing out of a paradigm reinforces its power. An analysis of two realist AFDs will illuminate the shortcomings of theories about AS that underpin *Curious Incident*—perhaps even the dangers inherent in its popular success. If this language seems hyperbolic, one might call to mind the theory that cold mothers cause autism and the misery that this psychological explanation caused in the mid-twentieth century. Jordynn Jack proposes that autism controversies use gendered stock characters for persuasive effect because they so effectively condense significant cultural information into easily recognizable packages. This information captures power relations; for example, in order to wrest power (even the basic power to speak) from the doctors who generated the stock character *refrigerator mother*, women generated the *hero-mother* type utterly devoted to saving her child from autism.[32] Jack argues that the *Aspie-geek* stock character "has limited popular and, to some extent, scientific understanding of ASD more broadly, by focusing attention away from females with ASD and away from features of ASD that do not conform to the geek profile."[33] Like *Curious Incident*, Mike Leigh's *Two Thousand Years* (2005) and Annie Baker's *Body Awareness* (2008) both use this stock character but, I will argue, torque it in interesting directions. The awkward sons at the heart of these plays provoke anxieties for their dysfunctional families. They seemingly lack social ties other than close but somewhat prickly relationships with their parents, and they have not found employment on a par with their considerable intellectual capabilities.

Although the twenty-one-year-old Jared of *Body Awareness* struggles against accepting the AS diagnosis that his mother and her partner urge upon him, he exhibits the requisite triad of impairments; that is, abnormalities in social relations, communication, and imagination. He scorns other people for their stupidity, speaks bluntly, and memorizes the *OED*. I will italicize descriptive terms and parenthetically identify the area of impairment drawn from the DSM's triad.[34] Jared displays *insensitivity to taboos on personal topics* (communication), contributing to dinner-table conversation with a stranger the comment that "I refuse to get naked in front of anyone" and joking that his family drinks their own urine.[35] He tries to demonstrate empathy but instead reveals his inadequate picture of other people's feelings:

> JARED: It must be hard to be a lesbian. Right? People make fun of you?
> PHYLLIS: Uh. Not that much anymore. Not to my face, at least.
> JARED: It must be hard to not be that pretty anymore. To get old.
> PHYLLIS: Are you trying to be mean?
> JARED: No! I'm telling you that I see how your life is hard. (39)

More outlandishly, *being overly literal* (imagination) leads him to *flout a social taboo* (social relation): he shows a girl his penis because the man to whom he has turned for dating advice has assured him that men's bodies are sexy, and feminist psychology professor Phyllis has asserted that penises are not ugly but beautiful. He then *fails to respond to others' emotional displays* (social relation), instead walking into the nearby pond when the girl screams. Jared's dictionary memorization is evidence of *obsessive interests that are circumscribed* (imagination), and he deals with anxiety by running his electric toothbrush over his gums, which one might construe as a *repetitive, obsessive behavior or compulsion* (imagination). Yet this last behavior might equally well be interpreted, along with his abnormally acute sense of smell, as evidence of typical autistic *sensory-motor, perceptual, autonomic, and affective characteristics*—the features of autistic experience that a primary focus on cognitive abnormalities tends to obscure.[36]

*Two Thousand Years* uses a central character and plot structure similar to *Body Awareness*. Josh, a brilliant twenty-eight-year-old intellectual, reads Kafka in the opening scene, has an advanced degree in math, and lives at home with his parents, never having held a job. His temporary embrace of orthodox ritual threatens his Jewish but nonobservant London family's sense of themselves as liberal and neutral in an increasingly fundamentalist world. In place of the forthright references to diagnosis that Baker gives us,

Leigh drops hints about Josh. We see him reading, moving from one part of the house to another and out into the garden, often with a book and a mug of tea, often on the periphery of the action. When his mother, Rachel, expresses some mild frustration and asks what he's planning to do, he offers the most minimal and concrete response: he's thinking and might go for a walk.[37] Josh's peculiarities could be construed as indicating AS or major depression. Or the problem might be simply that he has no job, as his father, Danny (a dentist), points out in anger:

> You live under our roof. We feed you, we clothe you, we don't complain. Your mother runs around clearing up after you, while I spend all day fiddling in people's mouths. We give you money, you buy books, you stay up half the night, you get up whenever you like, you're free to come and go. You've never had a job. Josh: you left university seven years ago with a First Class Honors degree in mathematics—the world was your oyster. We tried to bring you up decently and respectably, and now this *mishigas!* (22)

Josh's crotchety grandfather Dave needles him about living off his parents as well as about his failure to give a proper greeting, in a pattern that repeats several times and always culminates in an emphysema attack for Dave.

In her first scene, visiting after a trip abroad, Josh's sister Tammy asks him about his "welfare state" (26), the question soon revealed as a typical pattern of sibling sniping that brings on angry explosions from Josh. One might interpret him as just a moody slacker, but a quiet moment after he storms out on an argument indicates a difference that goes back to childhood:

> *Danny is holding up a small feather from a cushion.*
> DANNY: See this feather? It reminds me of Josh when he was a kid.
> RACHEL: Why?
> DANNY: The way he used to look at things for hours. Remember? Stones . . . clouds . . .
> TAMMY: Yeah . . . and the way the sunlight hit the wall. . . .
> DANNY: Yeah. And I used to do my dog.
> *He makes a dog shadow-puppet with his hand. . . .*
> TAMMY: Yeah, it's a shame he could never share it with anyone, really.
> (34–35)

That's as explicit as the dialogue gets, but I would argue for its significance. Josh prays alone at home; although he mentions seeing a rabbi during the first interrogation by his parents, that's the only reference that connects him to anyone outside of the immediate household. In the 2008 New Group production, Jordan Gelber played him with sufficient abruptness and physical awkwardness to reinforce the impression of AS. When the family argues—which is a great deal of the time—Josh either leaves the room or engages in an angry outburst to which the other characters react as overblown (*lack of normal response to others' emotional displays*, a social abnormality). He enters and leaves the room precipitously without observing any of the social niceties that others expect (*ignoring*, a communicative abnormality). After one particularly harsh comment, his mother tells a guest "I'm sorry. We try not to take any notice," indicating that rude behavior is typical (67).

Josh's embrace of orthodoxy upsets his family because they see themselves as having moved beyond a historical Jewish identity.[38] But his turn to religion is temporary—he seeks comfort and an identity for a time, and instead gets grief from every member of the family. In his final outburst, he says to his abrasive aunt:

> You think you're the only one who suffers, don't you? Well, you're not. We all suffer—life's about suffering! You think you're the victim in this family. Well, you walked away. I'm still stuck with it! My grandpa thinks I'm a waste of space. My parents see me as a religious freak! . . . My sister doesn't understand me at all! And let me tell you something. It's lonely! It's fucking lonely! (104)

When he returns to the room a few minutes later, it is without the yarmulke that he's worn for much of the play, and he's quietly crying (108). No one comments, but his parents move close to him and the others gradually take their leave. In the final scene, Josh plays chess with Danny and participates in a conversation about Hurricane Katrina with both his parents.

Given a world that seems to have no place for Josh, the core family unit provides succor unavailable from religion. The play does not explore his experience of the world, nor does it explore that of the other characters. Each can be seen as an aspect of Jewish culture, and Leigh throws them into conflict.[39] Josh represents the traditional Jewish embrace of learning and culture. This is what his liberal parents value and nurture even though there seems to be no place for him (or it) in today's world. The serious question underlying the play's veneer of bickering comedy is how to maintain these values without religion. Josh is no more impaired than his aunt or his grandfather: this dramatic world accepts a range of human quirkiness without invoking medical diagnosis and thus reifying any diagnostic category. *Body Awareness*, in contrast, puts Jared's disorder and his transformation at the center of its plot and gives him a voice, even though its central concerns lie elsewhere. If the cluster of characteristics that Josh and Jared share can shape a coherent character without invoking AS, what dramaturgical purpose does the diagnostic language serve? I propose that Baker's play reveals the ways in which popular AS tropes reinvigorate gender stereotypes—in particular, a cultural investment in female emotionality and male rationality that I would characterize as cruel optimism, a clinging to gender essentialism that is not good for us.

Asperger syndrome itself comprises a spectrum of cognitive and behavioral characteristics, yet just a few of these characteristics dominate public discourse about AS. In a program note for *Curious Incident*, prominent psychologist Simon Baron-Cohen explains the fit between Christopher and his own "psychological theory of autism spectrum conditions"; that is, "impaired empathizing alongside intact or even superior systematizing."[40] According to Baron-Cohen, Aspies do not learn the unwritten rules of social behavior because they have no "theory of mind"; that is, they cannot grasp other people's states of mind or adopt their perspectives.[41] Popular shorthand generally translates this concept as an absence of empathy. In this view, normal mindreading enables humans to attribute intentionality and emotional response to other humans, facilitating easy communication and social cooperation. According to some, the autistic mindreading deficit extends even to introspection, leaving an individual unable to reflect upon his or her own state of mind. Uta Frith and Francesca Happé propose that an autistic child's insensitivity to pain is a problem of self-reflection, for example: a young girl might experience the pain of appendicitis "in the same way as everyone else" but not complain because she is unable to attribute to herself the "emotional significance that normally accompanies pain."[42] Note that the construction of autism as a failure of mindreading, which includes the individual's ability to read her own mind, removes that individual's agency: she cannot interpret her own actions but must defer to the authority of neurotypicals.

Although Baker deploys familiar mindblindness tropes, *Body Awareness* simultaneously undercuts the notion that autism results from an empathy deficit and uses sexual disequilibrium to explore social and ideological questions. Baker sets her play during Body Awareness Week at the fictional Shirley State College in Vermont, in the household where Jared lives with his mother Joyce and her partner Phyllis. The artists invited to campus for this event stay with local residents, so Phyllis and Joyce host Frank Bonitatibus. Only after he arrives do they discover that he specializes in photographing naked women. Frank conceives of this as a kind of participatory therapy that raises his subjects' self-esteem—he thinks of it as a feminist project countering a cultural inundation with images of perfect female bodies. Phyllis can't see it that way and is horrified that she has invited him into her home. Joyce is more open to Frank and his work, which compounds Phyllis's principled disapproval with jealousy. The two women bring different personal histories to their three-year relationship: Phyllis "knew she was gay when she was in kindergarten," whereas she's Joyce's first female partner (20). After their first dinner with Frank, Phyllis tells Joyce, "I feel like you were kind of flirting with him. Do you miss male attention or something?" (36), and later tells Jared, "he wants to get in your mother's pants" (48). The play neither confirms nor disproves her suspicions, but Joyce is removing her clothes for a photo session with Frank at the play's climax, when Jared walks in dripping wet from the pond and shaking.

The play interweaves sexuality with AS right from its second scene, in which Joyce confronts Jared about masturbation—our introduction to both characters. The problem is not so much that he masturbates but that he's running up pay-per-view charges watching pornography. After some silences, Jared responds by returning the Tony Attwood book that Joyce and Phyllis have given him. (Atwood is a clinical psychologist who has published a number of very popular books about AS.) He denies that he fits the description for AS, and the desire to prove this point motivates his subsequent actions. Together with comical demonstrations of empathy and socially inappropriate demonstrations of irony, he sets out to remedy what he identifies as his social deficit:

> I know why you guys think I have Asperger's. . . . I've never had sex and you think that's weird. . . . The book says people with Asperger's have a hard time forging physical and romantic relationships because of their lack of empathy and social prowess and I know that's why you think I have it but you're wrong. I'm just shy, and introverted, and I have better things to do than go to a frat party and get drunk and make out with some stupid girl. (34)

As he describes the planned remedy in a moment of anger, "I'm going to get a girlfriend and I'm going to have doggy-style sex with her" (36). He seeks advice from Frank, who considers him spoiled ("You're not retarded. You're living with two women") and gives such sage advice as "I recommend eating the woman out before you actually try intercourse for the first time" (56)—hardly the most relevant strategy for a young man who has yet to ask anyone for a date. Jared's resulting misadventure at the pond puts an end to the photo session and the domestic upheaval, as Joyce and Phyllis comfort him and help him think through consequences and the right course of action. He demonstrates his mindreading capability: "It's just . . . if I were her? That would kind of be scary. . . . I would want that person to . . . It's so much better if the person admits to doing it, right? So then you don't have to spend the rest of your life thinking about it" (67). This goes unremarked, as does his admission that one needs a degree to be a lexicographer for the *OED*, suggesting that he will stop describing himself as an autodidact and go to college. Jared is the one who changes most over the course of *Body Awareness*. He finally accepts the diagnosis, although he articulates this as an excuse for stealing Frank's recorder because Frank took away his electric toothbrush.

Using AS to put empathy in the foreground works to highlight the mindblindness of all the characters—or at least the obstructed empathy that so often accompanies both political and artistic convictions. Frank can't see how his work can be objectionable in feminist terms. Phyllis can't see how removing one's clothing and being photographed could possibly help to validate a woman's superficial appearance and her intangible value. Joyce can't see how much her flirtation with Frank and his project is hurting Phyllis. In addition to complicating the play's treatment of empathy even while relying upon recognizable Aspie characteristics, Baker makes Jared central to the plot rather than being instrumental to the transformation of a neurotypical protagonist (the "sentimental savant" structure that Murray delineates); instead, the instrumental character here is Frank. Juxtaposing these two straight (and in the Atlantic Theater production, white) male characters with a lesbian couple further mitigates against easy stereotypes. Frank's brain may be part of a biologically male body, but he's not significantly better at systematizing or worse at empathy than the female characters, and his only common ground with Jared would seem to be their (presumably) male genitalia. As the play ends, he leaves the house unnoticed, snapping a family portrait.

Baker's reconfiguration of both the family unit and the Aspie character makes apparent the role that gender plays in many other AFDs, including *Curious Incident*, thus raising the question: Why is autism a significant locus for anxieties about the family and, particularly, women's place in the world? *Body Awareness* does not fall prey to the math-genius stereotype that both *Curious Incident* and *Two Thousand Years* deploy, instead giving Jared lexicographic inclinations as befits the profile for Asperger's Association of New England members, most of whom "are far better with words and images than they are with numbers."[43] Within popular culture, though, the stereotypical male Aspie geek, gifted with superior math abilities and computer-related skills, obscures other autisms. Monitoring by the Centers for Disease Control shows a statistical correlation between maleness and autism (1 in 42 for boys compared to 1 in 189 for girls), along with smaller differences according to geographical location and race/ethnicity, but "no data are available to support possible etiologic implications for these differences, including the sex difference."[44] Yet Baron-Cohen has gone so far as to characterize autism as an effect of the "extreme male brain," which is good at systematizing and bad at the empathy that supposedly characterizes female mental life, all characteristics that he considers to be hardwired in the brain.[45] Noting that Baron-Cohen's *The Essential Difference* targets a general readership and takes "much of its structure, tone, and style, as well as its rhetorical effect" from the self-help books that popularized a conception of women from Venus unable to communicate with the Martian men in their lives, Jordynn Jack provides an extensive analysis of this book's rhetorical structure, including the gender biases built into its quizzes and the history of research into empathic capacities.[46] As Stuart Murray points out, Baron-Cohen accompanies his controlled scientific research with an extended case study. Selecting the mathematician Richard Borcherds for this purpose enhances the authoritative aura of his argument, whereas an artist such as Andy Warhol or Larry Bissonnette would have required significantly different conclusions.[47]

The *Aspie geek* stock character began to take shape during the 1990s as the diagnostic categories introduced by DSM-IV interacted with a public focus on brain research, the new knowledge economy, and a revived discourse about emotional intelligence. As Jack points out, these cultural forces created a gendered tension between cognitive capitalism and the service economy to which working women were mostly restricted during the twentieth century.[48] Yet computer technology has largely displaced the pink-collar sector of the service economy. I would posit a further interaction as women increasingly entered the knowledge economy and neuroscience not only supplemented but largely supplanted psychoanalytic conceptions of mind and behavior in popular discourse. The demand for men as well as women to become aware of their own emotions and sensitive to those of others made common failures of emotional intelligence much more visible than they had been. Popular culture categorizes males who fail to meet these affective demands as Aspies, forgiving them for what seems to be a hyper-masculine cognitive style. This bastardized scientific language does little to soften the labels applied to comparable females. If they're good at system-atizing, then Baron-Cohen considers them to be women with male brains.

Angela Willey and her coauthors argue that this conception of an "ex-treme male brain" combines with "assortative mating" to heterosexualize autism, erasing what is "otherwise rather queer" about it and reinscribing conceptions of "sexual complementarity" that they call "neurocomplementar-ity."[49] The popular notion that autism diagnoses increased in places such as Silicon Valley because male geeks were mating with female geeks has little scientific support but "aligns with a range of social anxieties, including the role of women in the workforce"—particularly in historically male fields such as engineering and computer science.[50] The stock characters that pop-ulate autism rhetoric, the fictional characters created by autism fiction (in-cluding drama), and highly visible research such as Baron-Cohen's all work together to unqueer autism through "the erasure of queer implications and the eschewing of queer readings." This process makes autism intelligible by constituting "a particular kind of autistic subject, a subject who is symboli-cally, if not literally, white, straight, and male."[51]

Jack argues that gender features so prominently in autism discourse pre-cisely because so many gaps remain in scientific knowledge. She observes that "where knowledge or authority is lacking, gendered characters often fill in"[52]—as they do here in support of the mindblindness paradigm for au-tism. Alternative theories emphasize sensory abnormalities. Some autists describe hypersensitivities that render sensory input so overwhelming that it cannot be organized or sometimes even tolerated, or hypo-sensitivities that are sometimes but not always a secondary mechanism for screening out overwhelming input. These irregularities vary greatly between autists and also change for a given individual, depending upon circumstances—different sensory channels may shut down at different times, with awareness narrowed from a broad, unfiltered gestalt to a pin-spot focused on certain types of detail. Responding to the interpretation of an autistic child's insensitivity to pain as a problem of self-reflection, Victoria McGeer asks, "In what way could an autistic person really be 'having' a normal sensory experience of pain if the normal subjective accompaniments of that experience are not 'felt' by her as an experiencing subject?"[53] Taking the autist's subjective report of sensorial experience of the world "at face value" as representing a different experience rather than a mental state inadequately reported due to mindblindness, McGeer considers it more likely that sensory abnormalities prevent the young autistic child from the social interactions essential to developing normate social cognition.[54]

A focus upon sensory differences shifts the conversation away from empathy and reshapes the dramatic world of the autism family drama. The production of *Curious Incident* does this effectively in postrealist scenes that I consider its greatest accomplishment. Like the novel, the stage version uses presentational techniques from twentieth-century artistic experiments to intensify the impact of the narrative. For the novel, this is first-person writing, the inclusion of letters and similar documentary evidence, and intertextuality—Christopher explicitly models his investigation upon the adventures of Sherlock Holmes. For the theatrical adaptation, Treadaway's virtuosic movement engages spectators kinesthetically, facilitating a positive engagement with his performance perhaps less likely for a normate audience if he were to represent the character strictly within the bounds of realism as a physically and socially awkward Aspie-geek stock character. The staging shifts to evoke Christopher's sensory experience when he is either literally alone (searching for the notebook that Ed has hidden) or alone in public, overwhelmed by the sights and sounds of his journey. To create the train station in his hometown of Swindon, the ensemble crisscross the stage in formation, in step, and Treadaway has to navigate around and between them. The sound score here includes words and phrases that would appear on the station's signs, as though we're hearing what Christopher sees. When he sits down on the floor to calm himself and think of what to do—he's never even left his street on his own, let alone bought a train ticket—the signs' words are projected and move across the grid, indicating Christopher's split focus as he continues reading signs even while he interacts with a helpful policeman. Later scenes on the train make explicit this feature of his sensory experience—he is unable to screen from consciousness the details of perceptual experience that neurotypicals relegate to the background. As Christopher buys his ticket, the projected text continues moving calmly, and other actors walk slowly and casually through the space. As he moves to the train, though, this all speeds up. Now we hear his mother's voice guiding him and understand this to be happening in his mind, that he is remembering advice she has given him. The general lighting dims, a spot follows Treadaway, and red lights at the corner of certain grid squares guide him, creating a path that he can focus on and follow.

Following a brilliantly staged train journey to London, Christopher uses the same method to move through the even busier Paddington Station— at first following the red-light path on the floor grid and repeating "left, right . . ." as he steps. Then the projected signs proliferate, coming in from different directions, audible as well as visual. When he puts his hands over his ears, the projections and the sounds both slow down. He takes them off, and everything accelerates. The actors move through the space like busy commuters but also actively interfere with Christopher's progress: a woman putting her hands over his ears and slowing everything again, people lifting him through a front walkover, four of them picking him up like a piece of luggage and carrying him through the space. Finally, an imagined dialogue with his father (in his mind, audible to us) guides Christopher onto the platform and then into the subway train.

These movement-based scenes engaged me much differently than did the scenes of domestic realism. As the woman seated next to me at one performance suggested, any visitor to London would likely experience a moment of self-recognition during the Paddington Station scene, and I am also prone to sensory overload and overwhelmed by crowds. Yet my primary response was delight in the staging. These episodes function in much the same way as production numbers do in musical theater, providing a release from the dramatic situation into enjoyment of the performers' physical skill, the tightly coordinated responsiveness of the entire ensemble, and the cleverness of the representation. Christopher's adventures, both the detecting and the traveling, provide feel-good interludes that keep the audience engaged in the show despite its potentially difficult subject matter—a feature vital to commercial success. As with a standard book musical, these interludes also move the story forward and expand upon some aspect of a character's experience. We hear the parents' voices, which Christopher has internalized, guiding him through the scenes in which he navigates the world alone, and we see his success.

*Curious Incident* uses both realistic acting and postrealist staging to represent autistic disruptions of affect. These devices are beautifully designed to facilitate slippage and stickiness and to keep audience affect in circulation but also contained within familiar emotional categories. Consider the convention that the production establishes to represent Christopher's chaotic mental state: after an early confrontation, Treadaway quietly recites prime numbers to himself as projected numbers cluster on the floor nearby and float away, accompanied by the kinds of electronic sounds used in the production's opening scene. Then, in a later scene, Nicola Walker speaks the text of a letter from Judy as Treadaway silently reads it onstage, becoming appropriately overwrought in expressing her feelings of inadequacy as a mother and her reasons for leaving the family. This letter brings on a seizure for Christopher, which in Treadaway's performance seems to result from the onslaught of Walker's emotion as well as the content of the letter. Without the enactment of this scene, one would understand Christopher to be overcome by ideas that he can't quite comprehend or perhaps by the discovery that his mother is in fact alive—within the Theory of Mind paradigm that the narrative largely accepts, an Aspie wouldn't be able to imagine her emotions. Figure 5 shows Treadaway seated on the floor amid scattered sheets of paper, prime number projections swirling above him. This staging does not function in a manner similar to a musical production number, as I've argued the adventure scenes do; rather, this already well-established cue intensifies audience distress and then directs it toward Christopher in a flood of tenderness, just as cuteness does at other points. Tenderness works in frequent alternation with admiration at the inventive staging—which in turn echoes the wonder elicited by Christopher's savant-type capabilities.[55]

Although major plot points remain unresolved, the production draws one toward the hope that Christopher will succeed in some math-related field as Temple Grandin has done in the design of livestock-handling equipment. Just in case the lack of total narrative closure might leave audiences anxious, the production brings a live puppy onstage to channel affect into a coherent emotional response: Judy and Christopher are living in Swindon, and Christopher must spend after-school time at Ed's house but cannot trust or forgive him, so Ed buys him a puppy. Each of the three times that I saw the production, the audience responded to the puppy with an audible *aww*, the typical expression of tenderness that cuteness elicits. A puppy at the end of *Curious Incident* makes everyone feel better, just as the pinioned German shepherd at the opening creates a shock of distress. But Treadaway is cute, too, in his very skillful performance of autism. And Christopher is a relatively cute Aspie character who mostly does adorable Aspie things. Just as nothing really endangers him within the narrative, neither his physical

Figure 5. Luke Treadaway surrounded by prime numbers in *Curious Incident of the Dog in the Night Time* at the Apollo Theatre, London, 2013. Photo © Brinkhoff/Mögenburg.

fight with his father nor his hitting a policemen seem particularly dangerous to the other party. His disruptions of affective flow carry the plot through its complications, crisis, and resolution, but he does not disturb the audience's investment in the happiness of families. The production is limited by the novel's stock characters and tired paradigms.

## BEYOND HAPPY FAMILIES

Before moving away from realism, I consider an AFD that not only refuses the comfort of well-managed autistic sentimentality but also abandons cruel optimism with respect to the profoundly autistic young adult at its center. Deanna Jent's *Falling* (2011) stages a crisis in one family's efforts to care for a profoundly autistic son with no likely prospects for employment or relationship—a type of autist thoroughly elided by the geek profile. Like *Body Awareness*, *Falling* covers a brief time span, and it remains even more closely confined to the domestic interior. Parents Bill and Tami are exhausted by the work of keeping their eighteen-year-old son Josh at home rather than placing him in an unsafe and unloving institution. Their daughter Lisa wants out. When Bill's mother offers prayer as a solution, he tells her to "pray for programs and housing options and staff for people like Josh.... Pray that— that Lisa won't hate us forever. Pray that our marriage won't fall apart. Pray that people will stop just praying and take some action."[56]

Playwright Jent's production notes describe Josh's specific sensory issues in order to prevent mimicry of stereotypical autistic behavior: "His almost constant movement feeds his under-reactive nervous system the input to help him maintain balance. His delight in visual stimulation ... comes from a need to tune out unwanted noise and to control his visual environment" (5). The sensory difficulties combine with his limited expressive language to produce physical danger. When Josh becomes overwhelmed by noise or frustrated by changes in routine, he lashes out against the person closest to him. The aides hired to work with him always quit, and his mother bears the brunt of the violence. The large actor playing this role in the Minetta Lane production, Daniel Everidge, visually overpowered the other actors even at rest. When his hands closed around Julia Murney's neck, or he pulled her hair, I shared Tami's fear in sharp contrast to the tenderness that actors playing Christopher elicit in *Curious Incident*. Rather than presenting an Aspie-geek, *Falling* calls up the hero-mother and adds dimension to this stock character's heroism. The articulation of mother love seems retrogressive when Tami tells Lisa, "You can hate him. But moms don't get that choice. (*Her voice cracks.*) We can't help it—we just love our kids, no matter what" (35). Yet the play does not claim that all mothers are good and loving; rather, it shows that this one needs more help. She needs alternatives better than either institutionalizing her son or being exhausted and physically endangered by caring for him at home. Jent, who identifies herself as the mother of a profoundly autistic son (6), engages with autism from a different personal commitment than do the creative teams behind the other performances that I discuss in this chapter—at least, insofar as publicly available information would indicate.

No one improves in this play, nor does the situation. Instead of redemption for its neurotypicals or reassurance that the family will persevere, the plot culminates in the death of Tami's dream that her autistic son will have a normal life. After a dog barking outside the house triggers Josh to attack her once again and to also strike out at his physically disabled grandmother, Tami dreams that he has choked to death on popcorn and that a social worker visits the house to gather routine information on the death. The script specifies that this character, Lawrence, be played by the same actor who plays Josh. His questions insinuate that Josh may have been mistreated at home, and he asks Lisa whether she feels safe in the house. Lisa bursts into incredulous laughter and leads Tami into a joyous outburst of relief that Josh is dead, that they're no longer in danger and can lead a "normal" life. They pull a rope that tips feathers out of a suspended box, something that gave Josh so much pleasure when they would float down on him. Then Lawrence joins Tami under the feathers for a demonstration, and his gestural behavior begins to more closely resemble Josh. He fumbles in a pocket and drops three marbles, goes offstage with Bill to see the marble run in Josh's bedroom, and the fantasy ends abruptly with Tami left trying to sort it out as "reality" resumes. She tells Bill about the fantasy sequence just staged: "I dreamt that Josh was dead, and I thought maybe I really do want him dead. How awful is that? I really don't" (44). As Lisa, Grammy Sue, and Josh come in and out of the room, mixing conversation about how to improve the family's situation and about dessert, Tami interprets her dream:

Oh. It's not Josh . . . who's dead. It's not Josh. . . . It's the other one. . . . The man with the marbles. The one he could have been. (*Bill indicates his confusion with a gesture. Tami holds her stomach, remembering.*) That dream—you know. . . . That he'll go to regular school and sing in the choir and go to college and get a job and be . . . (*The grief hits her hard.*) It's dead. There's no dream for Josh. (46–47)

In this moment, Tami seems to accomplish what autist-activist Jim Sinclair asks of parents: that they go ahead and mourn for their expectations, for the child that they imagined having, but at the same time recognize that their autistic child is present, unique, and in need of help: "The tragedy is not that we're here, but that your world has no place for us to be."[57]

Rather than offering a resolution for this family, *Falling* makes an appeal. As Josh plays with his marbles upstage at the end of the play, Tami tells him she's "stuck," asks him "what will happen?" and they both approach the audience:

> (*She speaks to the universe, to God, to anyone listening.*) Okay. Okay. (*Her breath catches—afraid, but taking the plunge.*) Catch me? (*She spreads her arms as Josh tosses the marbles in the air—they land and bounce all over the stage as Tami surrenders and falls back into the couch. Feathers fall on the audience. Josh squeals and does his most happy of dances. Lights fade to black.*) (47)

Figure 6 shows this final moment, with Murney on the couch and Everidge dancing. The script is clear and direct rather than subtle in presenting its central problem and in calling for social change, then gentle in its brief final turn to the audience, using the fall of feathers to incorporate them within the nonfiction of the world presented onstage. *Falling* explicitly refuses cruel optimism about private solutions to social problems such as autism.

## ZANY LIZARDBRAINS AND IDIOTS

In 2008, Off-Broadway theaters hosted the remount of *Two Thousand Years*, the premiere of *Body Awareness*, and two collaborative postrealist theater companies using autism tropes to bring modernist literature into collision with the (un)happy family. Elevator Repair Service plays with autism's diagnostic predecessor in *The Sound and the Fury (April Seventh, 1928)*, staging the family's dissolution from the purposefully incoherent viewpoint of the "idiot" positioned as its only stable center, and with *Chekhov Lizardbrain*, Pig

Figure 6. Daniel Everidge and Julia Murney in *Falling* by Deanna Jent. Minetta Lane Theatre, New York City, 2012. Photo © Carol Rosegg.

Iron Theatre twists AS characteristics into a zany package to deconstruct the realist family drama.

Scholar/artist and former company member Telory Davies Arendell explains that Pig Iron proceeds by mixing "what appear to be incongruous ingredients to build original works that make bold and innovative statements about seemingly unrelated things."[58] For *Chekhov Lizardbrain*, they connected Anton Chekhov with brain science, turning the three sisters into brothers and the protagonist into an Aspie. The title refers to the theory that the human brain preserves earlier evolutionary stages within successive layers, a cold reptilian core surrounded by an instinctually emotional mammalian layer, both of them wrapped in the rationally conscious human neocortex. Temple Grandin, for one, relies upon this theory in the connections she draws between her autistic brain and the brains of animals.[59] James Sugg plays both the protagonist Dmitri and his alter ego Chekhov Lizardbrain, with mannerisms that clearly distinguish the two personae. Figure 7 shows him wearing Chekhov Lizardbrain's top hat and cutaway jacket over white boxer shorts. (In production, he generally puts the jacket on over his Dmitri costume, baggy brown pants and plaid shirt.) He stands before the red vel-

Figure 7. James Sugg as Dmitri/Chekhov Lizardbrain in Pig Iron Theatre's *Chekhov Lizardbrain*, 2008. Photo by Jason Frank Rothenberg.

vet curtain, which is opened to reveal the dark cave upstage that represents the inside of his brain. He separately articulates the extended fingers of each hand, the left raised near his hat and the right at his side.

The story seems to be that Dmitri, a socially awkward PhD botanist, has returned from Portland, Oregon, to his native Oswego, New York, and purchased the home of his childhood friends. This was an uncomfortable transaction, because these three brothers have in typical Chekhovian fashion disagreed about whether to sell the house after their mother's death. As a result, Dmitri didn't find out how to turn on the heat, and now he's suffering in the upstate New York winter, going over and over the chain of events that left him in this cold predicament. The play presents Dmitri's mental action within this situation, and the obsessive restaging of his interaction with the brothers gradually reveals both the recent events and key childhood interactions. The performance shifts back and forth between the historical present, with the brothers dressed in contemporary clothing, and the dramatized Chekhovian past, in which they wear long underwear, visibly false moustaches, and top hats.

Interactions between Dmitri and Chekhov Lizardbrain frame this remembered plot within the play. The piece begins in semidarkness as Dmitri makes his way around the red velvet rope that demarcates the playing space. Finally making his way inside the rope, he briefly poses with the manikin that holds his hat and jacket before rolling it upstage and disappearing behind the curtain. He reemerges as Chekhov Lizardbrain and sits at the table, preternaturally still except for his extending, moving, lizard-like fingers:

WELCOME

I know what you're thinking
who's that guy
no expression
such a bummer
what's wrong with him?
what's wrong with his head?
somebody help him
give him some medication
somebody help him out
he's in pain
that's where you're wrong

it's me
Chekhov Lizardbrain
Ta daaaaa.

I'm not so bad—I'm your host.[60]

He speaks mostly in a monotone, his mouth barely moving, but some words are overly dramatic. He pauses with an open mouth, his jaw slack. The show begins with this ironic presentation of an emcee's theatrical language and the performer's utterly untheatrical delivery. Dmitri interrupts this prologue, talking fast, blinking a lot, twitching:

DMITRI: Hey Chekhov Lizardbrain . . .
CHEKHOV LIZARDBRAIN: Yes?
DMITRI: Can I talk to you for a second . . .
CHEKHOV LIZARDBRAIN: Sure, Dmitri.
DMITRI: I don't want . . . I don't want anyone to hear me. . . . Is it time
    to—
CHEKHOV LIZARDBRAIN: Everyone can hear you right now, Dmi-
    tri. . . . Ladies and Gentlemen, Dmitri.
DMITRI: Oh . . . (to audience) Hi . . . um, let's see . . . oh, um . . . ladies
    and gentlemen . . .
    There's probably some things you want to know about,
    I want to know about some things, and the things I know about,
    um,
    The plants are very—
CHEKHOV LIZARDBRAIN: Whoa whoa whoa, Dmitri, we're doing a
    show here. We're on a very tight schedule.
DMITRI: I know. Let's keep going. I want you to keep going. I'm sorry.
    (77–78)

About halfway through the play, Dmitri explains the "lizardbrain" part of his alter-ego's name: "He's very in touch with his lower brain, you know, from the medulla oblongata, considering the theory of the three brains. That the upper brain is human brain and the middle brain is the dog brain and the lowest brain is the lizard brain. That's why they call him Chekhov Lizard-brain" (98).

Paul MacLean developed the triune brain theory in the 1950s, characterizing the brain stem and cerebellum as a primitive "lizard" brain responsible for the automatic fight-or-flight response to the environment; the so-called limbic system as a mammalian development responsible for emotions, memories, and habits; and the neocortex as a more recently evolved human brain, the locus of language, abstract thought, imagination, and consciousness. The notion that the reptile brain represents a more primitive base from which first the mammal and then the human brain evolved presumes an outmoded linear model for vertebrate evolution; that is, that humans represent the pinnacle of development and that studying the brains of reptiles and nonhuman mammals can reveal much about the functioning of these primitive regions preserved within our brains. In explaining the alternative radial (cladistic) model for evolution, Glenn Northcutt points out that modern reptiles and mammals have been evolving separately for approximately the same length of time; thus, "modern reptiles cannot be viewed as representing a more primitive grade of tetrapodal organization than mammals."[61] MacLean also consolidated previous work on the brain's involvement in emotion and memory to propose a discrete "limbic system" that developed in mammals. Neuroimaging research from the 1990s onward suggests that neither emotion nor memory are relegated to a discrete limbic system; instead, evidence suggests that general brain networks participate in emotional as well as nonemotional mental activity. In spite of its structural and functional imprecision, illustrations continue to use the concept freely, as does ongoing neuroscientific research.[62] Although the triune brain hasn't stood up to scientific scrutiny, it serves well as a concrete image for the Aspie-geek stock character: Dmitri's well-developed rational intellect is split off from his physical instincts, represented by Chekhov Lizardbrain. His emotional intelligence lacks personification. Dmitri can't turn on the heat.

The memory scenes occur in diachronic order, beginning with a chance meeting of Dmitri and Nikolai and progressing through his visit to the house and the change of ownership. In these memory scenes, Dmitri arrives at the house bearing a Japanese maple as gift, and he takes possession of the house. Clarifying the dramatic structure, Chekhov Lizardbrain explains "Anton Pavlovich Chekhov's 'Five Rules of Theatre'":

> One. Every play has four acts.
> That's simple enough. Four acts.
> Two. Keep the tragedy offstage.

I don't want to see that onstage. It's tragedy.
Three. Who owns the house?

...

Don't answer! It's not a question, it's a rule of theatre—has to be in
every play. Who owns the house.
Four. Every play has exactly one central symbol. Like a tree—

...

Five. Keep it clean, keep it civil.
That means no shouting, no taunting, and no cursing. (89)

Sascha, who lived in the house with his mother during her last years, wants
to remain but cannot buy out his brothers' shares. Each time their confrontation surfaces in Dmitri's memory, the scene disintegrates. The brothers
variously remind him that the memory being played out doesn't match what
happened, mouth his persistent question about the heat, steal Chekhov
Lizardbrain's brain and turn into a chorus of lizardbrain imposters dancing
around the space. Along the way, they also replay a childhood game of "Lost
and Lonely," a cruel hide-and-seek with Dmitri as "it" (94–95), left alone at
the end of the game and the end of the play.

In his last interaction with Chekhov Lizardbrain, Dmitri says, "Of course
I'm having trouble Chekhov Lizardbrain. It's cold and the heater broke and
the whole house is falling apart. It's just fucking falling apart and I'm all
alone" (123). To the suggestion that he's never alone, since he's the star of this
show going on in his brain, he objects that perhaps Chekhov Lizardbrain
should go play Lost and Lonely: "Only this time I won't come and find you.
I'll just let you sit there in the cave for seven fucking hours, all alone and crying, and somebody else will come find you and take you back to your own
home. And somebody else will come find you and take you back to your own
room and then you'll still just be sitting there all alone. And you won't know
when to stop" (123–24). This is Dmitri's state for his final run-on and mostly
incoherent monologue to the audience with no appearance by Chekhov Lizardbrain except for one last deadpan "ta da."

The production's costumes, stylized acting, and focus upon "who owns
the house" could qualify as camping up Chekhov, but I would argue that
the obsessive replaying of memory moves it into zany territory. Ngai defines zany as an aesthetic category and traces its frenzied, compulsive mimesis from the stock character of commedia dell'arte to the Lucille Ball
of I Love Lucy and Jim Carrey of The Cable Guy.[63] She focuses on depic-

tions of zany labor and proposes that "by turning the worker's beset, precarious condition into a spectacle for our entertainment, zaniness flatters the spectator's sense of comparative security, thus hailing her as a kind of phantasmagoric manager or implicit owner of the means of production."[64] The zany amuses its audience but produces a mixture of pleasure and aversion that I'm designating *eww*, because its "strained, desperate, and precarious" hyperactivity seems designed to activate "the spectator's desire for distance."[65] *Chekhov Lizardbrain* in fact resembles Ngai's theatrical examples, *Ubu Roi* and Dada cabaret, created just before and shortly after the modernist masterpiece that it parodies, Chekhov's 1901 play *The Three Sisters*.[66]

After all the zaniness, the loneliness of the ending leaves me with the uneasiness of a familiar feeling, not at a flattering distance but instead a bit too close for comfort, alone with consciousness, on a thin wire at the mental circus:

> DMITRI: don't look down dmitri this is the number one rule of consciousness don't look down and don't don't think about how thin thin thin thin the wire is this is the circus and everybody always goes home from the circus and at home some one broke in and stole everything and there's dirty handprints where the television set used to be and the paintings on the wall and the rugs on the floor and don't look down and see the empty house and that's the number one rule of consciousness don't look down or
> 
> *Pause.*
> 
> CHEKHOV LIZARDBRAIN: Ta da. (125–26)

This production presents the family as a sad object rather than a happy one. There's no sense in which the three brothers have something desirable. Their mother is dead. Sascha, who seems to have been close to her, hasn't fulfilled his potential, didn't go to college, cries about his uncertain future, and wants to keep the house. We don't learn much about Nicholas and Peter except that they have successful lives elsewhere—they mention Indianapolis.[67] The details matter only insofar as they establish a world that excludes Dmitri and does so actively. This is not a happy world, just a pattern of teasing partial invitations that end in rejection. Even Sascha rejects Dmitri's offer to stay on and share the house with him. Dmitri repeatedly exercises empathetic imagination, an effort never reciprocated. The play doesn't present his behavior as a problem to be solved—he's got a PhD, a career, and the money to buy the house. That's all we know about him except that he's cold and lonely. *Chekhov Lizardbrain* presents the family as something that needs cruelty to survive, that can't cohere except by placing someone else outside its velvet rope. The play presents a zany world working overtime to perpetuate a hopeless situation, the family, an exhausted structure. The deadpan Aspie is just trying to cope.

With *The Sound and the Fury (April Seventh, 1928)*, Elevator Repair Service (ERS) simultaneously presents, clarifies, and obscures the first chapter of William Faulkner's 1929 novel, the portion of its sound and fury that literally represents a tale told by an idiot.[68] Taking his title from Macbeth's description of life as "a tale / Told by an idiot, full of sound and fury, / Signifying nothing" (V.v), Faulkner conceived of Benjy as a subhuman creature stuck in mental infancy. He based the character on the son of a doctor in his childhood community. This man's "mind never developed" even as he lived into his thirties, chasing and scaring little girls, playing with his testicles "all the time," difficult for his family to control and requiring constant supervision.[69] Faulkner's neighbors apparently managed the situation more effectively than his fictional Compson clan, who castrate Benjy after he escapes from the fenced-in yard and grabs a schoolgirl passing by, "trying to say"—that is, attempting to speak to her but unable to do so.[70] The late nineteenth and early twentieth centuries interpreted an inability to communicate using language as an absence of thought and, influenced by social Darwinism and the eugenics movement, viewed diminished mental capacity as a cause of degenerate and criminal behavior. As Eyal and coauthors note, all sorts of socially undesirable actions could lead to institutionalization— "truancy, delinquency, epilepsy, alcoholism, sexual promiscuity, even masturbation."[71] People were supposedly institutionalized because they were "feebleminded . . . criminally inclined, psychotic, physically disabled, too young, demented," but the practice was in fact tied to class, ethnicity, and puberty: "From 1904 to 1945 the prototypical first admission to state institutions for the mentally retarded was a lower-class or immigrant 'moron' adolescent."[72] White middle- and upper-class parents such as the eleven families who brought their children to Leo Kanner for evaluation sought other alternatives well before their children reached puberty.[73]

The diagnostic category autism was not available when Faulkner created Benjy, epitomizing the situation of wealthy families whose money and social power made it possible to shelter a nonverbal family member at home.[74]

The novel chronicles the dissolution of this social structure by charting the decline of the extended Compson family. The pasture that Benjy roams in as a child provides a central landscape metaphor, sold and turned into a golf course, its caddies reminding him of his beloved sister Caddy, also gone. Faulkner had no insight into the mental life of a nonverbal person aside from imagining Benjy as an innocent, the still point around whom this formerly aristocratic Southern clan swirl with their various methods of self-destruction: alcoholic or suicidal men; neurasthenic or promiscuous women; incest, scorn, and thievery crossing the gender barrier. Two generations of an African American family live on the estate as servants who care for Benjy and enable their utterly dysfunctional employers to proceed from day to day. This sentimental proto-autist serves to index the moral character of each Compson in much the same way as the horses do for *Black Beauty* and *War Horse*,[75] his constructed innocence leaving space for neither his own moral capacity nor the reader's empathy. As Faulkner put it in an interview with James Meriwether, "You can't feel anything for Benjy because he doesn't feel anything."[76] Even seemingly sympathetic critics use this character to establish the boundary of not only normalcy but even humanity; for example, an influential early review by Evelyn Scott finds Benjy to be "beautiful as one of the helpless angels, and the more so for the slightly repellent earthiness that is his."[77] Maria Truchan-Tataryn contrasts Faulkner's objectification of Benjy with the agency and consciousness that he attributes to Caddy, noting that manuscript revisions progressively stripped away any "traces of agency or understanding in Benjy."[78] Somewhat paradoxically, Faulkner voices the first version of the Compsons' story as this inert object, Benjy. He then adopts three other voices, but Caddy, the agent with power to act upon her environment, never tells the story.

Assigning narration to a character who ostensibly lacks not only comprehension but language presents interesting medium-specific challenges. As a modernist literary experiment, Faulkner's writing demands patience and perseverance from its readers, who must appreciate the unusual narration of the first chapter or at least trust that the author will make reading it worth their while. Benjy's stream of consciousness jumps back and forth from the narrative present (his thirty-third birthday in 1928) to a few days before his fifth Christmas in 1898, touching upon multiple points in between. Whereas the novel clarifies the confusion of its first chapter by presenting the same events in subsequent chapters from the perspective of characters imagined to be more neurotypical, the ERS production clarifies by means of a chaotic acting out.[79] ERS performers literally read the novel aloud, by turns, as they enact what they're describing. The production follows a certain inexorable logic in placing everything—even the golf course scenes—within the confines of a shabby but ornate parlor, suggesting that this is the location for the chapter's action: Benjy, remembering. The actors compound the chaos by switching roles, playing cross-race and cross-gender, exchanging emblematic costume elements when a character passes from one body to another.

I saw the production for the first time at New York Theatre Workshop in 2008, more than twenty years after reading the novel with only modest understanding. In both cases, I needed to abandon any effort toward narrative comprehension in order to enjoy the experience. In the theater, my pleasure derived from the staging's odd cleverness, which also created suspense from the very first thwack of a golf club to the video "fire" within a sideboard rolled from place to place on the stage for different scenes—suspense related to staging surprises, not plot twists. The most memorable choices were ways of presenting the outdoor scenes within the scenic interior: the young Caddy climbed onto stacked-up furniture to peer over the set's back wall for the incident when she climbs a tree to look in through a window at Damuddy's wake, staying there for quite a long time as Benjy remembered other events; later, Miss Quentin clambered from the other direction over the same wall onto the stage to represent her escape out her bedroom window and down the same tree with a suitcase full of her uncle's money. After multiple subsequent viewings of video documentation and then another live performance of the slightly changed revival at the Public Theater in 2015, with additional reading of the novel along the way, I can follow the narrative quite well—but this seems beside the point. The knowledge that ERS used a hypertext version of the novel to position each passage within the fictional timeline and made shifts in casting each time the narrative made a jump in time engages my interest but affects my reception very little.[80] For one thing, any impulse to track these shifts quickly dissipates while watching.

ERS's adaptation gives Benjy an embodied presence that exceeds Faulkner's outlines. Aaron Landsman, who plays Benjy in a few scenes, presents him as both physically and vocally mute, a minimally reactive and pitiful object; in other scenes, Landsman plays Quentin, TP, and a golfer's caddie. As embodied by Susie Sokol at the heart of the production, though, Benjy guides the audience through the Compson world. Sokol is the first to read from the novel, and she alone takes on no other character, her Benjy

Figure 8. Elevator Repair Service's *The Sound and the Fury*, 2015, at the Public Theater, New York. Pictured, left to right: Kaneza Schaal as Caddy and Susie Sokol as Benjy. Photo © Paula Court.

most often positioned in a chair center stage and looking out at the audience. She observes the family, listens to the moaning attributed to Benjy but emanating from the theater's sound system rather than her body, attempts to follow the commands directed at Benjy: "Keep your hands in your pockets" causes her to shove them inside her pants, all the way down to the knees. In pursuit of a cuddle, she flings herself headlong and log-like across Mother's lap. Sokol's Benjy is silent (except in her initial reading) but wonderfully expressive, and I read in her face and body the same bemused incomprehension with which I watched the show, the same generally good-natured willingness to go along for the ride with these messy Compsons. Figure 8 shows Sokol in the chair, her hands emerging from the hem of her rugby shirt to grasp the backs of her raised knees, her gaze directed down, brows knit. The shirt's sleeves are tied together behind her thighs, restricting her movement like an odd, improvised straitjacket. Her feet rest on the shoulder of Kaneza Schaal, who kneels before her as Caddy, reaching toward her and speaking.

As Sarah Jane Bailes argues, all of ERS's works explicitly and intentionally fail as clear communication.[81] Rather than constructing a coherent narrative to unify a piece, the company disperses meaning among the various elements of performance much as it disperses authority among the creative ensemble (even while designating John Collins as director). The shows remain open even though the composition follows rules that an audience most likely cannot discern.[82] These rules generate material without a communicative intention, lacking central coherence, not adhering to communicative norms, paying extremely close attention to details that theatrical conventions most often relegate to a supporting function. The performers ostentatiously fail to display appropriate affect, at some times deadpan and at others wildly histrionic. Dance offers not only what company member Rinne Groff identifies as "joyous energy" but also, according to codirector Steve Bodow, a way to "focus exclusively on the musical composition of a non-musical element of the show."[83] Bailes observes that "in ERS shows, dances generally serve the function of 'ensembling' the group from disparate circumstances, changing the direction of the piece or neutralizing it before releasing them back into the fragmented montage of texts that make up a performance. But movement also functions as . . . a way of copying, translating, and reterritorializing material."[84]

The Sound and the Fury's dance intervals remove the performers from any character specification whatsoever: before the actors begin reading the novel, Ben Williams and Mike Iveson perform an Appalachian flatfoot routine; later, the entire company joins in at a point coincident with Caddy's wedding day—although without narrativizing the dance as part of the festivities. According to Olga Muratova, a video clip in the documentary Talking Feet (1987) inspired these dances, which were in turn foundational for the staging.[85] Noting that the dancers' bodies are fragmented just as Benjy's perceptions are, and their "faces wear an absolutely impenetrable and detached expression of not being involved in the act," she felt that the dances "rankled" Benjy even as they energized the audience.[86] Ben Brantley saw them as "a sensual metaphor for Benjy's watching social rituals without having a clue as to what they mean."[87] He enjoyed giving himself over to the ERS rendition of the Compsons' incoherence and praised the 2008 production, as did Hilton Als, but the clipping file in the New York Public Library's Billy Rose Theatre Collection held many negative responses, traces of critical irritation. Whereas Als observed that roughly a third of the New York Theatre Workshop audience left at intermission,[88] I noticed only one couple walk out of the intermission-free 2015 remount at the Public, which sold out and extended its run. A number of my companions dozed off. One who stayed awake but felt quite irritated by the production wondered whether they were trying to produce an experience of autism for the audience, given that the actions of the people on stage are clearly purposeful but remain mystifying, and the chaos at times builds to produce a sensory overload. All of ERS's work and, indeed, much postrealist theater would seem to produce this experience.

Yet these interpretations by my companion, Brantley, and even Muratova point back to the fundamental shortcoming of autism tropes. ERS builds this postmodern performance atop a modernist novel, and audiences respond to Faulkner's conception of Benjy. Truchan-Tataryn understands why the author would have taken this approach in 1929, although she refuses to condone it; however, she sees no excuse for subsequent scholarship that considers Benjy to accurately represent mental retardation or autism rather than recognizing and interrogating the "imaginings projected upon a population denied agency and voice by authors of public policy as well as narrative texts." She observes that even critics who argue with the diagnosis "idiot" fail to challenge the novel's validity as a representation of mental disability—a stasis in critical response to disability that contrasts markedly with the well-developed critique of Faulkner's constructions of gender and race.[89] His idiot figure correlates surprisingly well with its replacement, the autist as conceived by the Theory-of-Mind theorists, all too often similarly uninterrogated. As Melanie Yergeau argues, "Theories about ToM impact the autistic bodymind in material and violent ways. . . . [D]enying autistic selfhood and denying autistic corporeality and denying autistic rhetoricity reifies systemic abuse and ableism. . . . [A]utistic people have come to represent a tidily bounded limit case that signifies what it means to be inhuman—all in the name of empiricism, all in the name of ToM."[90]

Both *Chekhov Lizardbrain* and *The Sound and the Fury* stage a sort-of autist remembering. The hypercortical Dmitri has trouble understanding the behavior of the three brothers whose childhood home he now occupies. The nonverbal Benjy has trouble understanding, period. Both productions use these characters to position their audiences at the center of a zany compulsion to reconfigure both the family and representation, but the possibilities that they open are recaptured by the representational history of outdated autism tropes. In the midst of a noisy but incommunicative world, the audience is directed toward understanding modernist literature and the unraveled family rather than toward any sort of ethical engagement with autism.

Like all of the works that this chapter analyzes, they position autism prosthetically. *Body Awareness, Two Thousand Years, Falling,* and *Curious Incident* construe autism as a problem to be solved, center this problem in the family, and develop their complication and resolution dramatically. The family crisis connects metonymically to a larger social crisis, but only for *Falling* is this social crisis directly related to autism. *Chekhov Lizardbrain* and *The Sound and the Fury* construe the family as a problem to be solved and develop things theatrically. Both theatrical and dramatic in its structure, *Curious Incident*'s theatrical elaboration remains contained by its dramatic narrative and its reliance upon familiar AS tropes. Successful art can shore up faulty paradigms and through a looping effect perpetuate ideas beyond what they deserve. The greater the success, the more serious the impact and often, as in the case of *Curious Incident*, the more difficult to extract and analyze the underlying assumptions. Popular works on autism and representations in popular culture accept too fully the theory that the disorder has a unified cause, and that cause is a cognitive deficit, an inability to properly attribute mental states to other persons and to reflect upon one's own. This turns some of the difficulties most terrifying for autistic people, such as extremes of sensitivity and insensitivity, into second-order problems, or symptoms associated with a primary mindblindness. Furthermore, the predominance of Aspie characters elides the challenges of expanding the boundaries of the human in order to fully accommodate different types of autistic lifeworlds.

# CHAPTER 4

# *Performing with Animals*

As mentioned in chapter 3, *The Curious Incident of the Dog in the Night-Time* begins with the shock of a German shepherd corpse, skewered with a pitchfork, illuminated by a flash of light. The dead dog arouses an affective intensity that the plot directs toward the teenaged protagonist and his family, from the very start minimizing empathetic identification with the boy's father. This initial provocation accomplished, the dog recedes into the story's background, mentioned but not again seen. A living pet rat makes intermittent appearances, generally in a carrier and apparently a surprise hit both onstage and backstage for the Broadway production.[1] The fraught son-father and audience-father relationship moves to a sweet and reassuring resolution when the father brings a live puppy onto the stage. These animals, the live and the dead, channel audience affect and cue coherent emotional responses to particular characters. As befits a family-oriented production aiming for strong ticket sales, *Curious Incident* weights its affect economy very heavily toward tender concern and limits the shock of animal death to its opening punctuation.

Martin McDonagh's *The Lieutenant of Inishmore* (2001) follows a surprisingly similar trajectory: on the table in a Galway cottage at opening "lies a dead black cat, its head half missing," assumed to be the Wee Thomas beloved of Padraic, a psychopathic terrorist who has further splintered off from an IRA splinter group.[2] "Bits of its brain plop out" when Padraic's father and the young neighbor who has delivered the corpse pick it up (3), and their hands get bloody stroking it (7). Desperate to fend off Padraic's fury, they find a replacement cat, inconveniently orange, and coat it in black shoe polish (22–26)—to no avail. Upon his return, Padraic "shoots the sleeping cat, point blank. It explodes in a ball of blood and bones" (40). The cat action continues in this vein and remains disgustingly comic. Every single character expresses concern about the cat and cold disregard for the humans who are tortured, maimed, killed, and dismembered on stage, thus establishing the situation and providing ongoing gruesome humor. For the Atlantic Theater production, the beautiful, raked shale floor of the set literally ran with fake blood, eliciting a reiterated *eww* of disgust.[3] This chapter begins with stagings of animal death to elicit disgust; moves on to examine performances that lead their audiences across the borders patrolled by disgust, bringing them to interested engagement; and finally considers explicit efforts at ethical performance with companion species.

## ANIMAL DEATH AND DISGUST

After outlining the predominant evolutionary explanations for disgust, Paul Rozin, Jonathan Haidt, and Clark McCauley identify its consistent facial expression across cultures. Many (though not all) languages derive the words for disgust from eating, extending food-related terminology to other forms of aversion.[4] These researchers consider disgust to be an "affect program" as articulated by Tomkins and Ekman; that is, a very wide variety of inputs ("cognitive appraisals of environmental events") produce a quite consistent output ("behaviors, expressions, physiological responses"). From its original function of keeping dangerous substances out of human mouths, disgust has evolved to also limit conscious engagement with undesirable phenomena.[5] *Lieutenant* cannily combines and confuses core disgust, a visceral rejection of potentially damaging foods or sources of infection, with the moral disgust that prompts rejection of people, things, and behaviors. A live cat saunters into the carnage at the play's end: Wee Thomas was "out gallivanting" all along, and the kitty corpse was misidentified as his. This animate punchline not only underlines the pointlessness of the play's violence but also comforts the audience, encouraged by the plot to feel more warmth for the felines onstage than for the human characters. This *aww* response should ideally leave its audience less comfortable than *Curious Incident*'s puppy does, given that they've likely flinched but also laughed their way through a bloodbath and now feel a tenderness for Wee Thomas akin to Padraic's.

The approach is sweetly gentle in one case and viciously comic in the other, but in both plays the characters' affection for household pets high-lights their failure at managing appropriate human relationships. The eponymous animal of Edward Albee's *The Goat, or Who is Sylvia?* (2002) occupies a similar position, although she appears onstage only as a corpse, producing a shock at the end similar to that with which *Curious Incident* begins. Up to that point, the audience is cued to imagine Sylvia as a liv-ing creature around whom the play's conflicts swirl. Protagonist Martin's sexual relationship with the goat provokes the play's secondary characters to violence, first verbal and finally physical. The premise echoes Rochelle Owens's *Futz!* (1968), in which a farmer's carnal love for his sow provokes irate neighbors to kill her. Owens's brutal farce disgusted the critics, who also pronounced it overly didactic; for example: "*Futz!* is less likely to stir the senses than raise the gorge. Rochelle Owens' play is a sad saga of bestiality. Her preposterous moral is that people are beastlier than animals, particu-larly to a boy who prefers to make love to a sow. . . . Amanda [the sow] is never seen. Presumably, no pig was willing to take the part."[6] Reviewers in the 1960s did not deem it necessary to draw parallels to the public expres-sions of moral disgust at interracial and same-sex relationships that Owens was clearly satirizing only one year after *Loving vs. Virginia* and one year before the Stonewall riots. Thirty-four years later, *The Goat* more explicitly works out the reactionary logic according to which accepting same-sex mar-riage would lead inexorably to bestiality and incest.

Albee wraps his exploration of bestiality in a stream of brittle wit and intellectual discourse, generically closer to comedy of manners than to either the farce of *Futz!* or the tragedy with which it explicitly aims to engage. Re-ferring to "that jolly chorus of laughter that keeps rising from the audience," Ben Brantley discerned "a comfortable, self-congratulatory quality in the air, heard among people who are already in on the punch line of an elaborate joke."[7] John Kuhn notes that when Martin describes the participants in his bestiality twelve-step group during a long confrontation with his wife Stevie, "each new coupling [from dog to goose] is funnier to the audience and more infuriating to Stevie," who continues to make wisecracks even as she breaks pottery and overturns furniture. Sylvia herself remains an abstraction up until the final moment, when Stevie drags in the goat's corpse wrapped in a somewhat bloody sheet with the head exposed. Una Chaudhuri proposes that the corpse reanimalizes what has been for the audience an imagined (but living) creature.[8] Yet productions of any play that calls for a dead ani-mal will almost inevitably use an effigy; obviously, the prop presents fewer ethical problems and is easier to maintain over the course of a run. And as Peta Tait argues, the real presence of a fake corpse affects audience response:

> The use of a replica in human entertainment might draw attention to the species, but, paradoxically, such substitution could also be counterproductive for the living animal. . . . Prop replicas of birds, fish and animals in theatre represent realness that can be cognitively appreciated but deliver only limited bodily impact. It is possible to speculate that the replica might actually negate reactions to deadness, since the idea of realness can be received without visceral confrontation.[9]

Although viewing on video and advance knowledge of *The Goat*'s ending further dulled for me the visceral impact of its goat corpse,[10] it seems safe to assess its engagement with actual animal life as minimal.

Both McDonagh and Albee play moral disgust in a comic register. They keep the audience laughing, but laughing with some discomfort—a mixture common for core disgust as well. Rozin and coauthors observe that experiment participants generally react with a mixture of laughter and disgust expressions as they perform actions such as eating chocolate shaped like dog feces or drinking a liquid into which a sterilized cockroach has been dipped. Subjects also rate different situations on a disgust scale, and they are free to end the engagement when they wish. Most participants later describe the experience as "interesting and enjoyable"[11]—a parallel with this chapter's trajectory, by the way. Although many considerations of disgust limit themselves to the ways in which it pushes us away, Carolyn Korsmeyer elaborates upon its simultaneous power to attract:

> When disgusted one is almost wholly occupied with the sensory presentation or appearance of the intentional object rather than with its existential status. The intentional structure of this emotion is directed so strongly toward the properties of the disgusting object that it rivets our attention, even at the same time that it repels. This aversion actually searches out its object.[12]

Korsmeyer builds upon Aurel Kolnai's observation that disgust reaches out, in contrast to fear's inward turn, and "the tip of the intention penetrates the object, probing and analyzing it, as it were, and becoming immersed in its motions or in its persistence."[13] Because disgust is particularly sticky, "distinguished ... by the way in which it adheres to the object which is its cause,"[14] its object retains a disgusting patina long after the initial revulsion passes. Yet the disgusting object seems to stick to its viewer as well and thus lays the groundwork for fascination, for "there is contained already in its inner logic a possibility of ... touching, consuming, or embracing it."[15]

Albee both draws us in and pushes us away with moral disgust, whereas McDonagh uses elicitors such as freely flowing blood to bring core disgust into the mix, too.[16] Sam Shepard's *Curse of the Starving Class* (1977) engages more widely with core disgust, using a complex range of sensory stimulation. Unlike Albee's goat, Shepard's lamb appears on stage live as well as dead. The lamb remains peripheral to the plot although richly symbolic, representing—for a start—the land, the family, and the American dream. William Kleb enumerates some further referents: "innocence, need, disease, starvation, salvation, castration, rebirth, sacrifice, the Lamb of God, afterbirth, loss, death, meat, the civilized (inside), the uncivilized (outside)—and throughout, ... Wesley and his relationship with his father. Probably more."[17] Wesley is the teenage son of Weston, an alcoholic, and his estranged wife, Ella. His younger sister Emma completes the central family quartet. The symbolism proliferates well past any possibility of coherence—interpretation leads only to cliché, as Sheila Rabillard points out, likely a purposeful evasion in this highly poetic playwright's first flirtation with the elements of domestic realism.[18] Observing that everything about the play is teasingly ambiguous, beginning with the title—given the multiple referents for "curse" and perpetual hunger but certainly no "starvation"—Stephen J. Bottoms observes that "the progression of the piece is dominated by internal self-contradiction" and "mixes together clashing elements, particularly the comic and the horrific, so as to unsettle the audience by provoking conflicting emotional responses."[19]

Many of the play's emotional clashes inhere in the living animal on stage. Initially, Wesley is keeping the lamb warm in the kitchen of his dysfunctional family's rundown ranch house while he treats it for blowfly strike. Even if a production were to use a living lamb infested with blowfly larvae, unlikely for ethical reasons, the condition would not be visible to the audience; rather, the lamb's cuteness generally produces an *aww* response. As one review notes, the animal "looks adorable, makes noises when it has no lines and tends to relieve itself, albeit discreetly, in front of the audience."[20] The lamb upstages the human actors and registers as out of place both on the theatrical stage and in the fictive kitchen, where characters object to its presence:

EMMA: (*to* WESLEY) What's the matter with him?

WESLEY: (*watching lamb*) Maggots.

EMMA: Can't you keep him outside? He'll spread germs in here.

WESLEY: (*watching lamb*) You picked that up from Mom.

EMMA: Picked what up?

WESLEY: Germs. The idea of germs. Invisible germs mysteriously float-ing around in the air. Anything's a potential carrier.

TAYLOR: (*to* WESLEY) Well, it does seem that if the animal has maggots it shouldn't be in the kitchen. Near the food.

WESLEY: We haven't got any food.

TAYLOR: Oh. Well, when you do have food you prepare it in here, don't you?

EMMA: That's nothing. My brother pisses on the floor in here.

TAYLOR: Do you always talk this way to strangers?

EMMA: Look, that's his piss right there on the floor. Right on my chart.[21]

If staged exactly as scripted, the actor playing Wesley has by this point urinated on stage and his mother, Ella, has fried bacon.[22] Layered on top of these lingering odors, the script calls for boiling artichokes—the smell of which a secondary character likens to "stale piss" (174)—heating cof-fee, frying ham and eggs, and the scent of the lamb itself. Regardless of whether any individual smell pleases or disgusts a spectator, this olfactory dramaturgy likely grows unpleasant in the enclosed space of a theater, just as extraordinary as the live animal. Nicholas Ridout productively observes that live animals are out of place in the theater, which "is all about humans coming face to face with other humans and either liking it or not liking it. The animal clearly has no place in such a communication." Relegated by human convention to the realm "nature," the animal intrudes oddly in this place for "culture raised to the power of two"—in this case, as so often, a represented human dwelling (on stage) enclosed within another building (the theater).[23] Just as the animal's presence challenges the separation of illusionistic reality presented on stage from the "real" world that it repre-sents, smells (including the animal's odor as well as the foodstuffs) chal-lenge realism's conventional exclusion of the audience's sensory experience from the dramatic world. As Stan Garner notes, "Shepard's stagecraft here re-embodies his spectators by challenging the perceptual bracketing with which realism seeks to erase their sensory presence to play and stage. In so doing, Shepard implicates his audience in questions of hunger—actual and literal—that are attendant upon an embodied life in contact with his material and human environments."[24]

In dissonant counterpoint to the lamb's cuteness, the dialogue repeatedly invokes the maggots for which Wesley's drunk and disheveled father Weston recommends applying "some a' that blue shit" (159). After spending the second act offstage, the lamb returns at the start of the third. The stage directions specify that "*the lamb is heard 'baaing' in the dark as the lights slowly come up on WESTON at the table*," now sober and talking to the lamb as he folds clean laundry, effectively reborn thanks to an early morning reconnection with the land and a bathing ritual. After the reassurance that "there's worse things than maggots ya' know. Much worse. Maggots go away if they're properly attended to" (182), he shares a story about castrating lambs in the spring, throwing their testes up onto the roof of a shed for an eagle swooping down to eat them. Continued references to the maggots establish that Weston has gotten rid of them even as the descriptions become more revolting: "Didn't think he'd pull through. Maggots clear up into the small intestine" (187). Wesley unsuccessfully tries to effectuate his own renewal through bathing but comes back on stage wet and naked, carries the live lamb off, and then returns wearing Weston's cast-off raggedy clothes, announcing that he has butchered the lamb because they "need some food." Growing increasingly bewildered, he ravenously eats everything he can pull out of the now well-stocked refrigerator, "*throwing half-eaten food to one side and then digging into more*" (192), finally eating scraps from the floor (195). The reiterated maggots, the smells, the characters' hunger, and the actor's eating all elicit some degree of core disgust.

In the play's last scene, a pair of giggling thugs dump the "*skinned lamb carcass*" into the pen on stage (198), and Wesley and his mother complete the clearly well-known family anecdote that Weston had been telling to the lamb, with the eagle and a big tom cat tearing one another to pieces in the sky. This violent and somewhat puzzling animal imagery ties things together, as Bottoms points out, without creating any clear parallels: "The story could allude to the 'animal thing' of inherited masculine brutality, to the struggle of the animalistic predators for the farm deeds, or even to the helpless victimization of the lamb's (and by extension Wesley's) 'manhood' at the claws of disparate forces."[25] In addition to evoking blood sacrifice, the cute lamb has become horrifying almost-meat, a link back to the chicken that Emma describes (in the first act) having raised, killed, and cleaned—only to discover, as she prepares a 4-H presentation on properly cutting up a chicken, that her mother has already cooked and eaten it. Aside from those in the eagle-cat story, this play's animals remain more material than metaphorical, and the lamb ends as a carcass rather than a corpse, pointing toward the very material contribution that animals as meat make to human life.

*Curse* presents a practical, meat-producing rancher's view of animal life, but audiences respond to the lamb with tender concern. Preview articles for recent productions include information about how the lamb is being cared for, and reviews note that it upstages even the Wesley-actor's penis.[26] The sight of the carcass most likely repels the audience, a repulsion intensified by the pointlessness of the killing (Weston shouts, "THE ICE BOX IS CRAMMED FULL A' FOOD! . . . WHAT'D YA' GO AND BUTCHER IT FOR? HE WAS GETTING BETTER!" [191]) and the nonsensical final scene. Observing that the gangsters who bring in the carcass are "entirely extraneous to the plot" rather than serving as "some deus ex machina device," Bottoms describes their arrival as "a gruesomely hilarious intervention which assaults the audience with contradictory emotions: their giggling is highly entertaining, but should we laugh or weep? Is Emma dead? Where did they come from anyway? Look at that bloody lamb!"[27] The script fills the seven pages between Wesley's postbutchery entrance and the carcass display with a series of false cadences; that is, events and conversations that promise but do not deliver resolution. Wesley's dialogue ("I had the lamb's blood dripping down my arms. I thought it was me for a second. I thought it was me bleeding") produces not only a revulsion captured by his sister's response ("You're disgusting. You're even more disgusting than him [Weston]. And that's pretty disgusting" [195]) but also some sympathy for yet another pathetically ineffectual attempt on his part to affect the course of events. Both the stage directions and intervening events distance him from the death. Significantly, we do not see him dripping with the blood of the lamb, and for the final moments, he focuses elsewhere: "*ELLA is facing downstage now, staring at the lamb carcass in the pen. WESLEY has his back to her upstage. . . . They stay in these positions facing away from each other*" (199). The play's rich but rather opaque symbolism and unresolved plot combine with the cumulative olfactory onslaught and the sight of a woolly baby animal senselessly transformed into a bloody carcass, all of these together perhaps producing a powerful affective encounter that exceeds any discrete emotional category.

Albee's goat and Shepard's lamb participate in similar affective economies: killing the animal produces moral disgust directed at a previously sympathetic character without fitting that character neatly into the villain prototype. The audience understands the character's motivations, understands that the action is wrong, and feels an active confusion similar to what the character is meant to feel—yet for different reasons. Both plays foreground their experimentation with dramatic form—for Shepard, domestic realism; for Albee, tragedy—and refuse the customary resolution. But I would argue that *Curse* comes closer to accomplishing what Chaudhuri proposes for *The Goat*; that is, the reanimalization of an animal who is otherwise present as a carrier for human affective investment. I would argue that the fake lamb carcass has more impact than Sylvia's effigy, both due to the earlier presence of the live lamb and to the lingering odors of meat that has been cooked onstage.

I purposely use the term *effigy* rather than *prop* in order to mark the heavy load that these dead animals carry in their respective plays. As Joseph Roach explains, an effigy "fills by means of surrogation a vacancy created by the absence of an original."[28] At the simplest level, the animal effigy fills in for the corpse of an actual or fictional animal that once was alive—it fills a vacancy created not by death (as in the case of a king's effigy) but rather by the theater's reticence about bringing an actual dead creature onstage. But Roach extends the meaning of *effigy* beyond constructed replicas to include "more elusive but more powerful effigies fashioned from flesh." These performative effigies "consist of a set of actions that hold open a place in memory into which many different people may step according to circumstances and occasions."[29] When an animal steps into such a vacancy—or, rather, is *made* to step in—the resulting multilevel surrogation may still perform a similar function; that is, to provide coherence for the community that the act of surrogation gathers together. Here, the audience presumably coheres around opposition to the compulsory happy family.

## DEATH AND BARE LIFE

The impact of dead-animal effigies in scripted theater pales in comparison with Otto Muehl's *O Tannenbaum* (1969) and *O Sensibility* (1970) and Hermann Nitsch's six-day *Orgies Mystery Theatre* (1998), art performances with only minimal linguistic mediation. After moving to Germany when his notoriety made work in Vienna impossible, Muehl began performing live actions at screenings of his films, typically including sex acts, urination, and vomiting.[30] In a 1968 manifesto demanding "freedom for all members of the human and animal body," Muehl justified the killing of animals as part of these art actions: "in times gone by, animals and people were ritually tortured and killed. nowadays, animals are slaughtered en masse in order to fill the billions of gnome-stomachs. masses of gnomes allow themselves to be slaughtered for politically senseless objectives. should art alone be forced to look on idly?"[31] (Muehl habitually uses the German word for a garden gnome when referring to the petit bourgeoisie.) In keeping with this critique, he explicitly articulated his aim to create shock for "the audience, which is perverted in a traditional, conventional way, for those suffering from mental stagnation, for the masses bogged down in conformity."[32]

When Muehl's actions included an animal, he typically juxtaposed its slaughter alongside human nudity. *O Tannenbaum* featured a pig trussed up and butchered in a bed as a choir sang "Silent Night." Malcolm Green indicates that the action ended after urine, feces, and the pig's blood showered a naked woman.[33] References to the woman as "decorated" by these substances suggest a parallel to the Christmas tree onstage, which would normally bear tinsel, candles, and ornaments rather than the accumulated fluids and offal that eventually covered it here. Muehl specified that the pig be killed by a professional butcher in order to represent holiday indulgence, the obscenity of the act a metonym for the obscenity of bourgeois life. His scenario characterized the action as "a satire on marital life and the triviality of Christmas celebrations ('the festival of pious songs, gluttony and a brief ceasefire in Vietnam')." The three hundred spectators had been warned at the start of the action about exactly what they would see. Due to their "fairly lukewarm" response, Muehl abandoned the pig-scalding and -scraping that he had scripted. A secondary audience, not present, reacted more strongly: a petition on "Human Dignity" gathered 18,000 signatures, the university rector resigned, and further actions were banned in Germany. Charges were filed but then dropped because the event included no overtly sexual action, and no spectators actually walked out.[34]

Muehl's last action in Germany, *O Sensibility*, develops themes initiated by *Leda and the Swan* (1964), in which a woman engaged in sexual activity with a plastic swan.[35] *O Sensibility* begins with a woman and a man individually engaging in erotic activity with a live goose as it attempts to get away from them. (The bird seems less distressed by the woman's endeavors.) An orgy follows, during which one of the male participants inserts the bird's beak into a woman's vagina. Finally two men decapitate the bird over a masturbating woman, and one of them attempts to penetrate her with the bird's neck stub. Both the sexual uses of the goose and its decapitation may well have shocked and disgusted the audience, but they "heartily applauded" and public nuisance charges were dropped "because nobody complained and no offended spectators could be found."[36] A rather hilarious letter from Muehl depicts the second of two performances as an extended assault on the audience. The two female participants recruited men from the audience ("two new nudes") who then tried to engage the women sexually: "several people said the new nudes spoilt the action with their awkwardness. as if awkwardness wasn't one of our goals. one of them wanted to fuck mica, that wasn't exactly why she was there, as she said later, so i pissed on the bloke's back. malicious joy and laughter from the audience." The letter describes limited reactions to the goose, which Muehl claims to have hypnotised: "it was too much for one of the lads when the goose-blood spurted on to him," and "people stepped back, startled," when Muehl "swung the goose over [his] head, roared . . . and flung it at the wall." Yet in advance of this second performance, gallery owner Adam Seide had attempted to free the bird, who had spent the day "in seide's playpen as a plaything for his child" and was not as "gentle" as the first had been.[37]

Beginning with this attempt at goose rescue, people began to disrupt the actions and to remove the animals that Muehl intended to use. He had to cancel an event in Germany after threats to the gallery. A sheep to be slaughtered in Bremen for *Advent* was stolen, and "the audience of 1000 responded to the action by throwing eggs at Muehl and his two colleagues, storming the stage and breaking up the performance."[38] Author/actor Heathcote Williams stole the duck that Muehl intended to kill in Amsterdam for an event that generated protests, as did a planned chicken killing at the 1970 International Underground Film Festival in London for which the organizers would not permit his "expanded cinema" event although several others went forward as planned. Muehl and "his two well-trained girls" disrupted an action by Jeff Keen featuring his wife "in a G-string cavorting with a youth in a boiler suit topped by a pair of flashing red eyes." Muehl apparently considered this too tame, because he and his companions attempted to perform oral sex on the pair of performers.[39]

Muehl clearly advocated sexual liberation and, like so many others during the late 1960s and early 1970s, understood the release of sexuality from conventional restraints in revolutionary terms. Cecilia Novero argues that the intentional and explicit perversity of these actions "extends beyond the domain of the strictly sexual: it is a struggle against the order of the paternal law (or the Symbolic)."[40] Novero uses Herbert Marcuse's understanding of perversion to interpret Muehl's sexualization of the gooseneck:

> If in the history of Western culture and art the so-called individual has been reified and reduced—beyond its possibility of pleasure—to some function or another, so too have its organs been functionalized towards reproduction. Muehl exhibits this reification by using the body and its organs as mere things among other things and by reducing the body to the sex organ: the fetish of the pornography industry. The sex organ becomes the metonymy for a human reduced to a (paradoxical) animal machine.[41]

In other words, when Muehl "grabbed the goose and stuffed its bleeding stump of a neck into mica's hole, she screeched lasciviously, i had rolled a condom over the neck beforehand,"[42] the dying animal's body part took on the penis's "proper" function. He later identified the pig killed in Brunswick with his mother and the escaped Bremen sheep with his father; thus, he intended by slaughtering these animals to obliterate his own psyche's triangular, Oedipal structuring.[43] The pig and the sheep undoubtedly saw their lives in different terms and cared little for Muehl's psychic healing. As a corollary to Peta Tait's assertion that the use of fabricated animal-corpse replicas in the theater limits the audience's visceral response, pushing a scripted animal death more safely into the symbolic realm, I suggest that symbolism can never fully contain an actual animal's actual death. This becomes clear in Hermann Nitsch's *Orgies Mystery Theatre*, which—in spite of its complex investment in symbolism—gives dead animals pride of place.

In contrast to Muehl's sexualized Direct Art actions of the 1960s and early 1970s, which as Beth Hinderliter observes aimed "to inflict new injuries that would take precedence over preexisting social problems," Nitsch began during this same period to script theatricalized rituals oriented toward what he conceived as shamanic healing.[44] Upon initial examination, both Muehl and Nitsch appear to engage with animal death in pursuit of a Dionysian transcendence of social roles, individualization, and ego—a regressive abreaction aiming to transform the individual and ultimately society as well. Muehl largely abandoned art actions in the mid-1970s to focus on increasingly problematic experiments in communal living, and the critical literature—like his own writing—interprets his actions' symbolism as a satirical political commentary. Yet most writers elide the political implications of Nitsch's artistic engagement with animal death, which became much more elaborate after his wife used an inheritance to buy Prinzendorf Castle in Austria and he began to actualize the *Orgies Mystery Theatre* (OMT) that he had been planning since 1957, inspired particularly by Wagnerian opera and Greek tragedy. Nitsch's first manifesto stipulates in its fifth statute that "the o.m. theatre will breed its own cattle. no animal is to be killed on my account. in the o.m. theatre, only animals that have died of old age or have had to be put down will be disembowelled and rent." Yet the manifesto begins with the declaration "on 4 june 1962 i shall disembowel, rend and tear apart a dead lamb," unlikely to have died of old age. Nitsch understood this "Seventh Painting Action" as a sacrifice through which he took upon himself "all that appears negative, unsavoury, perverse and obscene, the lust and the resulting sacrificial hysteria, in order to spare YOU the defilement and shame entailed by the descent into the extreme." The manifesto's sixth statute further articulates a "wish to liberate humanity from its animal instincts."[45] However humanely Nitsch may have cared for the animals in advance of their "performance" in the OMT, and regardless of how painless the butchering, the actions routinely "liberate" these flesh-and-blood effigies from their animal life and transform them into anthropocentric symbols.

Susan Jarosi, who attended the first complete staging of Nitsch's *Six-Day Play* in 1998, characterizes its animal sacrifice as simultaneously symbolic and actual, with animal corpses calling to mind Greek and Hebrew sacrificial victims as well as the human sacrifice of Christian mythos—the lamb of God.[46] She details the materials required:

> 1,000 litres of blood; three live bulls slaughtered by professional butchers; slaughtered pigs and sheep provided by an abattoir; sixty stretchers and fifteen carrying devices; 10,000 metres of canvas for the painting actions; 1,000 kilos of tomatoes; 1,000 kilos of grapes; 10,000 roses and 10,000 other assorted flowers; 13,000 litres of wine; one bulldozer; and two Panzer tanks.[47]

The first slaughter, of a steer, capped the event's opening procession. Others followed, with continuously available wine abetting explicitly "Dionysian" activities throughout the six days.[48] Participants trampled and ripped apart all kinds of organic matter including the entrails that feature in so many images of the event, seeming to achieve the sort of ecstasy that Nietzsche imagined: "As the frenzy reached its climax, the participants became so mired in blood that their individual bodies were rendered indistinguishable, moulded into a collective mass of writhing limbs." Jarosi considered the effect to be more than mere appearance "as participants relinquished their individual identity and merged themselves into the organic movement of the mass."[49]

Video of the event's third day, the "Day of Dionysus," shows participants trampling tomatoes and lamb corpses; palpating entrails and stuffing them into an animal carcass or slathering them onto naked people—mostly but not exclusively male—bound to crosses both upright and supine; pouring foods, unidentifiable pulp, blood, and wine over the naked humans, at least one of these men massaging the pulp over his penis; pouring the substances onto a couple who seem to be engaging in hyperslow sexual intercourse. Accompanying the overlapping actions, the brass band playing Nitsch's musical compositions veers between the jolliness of a country fair and the atonal anxiety of a horror-film score. Approximately ten minutes into the video, a dozen or so white-clad participants huddle around a ripped-open steer carcass in a human circle that begins to rotate as others throw the diverse materials onto them. More and more people join the huddle, impossible to count during the two minutes that this action continues, backs facing outward, heads down, arms around one another's shoulders. The effluvia soaks the mass of people, eventually looking like the vomit that I can feel rising in my body from simply watching for sixteen minutes on a small laptop computer screen.[50]

Jarosi's description offers what the video cannot capture; that is, the effect of sensory immersion in these events, day after day, and in particular the sustained olfactory impact of blood and carcasses. Enclosed in a long and narrow space for a blood-painting action, for example, she struggled with "an increasingly powerful flight response, an instinctive compulsion to escape what seemed more and more like a space of violence and death," along with her consciousness "of needing to suppress this sense of urgent, visceral repellence" in order to remain engaged as a participant/observer.[51] For an outdoor event on the fifth day, two Panzer tanks repeatedly drove through a trench filled with entrails and blood while participants sent more eviscerated animal carcasses and more blood sliding down a wooden ramp into a concrete basin in the middle of the courtyard. For Jarosi, "the smell of blood and entrails proved literally overwhelming, provoking a response that can only be described as primal in its intensity," and she fought the urge to flee. In addition to capturing the event's atmosphere, Jarosi restores its political context and writes about the OMT as an ongoing critique of ongoing violence: "The revulsion engendered by the sight of the tanks as they ground over the animal entrails and of the carcasses as they slid into the pit almost inescapably called to mind the photographs and film footage of emaciated corpses of Jewish victims being bulldozed into mass graves at Nazi concentration camps after the close of the war."[52] She argues that the event uses "experiences of intensity, intoxication, and immersion" to reorient spectators' perception with the aim of re-presenting the ongoing trauma of history[53]—that is, to make experientially present the *human* trauma that belongs to the past but also continues.

To reduce any living being to "bare life," according to Giorgio Agamben, means to exclude it from both human and divine law; consequently, anyone can kill it without fear of punishment—the normal state of affairs for animals subjected to human domination, provided that the killing doesn't interfere with ownership rights. Religious bans against eating certain animals, such as the Hindu prohibition against eating beef, help to clarify the distinction between kill-able bare life and the sacred. Agamben initially takes his terminology from ancient Roman law but offers a medieval example more resonant with my argument: Germanic and Anglo-Saxon law that banned a man from the city defined him as wild—a bandit, a werewolf, *homo sacer* whose killing would not be homicide since he is "neither man nor beast" but, rather, *loup garou* "who dwells paradoxically within both while belonging to neither." Early humanist philosopher Thomas Hobbes premised sovereignty upon the savage state of nature, red in tooth and claw; that is, the sovereign's exclusive right to punish derives from his sole retention of a wolfish nature, with all citizens *homines sacri* to him. Modern civil society thus rests upon the "exclusive inclusion" of bare life.[54]

Muehl's and Nitsch's performative engagements with bare life circulate around an obsession with human sociality and mortality, sometimes appearing as a purposeful distraction from the latter. Whereas Muehl's disgust homes in on bourgeois sexuality and the family, Nitsch expands its target to encompass Western culture's drive for domination, much as McDonagh takes aim at political extremism. The connection between Nitsch's six-day play and Nazi atrocities clarifies the ethical stakes of performing animal death or, for that matter, treating animals metaphorically: the OMT's sensory onslaught and repugnantly compelling imagery thematizes human suffering and renders the death of its animal participants inconsequential. Although Nitsch wishes to position them as sacrifice, he constructs his spectacles within secular culture and lacks religious sanction for the killing. Possessed of no more than bare life, they might as well be dinner.

Animal rights activists responded to Nitsch's elision and metaphoriza-tion of nonhuman species trauma with ongoing protests throughout the six days, kept outside the property by police. As a result, OMT abandoned public slaughter for subsequent events yet continues to use animal carcass-es, body parts, and blood.[55] Like the "notes toward a definition of tragedy" that Albee offers as a third subtitle for *The Goat*, Nitsch's OMT reaches toward Dionysian (Nietzschean, really) epiphany through the bloody death of a nonhuman animal. Both of these otherwise quite dissimilar theatrical events conceive of tragic drama as the replacement for animal sacrifice—a commonplace notion that director Romeo Castellucci nicely articulates: "In the moment that the animal disappeared from the scene, tragedy was born."[56] Considering tragedy's vitality to now be depleted, post-Romantic artists such as Albee and Nitsch return the animal to the theater in order to infuse new blood into the cultural form, as it were. As Suzana Marjanić observes, the "animal stage victim" made way in antiquity for "*anthropocentric* tragedy," whereas the return of animal death to the stage in postmodernity brings about "*animal* tragedy."[57]

## FASCINATING, LIMINAL PIGS

If we accept Ridout's proposition that animals do not belong in the theater, a place where humans symbolize their conflicts rather than killing one anoth-er, and also accept that humans rightly wield the power of life and death over other animal species, then theater has no proper function in our natural-cultural relationship with them. Once that right to dominance comes into question, though, animals might appear in the theater on their own behalf rather than as surrogates for human concerns. Disgust shores up or per-haps even creates a border dividing the human from the nonhuman and at the same time attracts affect to that margin, where it may stick and fester. Yet this marginal disgust just as likely dissolves into interest and perhaps then further intensifies into fascination. Consider the following performa-tive encounters between humans and pigs that purposely dwell in the zone of indistinction where species blur. This purposeful entrance into the limen of human-animal distinction has the potential to run the anthropological machine backwards; that is, rather than forcing particular individuals or categories of human being into an extralegal state of exception where they have no human rights, or alternatively extending erstwhile-human rights to some or all animals, these performances forge—at least briefly—new indistinctions with a positive valence. Martin Puchner characterizes this process as a "negative mimesis" capable of "creating a kind of controlled breakdown within which the nonhuman can, negatively, appear."[58]

Between 1996 and 2000, Carsten Höller and Rosemarie Trockel created a series of encounters between humans and "hens, pigs, mosquitoes, bees, silverfish, rats, and pigeons," in order to explore the questions "What is an animal?" and "What precisely are we who ask this question?"[59] They have tended to work with despised animals and for Documenta IX in Germany created *A House for Pigs and People* (1997). Höller describes the human-pig relation as particularly complex "because of the way we treat these animals, as if they were senseless and emotionless meat production machines."[60] The "house" was a block-like cement structure that humans entered through a door on one side. Pigs were free to exit the opposite side of the building to access a yard with mud wallow and shade canopy, surrounded by a fence and further shielded by tall hedges. Humans could walk around the hedges and peer over the fence into this yard.[61] From inside the structure, visitors viewed the pigs through one-way glass but could not smell, hear, or touch them. The pig-side view was a mirror, so the swine saw only themselves even as the viewing environment seemed to turn them into "some hyperreal tableau vivant" from the human perspective.[62] The artists note that "the pigs actually liked to look at themselves in the mirror, and would occasionally do so for a quite a while."[63] Höller reports that visitors "were for the most part mesmerized to a degree that we didn't foresee. . . . There was an almost religious atmosphere inside the building, and visitors seemed to spend a long time on the inclined concrete platform" watching the pigs.[64] Daniel Birnbaum agrees that the interior was a surprising "place of calm reflection, meditation, even wonder."[65]

Although Höller seems uninterested in the gaze asymmetry, Birnbaum, Giovanni Aloi, and other critics make much of it. Christine Ross includes *A House* in her discussion of art that refuses intersubjective exchange.[66] Jean Baudrillard notes that spectators outdoors, "reaching up on tiptoe to see over a fence," saw both the pigs in their sty and themselves, reflected in the pigs' mirror, while those indoors saw the pigs and also "spectators unaware, or at least pretending to be unaware, that they are being observed." Baudrillard reads the arrangement as evidence that representation persists in the modern world only as a hoax: "The contract of signification—that kind of social contract between things and their signs—itself seems broken, like the political contract, with the result that we find it increasingly hard to represent the world to ourselves and decipher its meaning."[67] Ironically, this lucid albeit partial semiotic reading highlights the interpretive inadequacy of semiotics and the value of affect theory for grappling with what things feel like *in addition to* what they mean.

Rather than refusing affective engagement or putting an end to the production of meaning, these performative encounters with pigs raise questions that include the following: What might constitute intersubjective exchange with a pig? How does the social contract change if we include the pigs within its boundaries and recognize their subjectivity? Once we have entertained such questions, disgust has already lost its power to hold humanity at a distance from the rest of animality. Nonhuman animals reject certain foods, and certain simuli alert them to danger, but they do not wrinkle their noses or gag in disgust. Rozin and coauthors consider disgust to be a uniquely human capacity that thus doubly separates humans from other living creatures: "If humans are to convince themselves that they are different from animals," then in any area that elicits disgust, "work must be done to hide (as with defecation and menstruation for Americans) or humanize (as with table manners and funeral rites) biological necessities."[68] Recognizing the subjectivity and rights of other animals extends the bounds of William Ian Miller's observation that moral disgust clashes with the egalitarian ethos of Western civilization.[69] For a considerable number of ethically engaged spectators, though, the potential (or actual) mistreatment of an animal arouses moral and, in some cases, core disgust. Jennifer Parker-Starbuck, for example, reports the "visceral sensations of confusion" that she felt when musician Matthew Herbert's *One Pig* progressed from the acoustic register to the olfactory. His composition tracked the life of a pig from its birth on a farm to its consumption—by the audience. Whereas the sounds were recorded, processed, and difficult to identify, the cooking pork was concrete and unmistakable. Parker-Starbuck says that she, "a vegetarian, reacted with disgust while a clear sensation of pleasure swept over others around me whose hunger was piqued by the sudden smell."[70]

Pigs occupy a particularly rich border zone as a food source popular in many cuisines but taboo in certain religions. Even the use of piglets in ancient Greek purification rituals depended upon a negative categorization, although the Greeks enjoyed pork as a foodstuff. As Susan Guettel Cole explains, "the blood of the dead piglet, impure like the impurity it was designed to attract, was a homeopathic substance. Like a sponge, the blood of the slain piglet absorbed the impurity so it could be removed."[71] Elites in Egypt and Mesopotamia rejected pork, leaving it to the poor, and Judaism and Islam both made it taboo—Mark Essig notes that scavengers such as pigs become unclean by eating bloody meat.[72] Marvin Harris offers an environmental explanation, beginning with the fact that pigs competed with humans for food in the desert landscape; unlike ruminants, neither species can digest plants high in cellulose. Later, deforestation contributed to a continued taboo, because pigs don't thrive in strong sunlight.[73] Their susceptibility to sunburn and sunstroke abets the association with filth: deprived of shade, pigs will roll in mud to create a sunscreen; deprived of a clean wallow, they will create one by urinating in the dirt; deprived of dirt, they will roll in their own feces—which they can also eat, if need be, along with human feces and other waste products. And pigs retain an untamed streak.[74] Brett Mizelle likens the domestication from wild boar to domestic pig to that from wolf to dog, suggesting that the animals took initiative in choosing life with humans: "Because pigs are willing to move but do not need to be herded, only feed during some parts of the day, enjoy the company of each other and of other species, and are quite intelligent, perhaps domestication might best be seen as 'a treaty between consenting intelligent parties who entered into the agreement in a spirit of mutual self-interest.'"[75]

In medieval Europe, domestic pigs dwelt in forests where humans fattened them prior to slaughter by supplementing their normal forage. For a number of interconnected reasons, eating pork signified wealth and power: the (uncultivated) forests belonged to the nobility, who thus had access to pigs that the peasants did not enjoy; dining on pork emulated the Romans; domestic pigs had no function other than to provide meat; and the danger involved in hunting wild boars added status to eating the flesh of domestic swine as well.[76] During this period, the female (sow) carried negative connotations of filth and carnality, but the male (boar) represented ferocity and power.[77] Peter Stallybrass and Allon White offer a comprehensive analysis of human ambivalence about pigs, identifying distance from pigs (dissimilarity as well as disassociation) as a marker of bourgeois modernity.[78] Swine remained a common presence in daily life, even within cities, until the early twentieth century. By this time, direct contact with the animals had become associated with poverty even though pork did not disappear from wealthy diets.[79] Although the popular stage no longer features "learned pigs,"[80] porcine characters persist in children's literature, cartoons, and live-action films, and they make surprisingly frequent appearances in theater and performance art. This chapter could not encompass the complexity of the sow Bibi's performance in Jean-François Peyret's *Tournant autour de Galilée* (2007) or the appearance of Daisy, the potbellied minipiglet in Ann Liv Young's *Elektra* (2016), and will focus on two artists who position their skin as interface between woman and pig.

For Kira O'Reilly's first interspecies duet, the pig was dead. *inthewrongplaceness* (2005) grew out of a bioart project for which she planned to make living lace out of her skin. Practicing with the corpses of pigs killed in the course of asthma research in order to learn the skills required for biopsies and cell culturing, she felt a literally visceral connection when she made an inept cut into a pig's stomach and, spilling its contents, became aware of her own breakfast.[81] Rather than focusing on the gut's contents, *inthewrongplaceness* troubled the separation of humans from other animals by drawing attention to skin as both boundary and interface.[82] After donning latex gloves that were sprayed with ethanol in a gesture toward laboratory hygiene, participants were told that they could "touch both the human animal and the non-human animal" and led one at a time through an alley into a former social club that had "the aura of a seedy soho brothel or sex-cinema." There the lone spectator found O'Reilly and a recently slaughtered pig:

> Kira's limbs were entwined with the dead pig's, and because their skin colour was so close it wasn't immediately obvious which ones were hers. She moved slowly across the floor like a dancer leading a slightly smaller, more passive partner, rolling slowly over, occasionally heaving the heavy carcass up in order to move it. . . . There was still an intensity to the experience of watching it that was difficult to describe. The performance was too strange and too cold to be erotic. It was anxiety-provoking and a bit scary, partly because there was no boundary between performer and watcher, yet it still had a macabre beauty.[83]

This unidentified participant notes a "faint smell of blood," and O'Reilly chronicles other (nonpig) smells such as lilies in the room and ethanol on the gloves.[84] Along with the visual and olfactory, *inthewrongplaceness* also engaged the audience's sense of touch through the thin gloves. O'Reilly told Gianna Bouchard that the abattoir providing fresh carcasses for each performance removed the innards (standard practice in preparing an animal for consumption as food), and that many audience participants chose to explore this open cavity.[85] Finding in the continuously shifting positions of woman and sow in relation to one another a suggestion that "for us the animal is effectively always a discursively dead object to manipulate," Giovanni Aloi notes that the pig has no metaphorical function in this piece but "is a body, the body of the other."[86] Parker-Starbuck, though, sees here a "ritualistic symbolism of mourning and death" and suggests that the work's importance lies in its power to remind us "that these 'wasted' bodies were beautiful, were in fact, like us."[87] Among other pigs invoked in her meditation on waste, Parker-Starbuck engages with Melissa Martin's bubble-gum sculpture *Little Pig* (2004)—"made from waste, chewed and spat out" and "repulsive in its beauty"—and notes her desire to touch it.[88]

The cultural linkages between pigs and women, specifically, bring additional layers of meaning to O'Reilly's duet. Korsmeyer analyzes a similar blurring of sow/woman body in Jenny Saville's painting *Host* (2000), a classically reclining female nude resembling both pig and human. She proposes that "aesthetic disgust, in this case, plays a Janus role, revolting and enticing, both pointing to the compromised border between human and pig and teasing our curiosity about what lies on the other side."[89] Even more revolting/fascinating and very difficult to parse, Saville's *Torso 2* (2004) suggests to me a melding of hanging pig carcass and masturbating woman, bone ends of the foreshortened forelimbs visible, sinew resembling an extra arm reaching up into an opening at the crotch, back legs extending upward to the hooks from which they're suspended, rolls of meat at the bottom of the image rather than a head.[90] O'Reilly and her dead-pig partner trouble this species border by activating erotic engagement with their dance and thus with bodies identified as meat—whether literally, in the case of pork, or metaphorically, in the case of a naked woman offered for a different sort of consumption. O'Reilly describes one male audience-participant who challenged her personal boundaries:

> I didn't see his face.
> He put the gloves *on*
> and proceeded to touch, to feel out, was I
>     flesh, meat, body, lover, carcass, piece of
>     meat, who knows and what was she?
> He stayed off the erogenous zones, *just about.*
> Latexed and ethanoled hands opened
>     her between my legs with expert
>     determination.[91]

In a further species blur, O'Reilly writes *you stupid, stupid cow* to reiterate her shame or self-disgust—using this phrase first after the pig biopsy, then again after describing the performance.

The photographs in Miru Kim's series *The Pig That Therefore I Am* (2011) create a similar visual parallel between the skins of woman and pig.[92] The series title riffs on Jacques Derrida's meditation around species domination. Derrida points out that man's naming of the animals occurs only in the second version of Genesis, where it precedes the creation of woman.[93] According to this narrative foundational to Western civilization, woman emerges within an already-present rift between man and the rest of animate creation and then sets in motion—significantly, through illicit interaction with a snake—a long series of further alienations. Although feminism rightly objects to the patriarchal relegation of female humans to the animal-nature side of a binary opposition to man-culture, women artists often step back into the rift and consider the possibility of healing it. Pigs occupy a special position in this cultural equation. Höller and Trockel note that the Greek word for pig, *hys*, forms the root of *hystera* (uterus) and of hysteria, the "'neurosis arising in the uterus,' essence of the morbidly female." Rhetorically, they ask: "Does the Hebrew pork taboo originally represent a ban on cannibalism concerning above all women, since pigs are considered as sacrificial substitutes for women? Where pigs are eaten, are they being eaten instead of women? And does the pork taboo represent a patriarchally directed abandonment of the mother cult?"[94] These are only a few of the stream of questions with which they introduce the documentation of their pig installation.

Like O'Reilly, Kim performs unclothed. The similarity to photos of *inthewrongplaceness* comes through most clearly in the extreme close-ups titled "Compositions 1–10," the artist's skin smooth and the pig's hairy, but their tone and contours harmonious. In other photos, Kim poses among living pigs crowded into the pens of an industrial hog farm, her alien presence on all fours—of a size visually comparable to what must be young pigs although less than a third their weight—highlighting the cruelty of their living conditions. In image "MO1," she squats beside a long row of gestation crates, nose to nose with the sow confined in one; in "MO2," she walks away from the camera between two rows, the sows all facing away from her and unable to turn around, but one of them twisting to watch her. The rhythmic beauty of these photos' repeated shapes together with the haptic appeal of their soft colors and gentle, undulating curves contrasts ironically with the inhumane reality that they capture. The artist took these particular photos on a Missouri hog farm without permission, a risky undertaking similar to the earlier series *Naked City Spleen* (2007) that she shot in abandoned subway tunnels and industrial sites. Although she contacted farmers, supplying documentation of her work and proof that her aim was not animal-rights activism, she found only one who would give her access. Kim says that this farmer in Iowa "seemed to enjoy watching me work. Not many get to see a naked woman with their pigs.... It took about six hours to have them all lie down and get used to my presence."[95]

The artist's statement notes that the barn pictured in images "IA 1–5" and "Bodies (IA) 1–5" holds approximately 2,400 hogs who were initially frightened by her entrance and then eager to investigate, that they chewed on her hair and her heels, and that she was able to safely lie down among them when they napped in the afternoon. Kim's statement contemplates skin as an interface between the contained inner consciousness and the external world, a medium for registering sensations but also for displaying their traces:

> Both a pig and I carry our exteriorized memories on our cutaneous garment—scars, blemishes, wrinkles, and rashes that manifest markings of time, anguish of the soul, wounds of love and war. We all live at the same time, naked and not quite naked. . . . Born with a blank canvas enveloping us, we accumulate more and more brushstrokes of memories as years pass. . . . I put my flayed skin on display in the form of a photograph—a paper skin that is touched by light—from which emanates the aura of mingled bodies.[96]

These performative photographs arouse considerable curiosity about the circumstances of production, Kim's naked entanglement with mud and pigs eliciting disgust for some viewers. Journalist Joy Dietrich observes that "the impulse is to recoil in disgust, but you are easily drawn back by the stillness, the almost transcendental quality of the images."[97] Kim seems to accept this response as normal, describing herself as a "sanitary freak" in her daily life and much scrubbing after the photo sessions. As Elizabeth Cherry notes, "cultural attitudes toward boundary maintenance are so strong and pervasive that nearly any action toward a symbolic boundary serves to maintain it."[98]

But if the images' serenity successfully engages viewers, then contemplation may begin to alter the contents of a habitually revolting mental scenario. The situation seems to invert what Korsmeyer identifies as typical; that is, the photo's existential history may disgust, but its "sensory presentation or appearance" no longer does so.[99] Viewers such as myself, attracted rather than disturbed by the thought of getting muddy with pigs, find fascination in Kim's access to industrial pig farms. Although her description of the events, particularly her fear during the illicit photo sessions, evokes some unpleasant sensory images including remembered smells of travel through industrial hog country, these dissipate upon viewing the photos. I find myself drawn to the warm-looking pig bodies and morally disgusted at their crowding. Responses to the related photo installation and six-hour performance piece *Mudbath for Thick Skin* (Fokus Lódz Biennale 2010) and the performance *I Like Pigs and Pigs Like Me* (Art Basel 2012) seem to have similarly sided with the pigs. For the first, viewers peered through the small window of a basement room to watch Kim bathing in mud from a pig farm, accompanied by a video of herself with pigs; for the second, she spent 104 hours in a glass-enclosed pen with two pigs rescued from a slaughterhouse. Animal activists grew irate due to rumors that the pigs were sick.[100]

For both Kim and O'Reilly, the uncanny body-doubling of woman/sow seems to position them as equals and reminds spectators that they too are animals—according to Rozin and his co-researchers, a primary elicitor of disgust for (normate) humans who prefer to forget that they "must eat, excrete, and have sex, just like other animals."[101] For *inthewrongplaceness*, Rosemary Deller notes that this species-leveling effect might temporarily elide the fact that the pig's death was required for O'Reilly to animate its corpse.[102] Yet the public did respond strongly to the death. As was the case for Otto Muehl's actions in Germany, the secondary public, who neither participated in the event nor gave careful consideration to its documentation, responded with particular vehemence. Paul Rae notes that *inthewrongplaceness* brought the *Daily Mail* into surprising agreement with People for the Ethical Treatment of Animals that the event was "sick."[103] After performing six versions of *inthewrongplaceness* over four years and receiving a large amount of irate e-mail, O'Reilly responded to a correspondent's suggestion that she work with live rather than dead pigs by designing an experiment in coexistence, *Falling Asleep with a Pig* (2009). She and Delilah, a Vietnamese pot-bellied pig, occupied a specially constructed space for long enough to both fall asleep—thirty-six hours in the first version, indoors; seventy-two for the second, outdoors. The experimental nature of this performance highlights its shift in emotional focus from disgust to interest—as Johanna Linsley notes, O'Reilly engages with the scientific laboratory as a space of play.[104] In the case of *Falling Asleep*, the atmosphere remains gently playful, not touching any edges of discomfort. The installation experiments with a new relatedness through equal sharing of the temporary habitat rather than metaphorically equating the pig and the woman.

I would categorize these performances with pigs as "interesting," a feeling-based aesthetic judgment that, as Sianne Ngai notes, "ascrib[es] value to that which seems to differ, in a yet-to be conceptualized way, from a general expectation or norm whose exact concept may itself be missing at the moment of judgment."[105] To occupy a house "for pigs and people," even for the brief duration of a performance or art installation, takes one out of familiar territory. O'Reilly ties the relative brevity of *inthewrongplaceness* (only four hours) and even the limited duration of *Falling Asleep* (36–72 hours) to "the wrong 'placeness' of the gallery for life and living," proposing "that it really is a place for dead or inanimate things."[106] Yet engagement in such a space generates interest, which Tomkins defines as "a necessary condition for the formation of the perceptual world."[107] To categorize an experience as "interesting" means that one does not *yet* understand it and thus implies that one will return, either to the experience or to the memory, thus extending it through time unlike more fleeting experiences.[108] When one returns to the memory of a sublime experience, one most likely does so with interest rather than a reactivated awe. Ngai argues that "the interesting gets at the imbrication of the affective and conceptual that underlies all judgment, as a feeling of not-yet-knowing (an affective relation to cognition) accompanied by a lack of conceptual knowledge about what exactly we are feeling (a cognitive relation to affect)."[109] Tracing the ways in which interest "links heterogeneous agents or agencies together" within aesthetic, scientific, and sociological discourse, she observes the creation of "kinds of 'betweenness'—relays, conduits, associations—that in turn facilitate the circulation of ideas, objects, and signs."[110] Affect in general creates this sort of circulation, with interest distinguished by the calmness of its feeling and its compatibility with rational reflection.

What of the pigs' interest in the installation experience? Both Kim and O'Reilly needed considerable time to attenuate the pigs' interest in them sufficiently to permit sleep, whereas *A House* made the pigs' interest in themselves evident, as Höller observed. Criticisms of the unequal gaze exchange seem unaware that animals might find the presence of a human audience stressful—for this reason, zoos have largely moved away from display to favor immersive exhibits that shield the animals from direct engagement with human viewers.[111] The power to return the gaze of humans matters to humans but perhaps not to pigs. As John Berger puts it, in the eye-to-eye encounter with an animal, "man becomes aware of himself returning the gaze." Much as one may seek out this exchange in the zoo, however, one rarely catches the eye of any animal there: "At the most, the animal's gaze flickers and passes on."[112] Depending upon the animal, other senses may engage more steadfastly even as the human moves out of sight, which suggests the importance of coming up with less anthropocentric and ableist ways of understanding affective relation.

Donna Haraway points out that "human genomes can be found in only about 10 percent" of all human body cells; "the other 90 percent of the cells are filled with the genomes of bacteria, fungi, protists, and such."[113] She argues that there is no such thing as the human or individual, but instead a constant process of *becoming-with*, a relational dance between multiple "critters" of the same species or of different.[114] Rather than respecting a boundary drawn by human languages, she asserts that we are indeed "able to communicate with and to know one another and other critters." Even if the knowledge and communication remain imperfect, they create "mortal entanglements (the open) for which we are responsible and in which we respond."[115] She takes the notion of "the open" from Agamben, who describes a stopped "anthropological machine" that "no longer articulates nature and man in order to produce the human through the suspension and capture of the inhuman." In the resulting "standstill," he suggests that "something for which we perhaps have no name and which is neither animal nor man settles in between nature and humanity."[116] Rejecting both Agamben's separation of bare life (*zoë*) from *bios* and what she sees as his captivation by death and exclusion, Rosi Braidotti writes instead of a *bios/zoë* encompassing the "vitality of Life carrying on independently of and regardless of rational control" (*zoë*) inseparable from "the specific social nexus of humans" (*bios*).[117] Together, then, pigs and people can occupy a more positive "open" that Haraway describes as "the space of what is not yet and may or may not ever be; it is a making available to events," and she argues convincingly for the animal's rich openness to the world.[118]

## BECOMING-WITH ANIMALS

Haraway writes about the open that she enters through agility training with her Australian shepherd, and Holly Hughes shares her (and her poodles') engagement with this sport by talking about it in her solo performance art.[119] Others bring the animals themselves into theater and dance. As early as 1986, choreographer Ann Carlson "invited" animals into her rehearsals as an experiment to see whether they could be part of the process. She eventually kept some on stage for the *Animals* series of dances with goats, a dog, a goldfish, and a kitten. The nonhuman animals were present not as trained performers but as a challenge, and she stipulated that the performance would stop at any sign of their distress.[120] In each piece, Carlson performs as a nonhuman animal but also enters into composition with another animal present onstage. *Sarah*, for example, begins on a mostly dark stage, the light tightly focused on a goldfish bowl atop a black column. A male voice encourages the audience to wave their hands like they're splashing in the bathtub and then asks them to sing "just like this." They laugh when "this" turns out to be a whale's vocalization. As the light gradually expands to reveal Carlson's legs in black stockings and heels, raised in the air against the pedestal as she lies on the floor at its base, the voice refers to "her" as a little bit shy and asks the audience to try again. She begins to move, making fin-like shapes with the arms and turning the torso, and then rises to behave like a woman during a song about "Sarah, the man-eating whale." The song fades away, and she mimics a whale's vocalization. Then the two beings blend: the song and the whale voice, the woman movement and the whale movement. People laugh. The way Ann uses her facial muscles to make a whale noise resembles a scream, and by the time the trainer refers to "anything that's helpless," I think not of Sarah's prey but of the woman whose hands cover her eyes as her arms form a whale's tail.

For *Visit Woman Move Story Cat Cat Cat*, a kitten stands in for the pet that Koko, the famous gorilla trained in sign language, asked for, cherished, and mourned when it died. In this piece, Carlson unequivocally imitates the gorilla and dances naked, highlighting the similarity between human and ape physicality. Beethoven's String Quartet no. 16 underscores or even cues affect in this piece, joyful when Carlson lopes about the space and swings on bars, tender when she cuddles the kitten that she has taken out of its carrier, mournful when the kitten is gone and she retreats to a smaller portion of the space with repetitive hitting gestures and self-comforting movements. There's a level of whimsy in both of these pieces, teetering on the edge of cuteness, but here the *aww* does not reassure as it does with *Curious Incident*'s puppy. Awareness that the live animal (goldfish or kitten) is out of place on stage enhances awareness of the human who resembles another out-of-place animal as well as the connection to humans who don't fit neatly within established boundaries for human behaviors. Carlson considered dancing *as* another species to be a way for her to learn and communicate something about herself—as she told the audience at Dance Theatre Workshop, she considered her portrayal of Koko mourning her kitten to be "more about femaleness than humanness."[121] Dancing *with* other species was about reciprocity. Carlson told dance historian Janice Ross that she was beginning at this point in her career to conceive of the audience as offering "keen and loving attention, as opposed to critical judgment" and was concerned with "developing a correspondingly gentle internal audience within herself." The nonhuman performers offered this sort of nonjudgmental participation onstage and in turn needed the same quality of attention from their human partners in order to "function effectively on display."[122] *Scared Goats Faint* played most visibly with this balance. A dancer performing continuous falling phrases shared a fenced enclosure on stage with two pygmy fainting goats, a breed named for their heredity characteristic of stiffening and falling over when startled or overly excited. Both the dancer and the gospel choir arrayed behind the fence needed to calibrate their performance in order to avoid frightening the goats, whose response determined the piece's endpoint.

Carlson's choreography in the subsequent thirty years has extended a similarly gentle attention to all sorts of human participants, trained as well as untrained dancers, and has engaged with a wide variety of physical environments. Animals have moved in and out of her work, occasionally with polemical force. The video installation *Madame 710* (c. 2008), created in collaboration with Mary Ellen Strom, encapsulates a dilemma central to interspecies relations: regardless of intentions, the human cannot *easily* escape systems of commerce and consumption that exploit other species. In the video, Carlson wears only a clear plastic raincoat, its hem and hood stuffed with money but leaving her breasts visible in counterpoint to the udders of a dairy cow that take up a large amount of screen space during the first segment of the piece. She dances near and with the cow, seeming to parallel its opacity and to seek communication or mutual comfort.[123] In 2013, she created a photo version with a chicken—the entire coat stuffed with money this time, so that none of her body was exposed. Wesleyan University's Feet to the Fire Festival commissioned a version called *Green Movement* for four dancers and a cow in 2008 that Carlson described as "part Greek chorus, part Doris Humphrey movement choir, part tongue in cheek, part cynical take on the notion of 'green' . . . a ritual, a quirky, silent response to climate change. Maybe it could happen anywhere, at places where consciousness was being raised or needed raising around humanity's relationship with the Earth, and specific places on the Earth."[124]

Agility and herding competitions transform an archaic working relationship into sport. In their further transformation into art, dances with dogs, sheep, and particularly with horses open the relationship to audiences in a shared natureculture. The Equus Projects, under the artistic direction of JoAnna Mendl Shaw since 1999, has created forty works for dancers collaborating with local equestrians and horses, using "choreographic scores that allow for on-going dialogue with the horses."[125] Paula Josa-Jones created an interspecies company in 1998 to explore reciprocity and to extend equestrian dance in a direction compatible with the "intuitive, improvisational approach to the human-horse bond through movement and touch" that she teaches under the name Embodied Horsemanship.[126] In spite of their distinct structures and logic, the horse dances tend to look and sound somewhat similar, musical accompaniment swelling and swooping, costumed with elements of nineteenth-century dress, the eclectic combination of contemporary and nostalgic emblematizing the horse's troubled status in the Anthropocene era as touched upon in this book's second chapter.

Josa-Jones's *Ride* (2002) puts dancers on trapeze for some sections, creating mounted movement that resembles the riders on their horses, a similarity in carriage that also surfaces in the "Tango" section, spines and torsos still and erect, strong movement focused in the limbs. This evening-length work creates a vitality through which various facets of the historical relationship between women and horses flicker.[127] For the opening section, "Whips," dancers wearing full skirts and bodices with dangling elements of harness walk slowly into the space together with riders in black boots, tight jodhpurs, and camisoles. The riders flick long whips. In another segment, Dillon Paul dances with a saddle, at some points wearing it on her back, briefly becoming-horse in relation to the saddle but not imitating a horse—a distinction that I will discuss more fully in the final chapter of this book. The dancers become prey for "Allegra," hunted by rider Francesca Kelly and her horse Bijli, the only mare in the piece, a racing horse from the deserts of

India, lighter than the other horses, very fast and reactive, unpredictable. Here the horse mediates the representational relation between female rider in exotic costume as an Indian prince and the female dancers. The degree to which the rider physically mediates the relation between horse and dancer varies, from quite minimal involvement during an improvisational duet to a significant input for "Quadrille," which uses standard elements of dressage and also more tightly choreographs the six dancers to echo the four horses' movements. As Kim Marra observes, the "cross-species intercorporeal dynamics" of women and horses "are historically deeply queer, largely because the category boundaries that have defined and preserved 'straightness' . . . so readily blur through the sensuality, public spectacle, and supporting industry of horseback riding, a massively embodied and inherently dangerous and unpredictable practice."[128] Those who ride report experiencing with horses the kind of mutual emergence that Haraway describes in agility training with her dog.[129] A number of recent human-animal studies adopt from Karen Barad the term "intra-action" in order to recognize constitutive relationality.[130]

Josa-Jones describes skilled riding as "perfect communication" because the rider's guidance through legs, seat, and hands on reins becomes more and more subtle. Yet the horses' size and speed adds inevitable risk to equestrian dance. "To be with horses, we need to learn how to become a part of their herd"—the dancer needs to "enter horse-time" and become-with horse in a full awareness of all the ways in which she affects and is affected by the horse: "With their hyperspecific attunement to their environment, and because they perceive humans as predators, horses can discern in us layers of feeling and expression that we may not even be aware of."[131] She chronicles the process of learning to improvise with Escorial, a liberty horse who refuses to bear a rider and "will not perform unless the conditions meet his approval."[132] ("Liberty" means that the human and the horse work together without physical controls such as bits, halters, and reins. The trainer's two long whips give signals rather than blows.) Their initial attempt to dance with him failed because, as his trainer explained, he was "confused and frustrated by [their] lack of clarity." He had been trained to recognize a set of cues that the dancers needed to learn. After they mastered this shared language, then the movement could be varied. With his trainer's help, the horse trained the dancers, "insisting on a meticulous degree of clarity and precision from [their] movement."[133]

The horses approach the dancing quite individually; for example, Megan

Smith says that her horse, Judge, remains afraid of the *Ride* dancers, because the sweep of their long circular skirts makes him nervous. Her sister Lindsay's horse Roy Wind, in contrast, loves the dancers—she talks about the palpable electric energy when he dances with them following his own impulses, requiring no real input from his rider. The shared improvisation is most easily observed in the duets, particularly "Norman's Dance" with Ingrid Schatz. Norman is a five-year-old, very tall horse. Josa-Jones describes him in this duet as "completely light of [his rider Lauren Withers's] leg," meaning that she does not provide cues to movement through leg pressure, as she would commonly do in dressage. Instead, he and Schatz listen to one another and use all their senses to respond with "extreme delicacy and nuance." Withers speaks of the dance bringing both her and Schatz to tears, and one viewer reported weeping "when the dancer put her face to Norman's nostrils."[134] I would characterize the welling up of tears that I also experienced in watching it as an overflow of nonparticularized affect. The woman and horse often touch one another, move very closely together. They begin the piece walking sideways together, stepping slowly with full attention, the horse's head inclined toward the dancer. Later, Schatz goes to the ground on her knees and then arches back until she's supine, and Norman brings his nose down to her. As she comes up to meet his head, their foreheads gently move together and hold the touch. Figure 9 captures an embrace, the dancer kneeling on the ground with her full skirt pooling around her legs, her chest pressed to the horse's and her head arching back to meet his, which curves down over her back. The woman's eyes are closed. I am not certain whether the horse's eyes are open, but his nostrils reach down near to her waist. Josa-Jones describes this duet with Norman as a meeting "in this place of complete attention" that to her "feels like devotion to each other."[135]

The company developed a repertory for touring to appropriate arenas and has also donated performances "to help equine sanctuaries both increase public awareness and raise funds for their rescue, rehabilitation and education programs."[136] In 2012, Josa-Jones created a community-based, collaborative project at the sanctuary Little Brook Farm in Old Chatham, New York. Motivated by "a desire to make work that had a social-political dimension," she "wanted to do a piece with horses that weren't grand prix horses, that were not beloved companions, that were throw-away horses. They were all rescued from slaughter or had been discarded and found in situations where they were not cared for, starving, abused."[137] *All the Pretty Horses* accommodates their specific abilities and also those of the performers, some of

Figure 9. Ingrid
Schatz and Norman
performing *Ride*,
2002. Choreography
by Paula Josa-Jones.
Photo by Pam White.
Courtesy of Paula
Josa-Jones.

whom were dancers she had worked with extensively; others, riders from
the sanctuary's teaching program and children "who were around the barn a
lot." As with any community endeavor, the project also accommodated life's
events and pressures, past and present, for humans as well as horses. Some
of the horses couldn't turn easily, for example, or "would get too amped up
to go into a canter," so it was necessary to "find something else where the
relationship between rider and horse could be harmonious, integration
could be as full as possible." These discarded horses "were just as beautiful
and capable" as any other horse with whom she had worked, and they loved
the rigor of the work. Josa-Jones says that she saw the horses' "exuberance
and curiosity in the work" particularly during the difficult freestyle segment
that she choreographed for four horses and ten or twelve dancers—a human herd—"threading themselves through them and moving with them
and echoing their patterns." Whereas a horse may readily become a full par-

ticipant in a duet with a dancer, the dressage quadrille presented a particular challenge. Safety requires that the horses and riders always know where they're going next, and the horses "loved the formality" of this section with its very complex patterns. Josa-Jones wanted the performers "to feel like they were flowing like a river through rocks, all being carried along by the same current—dancers, horses, riders all part of the same river of movement . . . like a natural phenomenon."[138]

Real animals on stage simultaneously disrupt and participate in theatrical representation.[139] The playwrights and Aktionists with whom this chapter began elicit disgust with animal life and death, treating their animal surrogates as bare life/*zoë* in order to challenge human social organization/*bios* in the form of the unhappy family or bourgeois conformity. Humans performing with pigs in a purposeful zone of indistinction overcome disgust and foster interest in a shared, capaciously revised *zoë*. Yet critique of categories does not make them disappear, and Haraway argues that "living as species is non-optional. We have been worlded as species in a kind of Foucauldian sense of discourse producing its objects again. Two hundred years of what became the powerful world-changing discourses of biology have produced us as species, and other critters too."[140] Attention to the border as a zone of coemergence has the power to torque our worlding as humanimals, and performance offers a space for experiments in torque. The power of performance in this border zone becomes evident in the somewhat surprising opposition that it has recently engendered. In September 2016, the Vermont Performance Laboratory premiered *Doggie Hamlet*, Ann Carlson's multispecies exploration of "instinct, sentience, attachment, and loss."[141] Some of the sheep in the foreground of figure 10 gaze at the camera; others turn to look at the herding dog and five human performers walking away from them across a meadow toward spectators seated in the grass and a line of trees in the background. The performance incorporates herding, humans dancing with and without sheepskins, and sign language. Gia Kourlas reports that inspiration for the piece included sheepherding trials and a story about a hearing but nonspeaking boy who uses sign language to communicate with people and gesture to communicate with dogs.[142]

In December 2016, the *Washington Free Beacon* ridiculed the project in terms reminiscent of attacks on the National Endowment for the Arts in the late 1980s and early 1990s, observing that the piece "features no lines from William Shakespeare's *Hamlet*, only an older man and woman yelling at a sheep dog and a confused herd of sheep." The article ends with the

Figure 10. Ann Carlson's *Doggie Hamlet*, 2016. Photo by Kelly Fletcher. Courtesy of Ann Carlson.

sentence, "The *New York Times* has called Carlson's work heartbreaking," apparently intending this liberal newspaper's admiration to count as damning evidence.[143] A few months later, the *New York Times* published a defense of Carlson's work, surely reinforcing conservative opposition to this sort of frivolity but potentially attracting audiences and additional presenters.[144] None of the blogs or comment streams attacking *Doggie Hamlet* seem aware of the British *King Lear with Sheep* of 2015 (which did feature lines from Shakespeare), nor do they mention the flock of a hundred sheep that director Heiner Goebbels brought into the Park Avenue Armory in his staging of composer Louis Andriessen's *De Materie* earlier in 2016. But the first production did not leave the United Kingdom, and the second was created in Germany prior to its international tour. The attacks target the National Endowment for the Arts, which has supported *Doggie Hamlet* only indirectly by funding some organizations planning to present the work and, during development in 2015, through the National Dance Project of the New England Foundation for the Arts. Residencies in 2014 were funded by an independent organization, Creative Capital's MAP Fund. As Kourlas notes, attacks portray the piece as silly and frivolous, not dangerous like the performances by Karen Finley, John Fleck, Holly Hughes, and Tim Miller targeted by earlier attempts to defund the National Endowment for the Arts. Conservative critics mischaracterize interspecies performance as an inconsequential waste of funds. Perhaps this is because they fail to recognize its provocation as a deeply queer albeit nonsexual desiring machine. Or perhaps in the current political atmosphere they perceive ridicule as more effective than outrage.

## CHAPTER 5

# *Performing with Autists*

When he was a teenager in 1951, the savant skills that made Donald Triplett "legendary" in his hometown generated an invitation from a traveling mentalist to join him in show business, but his parents declined the offer.[1] His fame stems from an earlier encounter: in 1938, the Tripletts had brought four-year-old Donald for the first of four visits with psychologist Leo Kanner at Johns Hopkins, and Kanner described his behavior during these visits:

> He wandered about smiling, making stereotyped movements with his fingers, crossing them about in the air. He shook his head from side to side, whispering or humming the same three-note tune. He spun with great pleasure anything he could seize upon to spin. He kept throwing things on the floor, seeming to delight in the sounds they made. He arranged beads, sticks or blocks in different series of colors. Whenever he finished one of these performances, he squealed and jumped up and down. Beyond this he showed no initiative, requiring constant instruction (from his mother) in any form of activity other than the limited ones in which he was absorbed.[2]

Donald was the first of eleven case studies in Kanner's 1943 article, "Autistic Disturbances of Affective Contact," and Stuart Murray suggests that he should feature equally with Kanner and Hans Asperger in the history of autism.[3] The prognosis seemed grim—although less grim than if the boy had remained in the state-run institution where he spent the previous year, starting when he was only three, and from which his parents brought him back home against doctors' advice. They had sufficient money and self-confidence to seek out the most nurturing situations for their son, and their high status in Forest, Mississippi, helped the townspeople to accept him. Triplett earned a college degree in French, worked as a teller in the bank founded by his mother's family, has traveled widely, plays golf every day, and at the age of eighty-two (in 2016) was living on his own in the home that he formerly shared with his parents, supported by an irrevocable trust after their death. Given his class, race, family, and local culture, there was little chance that Triplett would pursue any sort of show business—although he did have a speaking role in the school play during his senior year of high school and seems to have enjoyed performing.[4] He recalls his most renowned feat, instantaneously counting the bricks on the wall of his high school, as a performance intended to impress the boys who posed the challenge; he simply picked a large number that they accepted without question. As John Donvan and Caren Zucker point out, this incident contradicts two of the most dearly held preconceptions about autists: that they're no good at deceit and that they can't understand social relationships.[5]

Through multiple, interwoven but not formally organized connections, a network of family, community, therapy, and education supported the flourishing of Triplett's unique interests, talents, and capacities. The same is true for poet, artist, and performer Christopher Knowles, who began his performance career in Robert Wilson's *The Life and Times of Joseph Stalin* (1973) when he was fourteen years old; went on to perform in *A Letter for Queen Victoria* (1974), which incorporated texts that he and other performers had written, and *$ Value of Man* (1975); and wrote much of the libretto for *Einstein on the Beach* (1976) but did not perform in it. In addition to these large-scale works, he and Wilson performed a number of smaller duet pieces such as *DiaLog/Network* (1978) and *DiaLog/Curious George* (1980). The various projects with Wilson included performances in New York and tours in Europe, Brazil, and Iran. Knowles went on to collaborate with a wider network of artists and performance makers as well as creating a body of work in various media.

The differences between Knowles's life and Triplett's seem more noteworthy than the similarities, although each was perceived to have a cognitive difference calling for early intervention and went on to live quite independently in the world. And as teenagers, each was invited to enter show business. Triplett's parents rejected this option, and Knowles's accepted.

The type of show business, the family, and the teenage boy differed considerably. Although Chris performs (socially) some typical savant feats such as rapidly identifying the day of the week for any calendar date (which his wife Sylvia Netzer referred to as a party trick when he calculated my birthday),[6] his most fully developed skills involve manipulation of language as simultaneously visual and auditory material, using unconventional structures to play with the words' linguistic meaning. Hilton Als and Anthony Elms describe him as "the only true heir to that great American writer who put standard English on notice—Gertrude Stein."[7] Knowles grew up in a significantly different milieu than Triplett did, nearly thirty years later and in New York City rather than a small town in Mississippi. The Tripletts were a banking family, whereas the Knowles family had a closer relation to the arts: Edward is an architect and Barbara, a graphic designer. And the invitation came from an avant-garde theater director on the cusp of fame rather than a mind-reading hypnotist who falsely claimed to have worked with Sigmund Freud.

The early portions of this chapter discuss diagnostic history at some length in order to abrade the edges of autism as a meaningful category. The life of autism's first child, Donald Triplett, has been far less grim than predicted. Knowles is well known as an autistic poet and artist, but the term does not appear in his archived medical records. His life has not been particularly grim, either. Quite likely some of Back to Back Theatre's actors are autistic, but the company does not use diagnostic labels. They make shows about issues they care about, including their own agency as persons with intellectual disabilities. The end of the chapter discusses opportunities for autistic actors in the theatrical mainstream and some recent projects more specifically focused on their creators' autism. Somewhat ironically, though, I discuss the psychiatric narrative in order to argue against its coherence even while recognizing the label's value for political self-advocacy. Noting the "ambiguous and elusive" nature of autism even within biomedical research, Majia Holmer Nadesan suggests that "perhaps autism is not a *thing* but is a nominal category useful for grouping heterogeneous people all sharing communication practices deviating significantly from the expectations of normalcy."[8] There is every reason to expect that research will increasingly recognize the diversity of both causes and manifestations not only among individuals but for any one person.[9]

## MAPPING POSTDRAMATIC WONDER

In 1973, Robert Wilson contacted Christopher's parents after a mutual friend passed along a cassette tape with the spoken word composition "Emily Likes the TV," and he invited the family to his twelve-hour performance *The Life and Times of Joseph Stalin* at the Brooklyn Academy of Music. When Barbara Knowles brought her son to Wilson's dressing room, he spontaneously asked the boy whether he would like to be in the show, led him by the hand onto the BAM stage, and began a precise replication of what he had heard on the tape: "Emily likes the TV. Em Em Em Em." Chris picked up with "Em Em Em Emily likes the TV. Because Emily watches the TV. Because Emily likes the TV. Because she likes Bugs Bunny. Because she likes The Flintstones. Because she watches it."[10] They improvised another duet during the first act. Wilson asked Knowles to start that one, and he performed variations on the syllables *hat hap hath* that when written down have a geometrical visual structure not likely apparent to a listener. When he tells this story, Wilson uses a whiteboard to illustrate and goes on to sketch the visual structure of *Einstein on the Beach*. He has repeated this performance essentially verbatim in many interviews and lectures both together with Knowles and alone, reproducing the vocal variations on the "em" sound.[11]

Christopher enjoyed his first theatrical experience, and his father telephoned Wilson the next morning: "He said they were astonished: Chris had seldom spoken and had never before initiated conversation. He was very excited about being in the play, and wanted to know if he could be in the next performance."[12] What had begun as an impromptu incursion into an otherwise carefully rehearsed work was repeated for all four performances. After visiting Chris at the school he was attending in upstate New York, Wilson convinced the family that their son needed more freedom and creative encouragement. Knowles moved into Wilson's loft in Soho for several months; they developed *A Letter for Queen Victoria*, which they toured internationally for ten months. Wilson had worked as a movement therapist with children who had learning disabilities, and his work with the large and loosely shifting performance collective known as the Byrd Hoffman School of Byrds aimed to rediscover unique individual ways of moving and behaving. But he worked with Chris as he had with Raymond Andrews, a deaf child whom he rescued from an altercation with a policeman and subsequently adopted. Bill Simmer explains that Wilson tried to adjust to both of these young men rather than expecting them to change.[13]

Wilson described his loft's milieu during the time that Knowles was living there and they were creating *A Letter for Queen Victoria*: "We had a TV and four radios on all the time. [Chris] also had tape recorders going, playing back things that had just occurred. He was making constructions out of what he heard."[14] Knowles's capacity with language fascinated Wilson:

> Everything he does makes sense but not in the way we're accustomed to. It has a logic of its own. His sense of organization and construction is fascinating. . . . He can remember complicated structures and repeat them word by word. At one time he was taking words and phrases and shifting every letter six places forward in the alphabet. And he's able to do it instantaneously, he doesn't need to figure it out with pen and paper the way you or I would have to. Chris constructs as he speaks. It's as though he sees the words before him in space.[15]

Knowles's textual compositions pervaded *Queen Victoria*, covering the drop brought down to obscure scene changes (referred to in the script as the break drop) with symmetrical arrangements of *pirup birup* and *ok ok ok spups*, square sections filled with *there*. The single squares with *is si* and *are* stand out by virtue of not being repeated.[16] Figure 11 shows Knowles and Sheryl Sutton seated at a table in front of the drop. The reversed *is* disappears behind Sutton's shoulders; fragments of *are* can be glimpsed through the chair legs. Sutton gazes at Knowles, her hands resting on the table. Knowles directs his gaze down toward his lap, his arms softly hugging his torso, the C-curve of his spine echoed by his sharply defined shadow on the backdrop.

This drop first came down after the opening section of act 1, with Wilson standing in profile at its stage-right edge, occasionally touching his mouth or scratching his head, and Knowles's voice repeating "pirup pirup" through the sound system, at one point saying "that's enough pirups."[17] Some of the words on the drop are familiar and others more private, but two stand out: *is* and *are*. Both interrupt the repetition of *there*—*are* standing alone, the singular verb *is* symmetrical with its reflection but alone within the overall composition. Musing upon this over the course of the drop's several appearances and then in retrospect, I relate *are* to things that fit into categories (*there are* these things) and *is* to singular things that don't fit the categories and yet find unique reflections (*there is* this thing, and *there is* this other thing that relates to it without being the same). Wilson's combination of theatrical slowness with enticing opacity invites such musing. As Telory Ar-

Figure 11. Christopher Knowles and Sheryl Sutton seated before the break drop in *A Letter for Queen Victoria*, 1974. Photo courtesy of the Byrd Hoffman Watermill Foundation.

endell observes, the layering of physical and verbal material "encourage[s] both his actors and audience to think simultaneously on multiple levels without distraction. In this multiplicity, a space opens in the brain that allows for dreamlike perception where the periphery becomes the focus."[18] Accepting the invitation to extrapolate from what I've seen without deriving a clear discursive message leads me to consider Knowles and Wilson as two singularities, drawn together reflexively but not becoming the same (*is* and *is* rather than *are*). This strikes me as a more positive description of their relation than some others—certainly more adequate than Stefan Brecht's characterization of the two as alter-egos "personifying genius" and "mental deficiency,"[19] but also more productive than to simply categorize this theater as autistic based upon its failure to become comprehensible within norms of communication.

Wilson was struck early on with the similarity between "the way [he] had been writing in [his] notebooks" and Christopher's constructs.[20] Knowles's unique manipulations of language manifest his distinctive perceptual and cognitive abilities. His mother refers to him in letters seeking therapeutic assistance and Social Security Supplemental Income as "brain damaged" and mentions congenital toxoplasmosis that presumably damaged the macula of both eyes.[21] When he was three years old, he didn't react to moving cars or other people, although she observed that he was able to navigate the world around him without difficulty and to see airplanes in the sky. In the supermarket, he liked to run back and forth with his eyes on a level with the shiny metal bars lining the refrigerated aisle, extremely close to them, and to stand for long periods gazing at colorful displays of large detergent boxes. He was fascinated with shadows and particularly loved to run over patterned sidewalks or tiles with his head down and sometimes holding the fingers of his left hand spread in front of his eyes. Play activities showed similar attraction to patterning: arranging blocks in repeating series; spinning things; arranging all of the family's shoes, in pairs, to form a long herringbone that duplicated some favorite paving blocks near his home.[22]

Wilson showed a similar love of pattern, at least once around age seven entering his family's kitchen during the dead of night to arrange every jar, can, cup, and glass according to size, shape, and color.[23] In early childhood, a central auditory processing disorder seems to have made it difficult for Wilson to process the connection between spoken language and meaning, although he could hear. Dr. Cecilia McCarton explains that "it is difficult for children with this disorder to organize their expressive language; they are usually late talkers and are often labeled as stutterers. Eventually, the children acquire language through visual cues, gestures and repetition."[24] Feeling isolated and embarrassed at school, Wilson preferred to be alone at home and says that he "drew and painted all the time."[25] Working with dance teacher and physical therapist Bird Hoffman helped him overcome the language disorder and also influenced him in other ways. Relaxing and speaking more slowly made it easier for him to express his thoughts.[26] At age six, Knowles began an intensive program of therapy supervised by the Philadelphia Institute for the Achievement of Human Potential and largely carried out by his parents at home that involved creeping and crawling on a textured floor surface for at least an hour every day, at times with a patch covering the dominant eye and incorporating visual clues; various types of cross-patterning to develop bilateral opposition; and visual techniques to correct misalignment of the eyes and encourage visual convergence.[27] By the end of this therapy, he was speaking more, learning to read, and had gained in all areas. Tape recorders, which became so significant for him artistically, played a therapeutic role.[28]

Neither of these children was diagnosed as autistic, a category that only gradually assumed its current shape and continues to change. The American Psychiatric Association began developing standard classifications prior to World War II in order to diagnose severe neurological and psychiatric problems among hospital patients. By the time the organization published the first DSM in 1952, returning servicemen and veterans had increased the need for outpatient diagnosis.[29] Autism remained a subcategory of childhood schizophrenia until 1980, when DSM-III redefined it as a subcategory of a new grouping, pervasive developmental disorders. The diagnostic criteria kept it rare, requiring onset before thirty months of age and "*complete lack* of social responsiveness," but downgraded it from illness to disorder. Then by dropping early onset and relaxing the definition to "*abnormal* social responsiveness," DSM-III-R in 1987 made the diagnosis applicable for more cases.[30] Wilson was born in 1941, only eight years after Donald Triplett, and was two years old when Kanner published "Autistic Disturbances of Affective Contact." He would not have fit Kanner's conception of autism, and his childhood cognitive and behavioral profile would never have prompted institutionalization as "feebleminded," the threat that led parents such as the Tripletts to seek psychiatric consultation at that time. Nor did he remain socially isolated for very long. His sister and a Waco neighbor both recall his ability to organize the neighborhood children for various activities, including putting on shows.[31] By the time he was very briefly institutionalized after a suicide attempt in the mid-1960s, he had attended the University of Texas at Austin, earned a bachelor of fine arts degree from Pratt Institute in Brooklyn, and reached a creative crisis prompted by a show of his paintings in New York.[32] No psychiatrist would have considered diagnosing a college graduate with a type of childhood schizophrenia.

Around the same time as Wilson began experimenting with performance in downtown New York, Knowles (born in 1959) was early in the therapeutic interventions for what his parents clearly considered to be serious impairments. Although spinning, lining up objects, lack of interest in other children, and language delays now feature prominently in conceptions of autism, the disorder was more narrowly defined in the 1960s and often viewed as a psychogenic mental illness caused by maternal coldness. The Knowleses and the doctors whom they consulted attributed Chris's atypical development to an organic cause. After finishing elementary school in Brooklyn, Chris lived for most of a year with an aunt in upstate New York, where he first attended special education classes at Oneida Junior High and then a day program at the O.D. Heck Developmental Center.[33] Although he was never actually institutionalized, the notion that Wilson rescued Knowles from a mental hospital fits two stock characters into a standard scenario, making it easily accepted by anyone not specifically concerned to present Knowles as a complete and complex human being.[34]

Children classified as retarded or emotionally disturbed—the categories available at the time—were still commonly sent off to live in institutions during the 1960s, but these facilities began emptying in the early 1970s. Outrage directed against the Willowbrook State Developmental Center in Staten Island provides an indicative timeline: in 1965, Senator Robert Kennedy brought this "snake pit" to national attention, but little changed. At its peak of overcrowding four years later, facilities built to house 4,000 children and adults warehoused 6,200 residents. A television exposé in 1972 prompted a lawsuit that was settled in 1975, with new standards of care in place. The goal of reducing the number of residents to 250 was never achieved, but the facility closed in 1987.[35] The O.D. Heck school did not close until 2015, part of a general transition but following lawsuits prompted by the mistreatment of residents.[36] Eyal and coauthors argue that deinstitutionalization blurred the categories that had served institutional needs ("moron, imbecile, psychotic, idiot, feebleminded, mentally deficient, mentally retarded—whether deemed educable or trainable, or neither—emotionally

disturbed, psychotic, schizophrenic child, and so on") into "a great undif-
ferentiated mass of 'atypical children.' . . . Then gradually, new categories
began to be differentiated within a new institutional matrix that replaced
custodial institutions." Along with new therapies and new experts came "a
massive change in the social organization of expertise," a shift from psychiatry to "special educators, occupational therapists, behavioral psychologists,
activist social scientists identified with the anti-psychiatry movement—and
parents."[37] The Knowleses' pursuit of therapies intended to help Chris live as
full and independent a life as possible were near the leading edge of trends in
the mid-1960s. Parents had begun to organize, seeking appropriate accom-
modation and therapy for their atypical children, who increasingly lived at
home with their families and attempted—with varying degrees of success—
to attend school. The National Society for Autistic Children, founded in
1965, was only the first of many such organizations that generally coalesced
and split apart in support of a particular therapeutic approach.[38] Diagnostic
terminology changed along with therapeutic goals, responding to pressure
from parental activism.[39]

By the time DSM-III redefined autism as a disorder rather than a mental illness in 1980, Chris Knowles had passed his twentieth birthday. He had
been performing with Robert Wilson for six years; for five, he had been living with performer and vocalist Cindy Lubar—they became a couple while
working together in *Queen Victoria*. He was twenty-seven when DSM-
III-R widened the diagnostic criteria. During that particular year (1987),
Chris performed the lead role in Wilson's *Parzifal* at the Thalia Theatre in
Hamburg, House Bebert in Rotterdam published an edition of *Christopher
Knowles Typings*, and the Holly Solomon Gallery had been showing his visual art for ten years. The conception of autism had shifted in ways that might
have fit his neurological and behavioral profile, but the diagnosis would have
served no more purpose at that point in his life than would a diagnosis of
Asperger syndrome for Robert Wilson when DSM-IV was published in
1994. The primary purpose of diagnosis is to obtain appropriate medical,
psychological, social, or financial support, and both of these men had alternative pathways in all of these areas. The therapeutic interventions during
their childhoods responded to specific physiological and neurological issues
rather than seeking to remedy, as Nadesan puts it, a "lack of 'normal' communication skills defined in the broadest possible way."[40]

The neurodiversity movement shifts emphasis from behavioral differences to the underlying sensory experience. As Amanda Baggs forcefully

demonstrates in her video performance *In My Language*, for example, what neurotypicals tend to dismiss as meaningless stimming comprises a nonsymbolic language that she describes as "being in a constant conversation with every aspect of [her] surroundings"—she sings along with running water, a drawer pull, a piece of paper, a slinky, a chain, a magazine. Baggs counters the neurotypical interpretation of these behaviors as being locked in "a world of her own" with the assertion that she reacts to a much larger portion of the world than what they recognize as worthwhile and does so with all of her senses. Yet only when she translates something into neurotypical language is her thought recognized as thought.[41] She writes that "my biggest frustration is this: the most important things about the way I perceive and interact with the world around me can only be expressed in terms that describe them as the absence of something important."[42] Tito Rajarshi Mukhopadhyay also describes the richness of his interaction with his surroundings and writes (with considerable sarcasm, I think) that when he first heard the term "autism" as a label for his way of being, he made up "a whole list of things" that he classified as autistic, such as curtains, leaves, and bits of paper "because they flapped, because they would not respond to any blocks, because they did not talk, and I was sure that they would not be able to imitate the clinical psychologist."[43] Both of these individuals communicate with neurotypicals by typing rather than through speech, and they argue for their human rights. To paraphrase a line from *small metal objects* by Back to Back Theatre to which I will return, they want people to see them, and to see them as full human beings. Mel Chen argues for the importance of expanding our conception of sociality beyond the human or even the animate, particularly in order to adequately account for autistic social relations.[44]

Much as I wish to trouble the category, I must acknowledge that Christopher Knowles is central to this chapter precisely because the adjective "autistic" has so often been used when referring to him. The references begin casually, perhaps as attempts to describe Knowles's distinguishing characteristics in anodyne terms. Theater critics initially mark his apparent divergence from behavioral norms and simultaneously cast Wilson as rescuer. A 1974 review refers to Chris as "what society is wont to call 'abnormal'" and observes that "for Wilson he is clearly no specimen, but a fellow creature, and Wilson is onto his wavelength."[45] Bonnie Marranca asserts in 1977 that "Knowles is *clinically diagnosed* as autistic though Wilson firmly believes he simply has other perceptual powers than those considered 'normal' in our society." She specifically picks out *A Letter for Queen Victoria*'s entr'actes for

"their incorporation of behavior patterns of autistic children in the theatrical performance: repetition, echolalia, wordplay, imitation."[46] Writing after
DSM-IV brought autism into common parlance, Arthur Holmberg characterizes Knowles as an "autistic poet," acknowledging him as author of some
portions of *Queen Victoria*'s text but not as creator of its visual treatment of
language, which he likens to "concrete poetry." Holmberg perhaps inadvertently suggests the transformative potential of neurodiversity: "Language is
one of society's most potent weapons to control its members; its rules are
mightier than any individual. . . . What happens when one radically violates
the rules that govern communication? One withdraws from society into autistic isolation. Language binds us to a community. By turning one's back
on speech conventions, one turns one's back on society."[47] Holmberg likens
Wilson and Knowles to "a speech community of two" establishing their own
norms in the entr'actes, but this description does not take into account the
fact that they are engaging in this communication before, for, and with audiences who view a performance rather than glimpsing a secret world.

For the performance videorecorded in Paris, Knowles and Wilson begin
the first entr'acte on opposites sides of the stage, clapping wood blocks together and shouting at each other. They continue this activity while reclining on the floor, shouting directly into the microphones positioned there,
the sound growing loud and assaultive. The interaction becomes differently
discomfiting when they stop clapping the blocks and stand up again. Wilson
keeps asking "what are we doing?" and Knowles gives concrete answers, such
as "the four acts . . . *A Letter for Queen Victoria* . . . the play." Wilson eventually walks across the stage and shouts into Knowles's face. This happens a
couple of times, and then their roles reverse. They finish with a repetitious
dialogue: one says "and you sit on the bench," and the other replies "and you
wait for me." They switch lines after awhile, then fragment them and repeat
the fragments in unison, eventually recombine them and add "till I come
back" (72). The second entr'acte echoes the estranged intensity of the first
with what the script describes as a "scream song by Robert Wilson" (89):
he crosses the stage in front of the break drop in a two-dimensional walking dance, emitting screams but also vocalizations that resemble words and
song without resolving into either. The final entr'acte isolates Knowles in a
spotlight, spinning and repeatedly informing the audience how much time
remains until the next act. His movement echoes the continuous spinning
on downstage ramps of dancers Andy DeGroat and Julia Busto that frames
most of the performance. As auditory backdrop, Knowles's taped voice re-

peats "and you sit on the bench and you wait for me" over and over, finally developing into "and you wait for me when I come back" (92).

Continuing to collaborate on performances similar to these entr'actes, Wilson and Knowles performed the flexible *DiaLog* pieces internationally from 1975 to 1980. To begin each of the twelve sections comprising *Dia-Log/Network*, Knowles logs a specific time on the afternoon of August 30, 1977, in New York, and his taped sound collage mixes fragments of dialogue from the film *Network* with pop music recorded from the radio and ambient sound that includes a dog barking and multiple alarm clocks ringing. Wilson and Knowles speak over this, live, and add more layers of sound such as the loud rasp of Wilson filing his fingernails next to a microphone. The two of them variously lie on a mattress and pace in geometrical patterns.[48] Neurotypicals most commonly dismiss an intense interest in a topic (such as a particular film) as maladaptive perseverance, an engagement both flat and empty. But here Wilson instead engages with the film as Knowles does.

In watching the eighty-four-minute video documentation, I gradually began to see the performance as a cultural prism channeling a mainstream film and fracturing it into separate rays. I heard the film's language as sound, as music; heard it harmonize with other soundtracks, whether rightly identified or not; perceived an auditory landscape evoking a past August in New York; in a sonic pentimento, heard the Grateful Dead's "Sugaree" and the Eagles' "Take it Easy" seeping up through the surface of *Network* dialogue; saw Wilson and Knowles echoing every vaudevillian duo and dance team as well as Didi and Gogo in Beckett's *Waiting for Godot* or Hamm and Clov in his *Endgame*. *DiaLog/Network* offers a microscopic view of the cultural reworking that all of our arts and entertainments practice to some degree. This refraction of popular culture carries across Knowles's work in various media—performance, poetry, visual, and audio. As Lauren DiGiulio notes, for example, Knowles "maintains a keen interest in using cassette tape players to break apart and reconfigure the aural components of spoken language," a practice that he began when he was eleven. For the audiotape "Popular Songs A" (1984), he recorded on each of fourteen days snippets of the songs from *Billboard*'s Top 20 songs for that specific day between 1957 and 1971 as played on an oldies radio station in 1984. "This temporal layering," DiGiulio says, "creates a folding effect that draws sonic connections across moments in mid-twentieth century popular music. . . . As listeners, we are invited to tune in to the soundtrack of Knowles's everyday world, and to shift effortlessly with him across these carefully measured distances."[49] The archaic technology—broadcast radio and cassette recorder—anchors the sound in its material circumstances of production and lends a unique texture to the analog sampling.

In contrast to Wilson's spectacular, large-cast operas, these two-man performances were flexible, inexpensive, and easy to tour. For *The Life and Times of Joseph Stalin*, more than one hundred people were on stage; *Einstein on the Beach*, with its smaller cast of performers who were better compensated, left Wilson deeply in debt but also secured his reputation as an artistic genius and his ability to raise funds for future projects. Certainly this growing renown made the *DiaLog* performances possible; in turn, they kept him in front of audiences while he developed the larger works. Knowles was a collaborator both comfortable and generative—Wilson describes him as the person with whom he has worked to whom he feels closest, saying that they think alike.[50] Prior to working with Chris, he created silent operas that followed a dream logic. I propose that Knowles's particular sort of verbal play gave Wilson a way to incorporate language without blocking wonder, an emotional state related to both interest and awe. Wilson's long and slow-moving productions seem the antithesis of interesting; rather, they challenge audiences to persevere through their boredom and attain the wondrous response, *ah!* Delight suffuses the wondrous, rather than the fear that may shade the aesthetic sublime. Whereas the awe-inspiring puppet spectaculars that I discussed in chapter 2 strategically build anticipation in order to elicit tears or gasps, Wilson's postdramatic theater bores its audience to produce a sigh. In English, as Philip Fisher observes, the action of wondering and the judgment that something is a wonder connect intellectual curiosity with the pleasure of discovery.[51] Puzzling over a conundrum and then suddenly "getting it" produces wonder, which Fisher argues is by definition extraordinary, a response to something suddenly and unexpectedly seen for the first time. Narratives, which by their very nature rely upon memory and expectation, produce surprises but not wonder.[52] Language itself tends to block wonder because "small scale syntactic and grammatical expectations are nested within other structures of ever larger scale which are fundamental to narrative itself, with the expectation controlled and played with at every stage."[53] This is true of normate language use, but Knowles brought to Wilson ways of canceling out syntactic and grammatical expectation.

Hans-Thies Lehmann describes Wilson's theater as a continual "metamorphosis [that] connects heterogeneous realities, a thousand plateaux and energy flows," its actions seeming unmotivated by the humans present on stage, its spaces not unified, its elements unsynthesized, interpretation impossible. "Through the montage of juxtaposed or imbricated virtual spaces, which . . . remain independent from one another so that no synthesis is offered, a poetic sphere of *connotations* comes into being."[54] Instead of the narrative that organizes dramatic theater into a representation, Wilson's works draw upon "a kind of universal history that appears as a multicultural, ethnological, archaeological *kaleidoscope*." In a kind of "playful delight," Lehmann argues, "mythical imagery here takes the place of action, satisfying a 'postmodern' pleasure in the quotation of imaginary worlds whose time has passed."[55] Somewhat paradoxically, this abolition of both dramatic action and linguistic expectation produces a refreshed experience of time. *Ah!*

Knowles is a framing presence throughout *Queen Victoria*, easy to pick out among the four performers who read the eponymous letter even though they look very much alike.[56] His gray pants and blue jacket set him off against their black suits, as does his contrapposto stance. Wilson, Brecht, and Kathryn Cation remain erect and still, as formal as the performer representing Queen Victoria who stands nearby, but Chris moves quite a lot—putting his foot up on a Plexiglas cube, scratching his head, leaning on the wall, putting a finger in his mouth, looking at his watch. According to the stage direction, "Christopher Knowles reads his letter, and three members of the cast simultaneously read the other letter" (52). Chris has a more coherent version of the letter that he reads rather calmly ("I have the scarcely forgivable presumption of addressing myself to you, knowing fulwell the positive dismerit hereof on the part of one . . . ," 53) while the other performers essentially shout theirs ("I have the scarcely forgivable of the presumption of addressing myself to you, knowing fulwell the disposisore of this merit of this posital of of that in in in in into the spotless lights . . . ," 52). During part of the second act, he reclines with a cassette tape recorder on the floor near a microphone downstage, according to Brecht "laughing much of the time, recording the ongoing dialogue and an occasional loud 'burrup' . . . from himself, and replaying what he has recorded."[57] Later, he slowly flies across the stage dangling from a harness, saying at one point "I'm an airplane" and occasionally uttering "scarf." Often present but always set slightly apart, Knowles's behavior and presence seem more relaxed and natural than anything else happening onstage. During the chaotic fourth act, he reclines on the floor downstage, watching, occasionally saying "tape recorder." When everything suddenly stops and the lights return to normal, he says, "Will you all return please at 8 o'clock" (101).

As Holmberg observes, the "Chinaman" (performed by Cindy Lubar) articulated a sort of explanation in the fourth act:

A person appears in a place for a length of time, interacting with others, and goes—nothing unusual in that. . . . A person appears in another place for the exact same length of time, interacting identically with the same number of people down to the smallest details—Who can know that one is part of the other? . . . Who can recognize the same names, the same faces, the same course of events? Only one with a view of sufficient breadth and patience. (93, ellipses original)

Wilson seems to advocate adopting this perspective when watching *Queen Victoria*, as quoted in a review of the (spectacularly unsuccessful) Broadway performance: "If a child wants to go to the window and watch the sky change for six hours, that's considered autistic behavior. Well, I believe in autistic behavior. I believe in alternating it, but also in reinforcing it."[58] But if the Chinaman and Wilson offer rational guidance, Knowles remains the spectator's affective guide. Late in the first act, he enters the stage on a bicycle and hovers near two men with newspapers, seated in club chairs, exchanging utterances about *Butch Cassidy and the Sundance Kid*. Occasionally he interjects "spups spups . . ." (67). He strikes me as a kindly spirit watching over Victorian gentlemen who would never adapt to the drastically changed landscape behind them, at the same time watching over actors struggling to carry on a conversation that is not one.

This scene exemplifies Knowles's performative landscapes as distinct from Wilson's, although they overlap and influence one another. Chris performs a landscape of popular culture, with little of the natural world, dream world, or high culture that—especially more recently—appear on Wilson's stages. The *DiaLog* performances develop this landscape further, as did Knowles's collaborations with Cindy Lubar.[59] More recently, *The Sundance Kid is Beautiful* (2012–15) presents a culmination in solo format, initially commissioned by Frank Hentschker of the Martin E. Segal Theatre at the CUNY Graduate Center with dramaturgy by art historian Lauren DiGiulio and direction by Watermill Center's curator Noah Khoshbin, all of them drawn together through Wilson's Watermill Center laboratory, which Knowles attends every summer. Hentschker observed that working with Knowles allowed his collaborators to move slightly out of Wilson's shadow, to be creative, and to discover something that they hadn't known before.[60] The Segal Center presented a thirty-minute premier in 2012. Knowles has performed subsequent versions, expanded to one hour, at White Box and the Performing Garage in New York, the Musée du Louvre in Paris, the University of Rochester, and in conjunction with the 2015 retrospective *Christopher Knowles: In a Word* at the Institute of Contemporary Art in Philadelphia.[61]

The walls, floor, folding chairs, and a small table are all plastered with sheets of newspaper, creating a paradoxically expansive claustrophobia. Like Knowles's smaller-scale word constructs, the newsprint transforms text into visual pattern, with several repetitions of the same large "NO" the only word legible from a distance. Pools of light sometimes isolate the chairs and table, as at the beginning of the piece. At other times, the entire space is brightly lit, or a spot picks out Chris only, or the lighting (by John Torres) picks out a smaller area. During one extended section, everything is dark except what Knowles illuminates with a flashlight. A window frame, made of bright green Lego blocks, suspended up high throws its shadow on the back wall within a rectangle of light and at one point on the floor as well. The basic materials are mass produced but manually worked over and made strange. Three cones decorated with Chris's marker designs disrupt both the newsprint and the sense that this is a room, the shapes suggesting (to me) manicured shrubbery. The recorded soundscape incorporates audiotape compositions, popular music, and a number of his poems including "This is Chris His," "These are the Days," and "Mister Bojangles," accompanied in some cases by the music from their original performance source such as *Einstein on the Beach*.

Knowles physicalizes each section differently; for example, during Harry Nilsson's song "We Can Make Each Other Happy," he walks deliberately—or for one transit skips—from chair to chair, bending to touch each seat, ending this section slowly spinning in place. The sound of a heartbeat precedes this song, and after it he crosses the stage on a diagonal, saying, "Stop . . . Look. Listen to your heartbeat." This is one of the few times that he speaks. He sits on a chair for a recorded sound collage from the film *Network*, gazing up at the window that leads only to the same newsprint that covers every surface except his body and the cones. In the 2015 version, the film's "mad as hell" dialogue resonates with the word "Trump" on one of the cones. After this he picks up a newspaper and speaks again, a few lines from the 1977 performance of *DiaLog/Network*—"Every time I turn around . . . I'm tired of all of you to say . . . and I'm tired of this madhouse"—folds, crumples, and throws away the newspaper. Then he burrows under some of the newspaper on the floor, pulling a big patchwork sheet of it up over his back, and crawls on hands and knees repeating variations on "pirup" and "spups." (Although I found this utterly delightful, on the video at least one person could be seen leaving.) He emerges with a portable radio, pulls out its antenna, and slowly crosses the stage as fragments of the song "Can't Take My Eyes Off of You" play in what seem to be infinite versions with brief static in between, as if he's dialing the radio and every station is playing a version of the same song, forever—except that at just one point, there's a bit of the "oh oh" refrain from "We Can Make Each Other Happy." Reaching the table, he sits down, looks out at the audience and in a sly exercise of power very slowly opens, pours, and drinks a soda. Here the audience stops fidgeting and looks at him looking at them, in contrast to the visible restlessness while he embodied the crawling newspaper beast uttering incomprehensible phonemes. When he has finished, he says: "Ladies and gentlemen, the intermission is over. Will you please take your seat." I find this pretty funny, since he's the only one who has enjoyed an intermission, and this marks the end of the performance. In figure 12, sharp-edged pools of light pick out three newspaper-covered chairs; the window frame's shadow on the back wall; and a central cone striped in red, white, and blue; as well as Chris lying on his back, the newspaper pulled up to his waist like a blanket, an alarm clock by his downstage shoulder and another upstage of his head.

When I first saw *The Sundance Kid is Beautiful* at White Box in 2013, I knew only that Knowles had worked with Wilson and that *TDR: The Drama Review* articles I recalled reading in the 1970s mentioned brain damage. I had not yet seen any of their collaborative work. I wondered what Knowles's life was like, to what extent he communicated with others, who the producers and audience were, and why they were present. DiGiulio noted the extent to which the audience for the first few versions of *Sundance Kid* expressed their anxiety, asking for example how many of the performance choices were his and how many came from his neurotypical collaborators. She suggested that spectators redirected their own anxiety about watching onto a concern about whether Knowles was being exploited and controlled like a puppet figure. Audiences primarily comprised people who already knew either Knowles or Wilson, although the connection to Gavin Brown also brought in a younger audience engaged with the visual arts scene. Those who didn't know Knowles or who knew him only through the *Einstein* libretto or his visual art seemed the most unsettled.[62]

I will return to this issue but note for the moment that a dramaturgical

Figure 12. Christopher Knowles in *The Sundance Kid is Beautiful* at the Museé du Louvre, 2013. Photo © Julian Mommert.

attempt to work on misrecognition informed more recent residencies with *Sundance Kid*, and responses to the performance at the Institute of Contemporary Art in Philadelphia evinced less anxiety. The performance context was helpful, and some spectators responded to it as an extension into three dimensions of the visual art exhibition.[63] One can view (or buy) paintings, typings, or audiotapes by Christopher Knowles as indices of cognitive strangeness, bringing the object well inside human culture but continuing to position the person who created it on the periphery.[64] In performance, though, Knowles's bodily presence within this media landscape makes it difficult to consider him a distant and inscrutable outsider. Knowles is certainly not outside the art market or avant-garde art scene; indeed, he has grown up and developed his wide-ranging practice at its very heart. His close working relationship with Wilson began when he was fourteen years old and spread into a living, shifting network. DiGiulio argues that the popularity of Knowles's work, his sustained creative output across different media, and his influence upon other artists belie any categorization as an outsider artist: "Historically, he's known as a cult artist in either theater, poetry, or art, and not for his entire body of work. What we're doing with [*The Sundance Kid is*

*Beautiful]* is bringing all these fields together to show the depth of his work and that he's an artist whose work should be taken on his own terms. He has a detailed mind that allows him to see things we typically don't see."[65]

Watching Knowles perform makes it impossible to entertain the Romantic fantasy of isolated genius precisely because this network remains visible. Wilson is equally embedded in a network of support and collaboration, working with other artists, dependent upon tremendous fundraising efforts—all of which easily recedes from view, overshadowed by his presence and reputation. Responding to Barbara Knowles's concern for Chris's future at the time he left O.D. Heck, Wilson said: "'What if we have to support him all his life? Does he have to be like you and me? Don't put him under that pressure.' . . . And what happened without trying to make it happen— he did become independent."[66] Yet that independence cannot be complete for any of us, and Mukhopadhyay aptly questions its value:

> A farmer who grows food is dependent on a baker, a barber, a doctor, and so on. A doctor is dependent on other people of different professions in order to survive. I am dependent and will be dependent on certain caregivers and therapists. Those caregivers and therapists need people like me to earn their bread and butter and draw their salaries. . . . The question of independence is a totally relative experience. We like to think that we are independent living things, forgetting how bound we are to our physical bodies, with their own packages of diseases and emotions.[67]

Chris's relational network includes vital links with many humans but also with alarm clocks as well as his primary media, typewriters and markers, and the tape recorders that he began composing with as a young teen. These objects retain their own agency, participants in an expanded sociality not limited to the human or the animate, kept in the foreground like the objects and forces with which Amanda Baggs demonstrates her ongoing nonsymbolic conversation. Even considering humanity alone, though, the affective linkages reach in every direction—Knowles has also supported the flourishing of others and significantly torqued their work and lives. Were power relations and preconceptions different, critics might have commented about Knowles's influence upon Wilson's performance as an old man engaged with tape recordings of his life in Samuel Beckett's *Krapp's Last Tape*.[68]

## SHAME AND SHAMELESSNESS

The anxiety of spectators expressing concern that performers such as Knowles are being exploited derives in part from the potential that exposure on stage might shame the performers for their perceived cognitive difference. When Wilson shouted questions into Knowles's face during the first *Queen Victoria* entr'acte, for example, familiar viewing habits led me to initially see anger and frustration on Wilson's part and, in Knowles's spine sagging away into a C-curve much as Luke Treadaway's did in *Curious Incident of the Dog in the Night-Time* when confronted by his father, to perceive a shrinking away from aggression. (Figure 11 also shows a dropped head and gaze that the shadow exaggerates.) According to normate face- and body-reading practices, this posture could be interpreted as extending into the entire body the shame–humiliation response, as Silvan Tomkins describes it: "By dropping his eyes, his eyelids, his head and sometimes the whole upper part of his body, the individual calls a halt to looking at another person, particularly the other person's face, and to the other person's looking at him, particularly his face."[69] Shame is ambivalent rather than being totally negative, as Sara Ahmed points out, because it requires a potentially positive relation to the person before whom one feels shame.[70] Tomkins stipulates that one must already be interested to respond with shame, which inhibits interest and enjoyment, and an increase in excitement or joy can in turn inhibit the shame response.[71] Tomkins devotes less attention to the positive affects, describing the facial signs of the continuum interest–excitement as "eyebrows down, track, look, listen" and of enjoyment–joy as "smile, lips widened up and out," going on to note changes in breathing that accompany visual exploration of exciting objects; that is, either a suspension of breath or rapid breathing.[72] To pursue the reading by Tomkins's criteria, then, one might interpret Knowles's repeated grins and looks with lowered eyebrows over the three hours of *Queen Victoria* as evidence that his interest overcame his shame.

Yet other difficulties with communication and looking produce behaviors that closely resemble the shame response and create confusion for a spectator who misreads a retreat from sensory flooding, whether in a social situation or on stage. In *Queen Victoria*, the action's reversal provides important clues. Knowles's loud questions to Wilson, also delivered at close range, seem pressured but not angry; moreover, his slight grin leads me to read pleasure into his loud and intense questioning of Wilson and then, further, to reassess Wilson's shouting, erasing the negative affect in both cases. Perhaps Wilson was trying to match Knowles's delivery and inadvertently added behaviors that read as anger. Arendell proposes that *Queen Victoria's* "distillation of language . . . transformed Wilson's non-autistic performers into automatons, while Knowles was fully present and fluent in the abstract phrases he helped create. . . . Wilson's non-autistic actors borrowed this stereotype of affectless speech to create a group phenomenon of automatism on stage."[73] In echoing familiar emotional situations, this entr'acte initially made me anxious that the piece might subject Knowles to humiliation and caused me to seek reassurance that this was not the case. Knowles's calm and direct gaze during the Coke-drinking section of *Sundance Kid* offered similar reassurance and, significantly, came shortly after his retreat under the newspaper. Watching with openness and waiting for the *ah!* of wonder leaves spectators vulnerable to a sticky residue of shame adhering to the covering-up action and thus to their own anxious feelings. The performance in no way signals that a spectator should reflect upon the *Network* context in order to arrive at an interpretation such as the following: the performer grows increasingly disgusted with and overwhelmed by the media that the newsprint represents, and he retreats from it by going underneath or is completely absorbed by it, crawling around until he emerges with music. This interpretation is perfectly reasonable but in no way essential. In both of these performances, misreading—even if subliminal—creates anxiety, and Knowles's interested facial expression relieves it.

Theory of mind explanations for autism militate against this sort of relief by casting doubt upon the autist's ability to recognize his own emotional states. I discussed one example involving pain in chapter 3 and note that the terms of debate shift a bit when transposed to address shame: If the autist cannot identify his own state of mind, which includes emotional feelings, to what extent can he be said to feel shame?[74] (I will use the masculine pronouns here simply because the performers I discuss in this chapter are male but wish to mark this conformity to stock character types.) Considering him to be shameless both returns the neurotypical spectator's anxiety to the picture and denies the autist's full humanity. Tobin Siebers raises the question "who gets to feel shame?" and argues that "having nothing to be ashamed of . . . is not a sign of either moral integrity or moral failure. It is a sign of social worthlessness." Rather than being recognized as persons, "people with disabilities are cast as objects of mourning. The feeling of grief directed at them exposes the idea that they have somehow disappeared— that they have become nothing, that they are dead."[75]

Even Tomkins's observation that infants begin to manifest the "shame face" at failures of reciprocation between three and seven months, after they have learned to recognize the caregiver's face and to mirror facial expressions, depends upon normate development with which sensory processing disorders could interfere. Michael Lewis, who distinguishes self-conscious emotions such as shame and embarrassment from basic emotions because of their complex relation to standards, rules, and goals, classifies shyness as "a dispositional factor not related to self-evaluation" but, rather, to fear and social discomfort. He further distinguishes the type of embarrassment that results from public exposure, even in the absence of negative self-evaluation, from the type of embarrassment more closely related to shame.[76] This more nuanced taxonomy of emotions seems better able to accommodate different cognitive styles; however, affect theory's general reliance on Tomkins (particularly as conveyed by Eve Kosofsky Sedgwick) captures important trajectories for audience response even if the theory may not be fully adequate to the emotional phenomenon. Ridout, for example, develops at length an analysis of shame and embarrassment as not only psychological (per Tomkins) but also political (per Agamben, who describes the flush of a prisoner selected at random to be shot during a forced march from one Nazi concentration camp to another and thus reduced to bare life/*zoë*).[77] As Michael Warner notes, because "shame is a kind of social knowledge," we must always take its "social contextualization" into account:

> But it is infinitely complex, perhaps especially in the Anglophone North Atlantic cultures, where shame encompasses in some sense guilt, degradation, abasement[,] abashedness, bashfulness, shyness, embarrassment, self-consciousness, modesty, dishonor, disgrace, humiliation, mortification, low self-esteem, indignity, ignobility, abjection, and stigma. It's like having thirty-two words for snow: the fine discriminations of the vernacular suggest something like a fascination.[78]

Ambivalently social, this fine-grained and amorphous affect appears particularly contagious. Sedgwick notes that "a shame-prone person" experiences a flood of shame when witnessing another's humiliation: "Shame floods into being as a moment, a disruptive moment, in a circuit of identity-constituting identificatory communication."[79]

Douglas Crimp suggests, though, that shame contagion tends to reinforce separateness rather than overcoming it. He argues that one does not in this case vicariously take on the other person's shame but, instead, revives one's own. One identifies only with the other person's vulnerability to shame; thus, "the other's difference is preserved."[80] If this is the case, then my anxiety that a performer might be humiliated makes me anxious that shame might also flood me. And spectator concerns about exploitation and agency may also derive from the potential for shame at being caught watching a latter-day freak show, something that the Theater HORA/Jérôme Bel collaboration *Disabled Theatre* (2012) explicitly acknowledges when performer Damian Bright reports that his mother "said that it's some kind of freak show, but she liked it a lot."[81] *Ganesh Versus the Third Reich* (2011) addresses this anxiety directly as it presents a fictionalized version of Back to Back Theatre rehearsing a play about the elephant-headed Hindu deity Ganesh traveling to Germany in 1943 to retrieve the swastika, which Hitler took when the gods weren't paying attention.[82] This Australian company got its start in the 1980s, a time of deinstitutionalization when the arts seemed to offer paths toward normalizing people with disabilities. Artists working with Corilong, a disability service provider in Geelong, soon began to move the company toward professional independence, which it accomplished in 1997 although the fight for legitimacy continued.[83] In the early 2010s, they were "the only full-time professional acting ensemble in Australia."[84] Petra Kuppers refers to them as "one of the most recognized exports of the Australian culture industry."[85] Back to Back practices a reverse integration; that is, ensemble members without disability adapt themselves to the central core of "professional actors considered to have an intellectual disability."[86] As executive producer Alice Nash puts it, "the ethos of Back to Back Theatre was deftly drawn from the company's inception to focus on the idiosyncratic genius of each ensemble member."[87]

Arriving first at Auschwitz, Ganesh encounters "angel of death" Josef Mengele and befriends a prisoner named Levi, who tells him, "I am alive now only with the help of my mental retardation. . . . Dr Mengele saved me when he saw my appearance. Despite his many painful experiments on my body I have remained alive" (168). Yet when Ganesh inquires about his "retardation" and its "effects upon [his] body" that have fascinated the Nazi doctor, Levi instead describes an enhanced mental capacity: "As a child every thought and image stayed with me. Books I had read years before I could recall as if I had just read the page. I came to realise my memory was photographic. I have forgotten nothing" (168). Paradoxically, a perceived impairment has kept Levi alive when the rest of his family were exterminated; doubly paradoxical, the request to describe a disability produces a description of ability.

Figure 13. Brian Tilley as Ganesh, Simon Laherty as Levi, and David Woods as Dr. Mengele in *Ganesh Versus the Third Reich*, Tokyo, 2013. Photo by Jun Ishikawa. Courtesy of Back to Back Theatre.

Ganesh's unusual appearance also accompanies advantages not apparent to Mengele, who sees only the mixing of human and animal but misses the supernatural. Having patiently explained how he came to bear an elephant's head, Ganesh responds to Mengele's repeated question "How have you an elephant head?" with an outburst beginning "It is only through my favour you have seen me, for my true form is smaller than the atoms and greater than the heavens" and ending "I am the maker, the destroyer, the leader of all. I am the father" (163).[88] Mengele drops the table knife with which he has been menacing his captive, as shown in figure 13, and falls to the floor. The two prisoners thus share an extraordinariness, on the one hand (or head!) a species mixing; on the other, an ambiguously valued cognitive capacity. They escape the extermination camp and travel together incognito, on foot and by train, eluding Nazi pursuers. Ganesh confronts Hitler in Berlin, Levi heads for Switzerland; Mengele briefly reappears with Levi as hostage but drops dead at Ganesh's roar.

Interesting enough in itself, and beautifully staged with an impressively low-tech combination of lighting and scenic backdrops painted on multiple layers of plastic resembling shower curtains plus an absolutely gorgeous elephant-head mask, Back to Back presents this story as a play within a play in which the actors represent themselves rehearsing. Although the ensemble collectively developed the script through long-term improvisation, Brian (Tilley) plays the script's author within this metatheatrical frame as well as playing Ganesh. (The script uses the actors' first names to identify their characters in the framing scenes. This does not mean that they are "being" themselves. As my discussion progresses, I will use the last name to refer to the individual as distinct from the character.) Simon (Laherty) begins by negotiating with Brian to secure parts for himself and Mark (Deans). Initially, Brian assigns them to represent "Jews on the run from the Nazis" (160), and Simon does play Levi. But Mark doesn't join in, and Simon complains: "I've had to do all the Jewish stuff. All of it. Your part and my part. It's really hard being a Jew" (165). In the end, after the show has fallen apart, Simon steps up to fill a crucial gap, pressing the moustache onto his lip and playing Hitler. Scott (Price) plays an SS guard, acts as stagehand, and most important offers an ongoing critique of the show, the performers, and the director played by David (Woods), who also takes on Vishnu, Mengele, and a stocking salesman encountered on the train in a scene reminiscent of *Van Ryan's Express*.[89] The company brought Woods in about ten months before the premiere, after they had been at work on this piece for several years while also creating and performing *small metal objects* (2005) and *Food Court* (2008). They specifically wanted a nondisabled person in the role because the framing scenes respond directly to comments from audiences, the director of a festival, and disability arts organizations expressing skepticism about the creative capacity of the Back to Back actors.[90] After a 2009 performance of *Food Court* in Brussels, for example, an audience member said that he didn't believe that the people he saw on stage had actually made the work: "I have worked with people like this and I don't think they are capable of it." Price jumped up to reply, "Well mate, you can just get out of here because what you just said is so wrong and so offensive."[91]

In *Ganesh*, Scott similarly speaks his mind, repeatedly raising ethical concerns in an increasingly forthright manner. He begins by telling Brian that Hindus may object to the appropriation of their gods, and that Simon and Mark "have no idea about the content" of the play because they have no connection to Judaism (169). When Brian misses the point and turns the conversation to *King Kong*, Scott thanks him "for the chat" and smacks his forehead in exasperation (getting quite a laugh from the audience for the videorecorded performance that I watched and from me as well). He approaches David next: "Not all the actors seem to understand the gravity of what they are playing. I'm concerned. Brian is playing an Indian deity. Do you think that's OK?" He then asks Simon: "Do you comprehend what it is to represent a Jew in the Holocaust?" to which Simon replies: "Fuck off Scott" (170). David holds a meeting to address these concerns, but instead of discussing the actors' comprehension or right to play with sensitive cultural material, Scott attacks David's direction—"I think you have been doing a crap job directing and the show is a piece of filth"—and accuses him of manipulating everyone. This time, the generally silent Mark says, "Get fucked Scott" (180), getting an even bigger laugh than Simon did. Scott's behavior to some degree forestalls objections related to cultural appropriation by explicitly acknowledging them and also brings to the table the issue of a neurotypical director exploiting performers who "nominate themselves as being perceived to have intellectual disabilities" (185)—David, the supposed exploiter, offers this description. In fact, David's repeated and largely unsuccessful attempts within the rehearsal scenes to manipulate the actors provide the predominant source of humor throughout the piece, and he comes off as an egotistical jerk.

The company leaves the precise nature of its members' cognitive differences largely unspecified, although they all qualify for disability pensions during the periods when Back to Back does not pay them a full salary.[92] Several of them have the precise and detailed memory characteristic of some autists. Bruce Gladwin mentions that Laherty, Price, and Tilley "have a huge capacity for memorizing text," and Price "can memorize text faster than any actor [he's] ever worked with."[93] Price identifies his formal diagnosis as Tourette's syndrome,[94] and for *Ganesh* he presents a version of himself characterized by neglect of social niceties and what might be considered an obsession with following the rules—in this case, ethical rules. The inability to restrain speech that characterizes Tourette's here is transformed from a source of shame into brutal honesty, and the piece uses Scott to align the audience in a skeptical position with respect to the show. David seems to conflate the audience with Scott, reacting to the critique of his direction by attacking them instead. He addresses a row of empty chairs and imagines the audience who will fill them, accusing them of being "perverts" who have come "to see a bit of freak porn" (183–84).[95] In performance, of course, actual spectators fill the chairs and receive this challenge. Scott has proposed that Mark be removed from the show because "he doesn't understand what is fiction and what is not" (182). David now says that his imaginary audience has "problems with us blurring reality and fiction because [the actors] are a group of people with intellectual disabilities" (184), whereas "they don't have an issue with non-intellectually disabled actors blurring reality and fiction—being deluded, being mad" (185). Helena Grehan observes:

> As a spectator the feeling is one of shame ... and an emotional reaction as if we have just been punched or slapped. *Ganesh Versus the Third Reich* has taken spectators on a difficult journey where they are encouraged to connect emotionally with the performers.... Yet all along this was a ruse or at best only part of the story. The frameworks that we went along with have ultimately led to a limiting engagement with the show, because we would not have employed them if the actors had "merely" been "mad" or "deluded" as David points out.[96]

The audience's shame derives from the ambiguity of spectating, made briefly explicit here as it was in *Disabled Theatre*. This is the point at which *Ganesh* looks back at the audience whom it positions as "an embodied reflection of mainstream society," as Grehan and Peter Eckersall note, reminding them that "while the space is shared it is shared unevenly.... We realize that not only is the work looking back at us but that we were under surveillance all along."[97]

Yet this metatheatrical acknowledgment of shame lets the audience off the hook sufficiently to continue watching. As the piece progresses, it's David who loses his grip on reality after Scott cannot adequately physicalize being shot. The confrontation begins with verbal insult and, after Scott blurts out "go and get fucked cunt," escalates to a physical assault (191). The "director"—wearing his Mengele costume throughout this scene—goes wild, ripping down scenery and dragging Scott onto the floor where he curls up in a ball, screaming, as the rest of the actors pull David away and throw him out of the room. Simon then puts on the moustache that the other actors have refused and joins Brian to enact the final confrontation between Hitler and Ganesh. That the disabled actors have removed the neurotypical director before proceeding to do what's required to complete the show cancels out any doubts about the Back to Back actors' agency—at least, within the fictionalized rehearsal situation.

*Ganesh* also makes shrewd use of a Down-syndrome stock character, initially placing him in opposition to Scott and then aligning the two against David. Mark's actual correspondence with Deans himself must remain ambiguous, as must the relation between Price and his character. For Petra Kuppers, Mark grounds the performance like a Greek chorus, remaining largely uninvolved in the Ganesh play within the metatheatrical frame but from the margins "project[ing] an attunement to the emotional field that develops."[98] He does not, however, function as affective guide in the way that I've proposed Knowles does for *Queen Victoria*, and the fields that the two works establish are quite different. The audience for Wilson's postdramatic landscape could follow Knowles into a practice of watching without discursive interpretation, whereas *Ganesh* plays Mark and Scott against one another to help its audience navigate both drama and metadrama. Scott's skeptical ethics repeatedly encounters Mark's unflappable affect and bounces off, ricocheting toward some other target. Consider again the confrontation that prompts David to attack the audience, which begins with Scott insisting that Mark should be removed because he doesn't understand the play within the play: "Mark's mind is probably, OK like, working like a goldfish" (182)—a rather horrifying and potentially humiliating assertion that David proceeds to push directly at Mark, presumably to shame Scott for shaming Mark:

> DAVID: I think I can answer your quibbles with the help of Mark. Mark, do you think of yourself as having the mind of a goldfish?
> MARK: Goldfish, whale, penguin . . .
> SCOTT: See, what did I tell you . . .
> BRIAN/SIMON: Hang on . . .
> DAVID: Let him answer. Let him answer. Yeah, go on, Mark.
> MARK: Octopus, seal, whale, shark, Sea World. (182, ellipses in original)

The moment is funny, transforms an insult into a list of sea-related creatures pleasant to observe, tells us absolutely nothing about what Mark thinks or feels, and certainly tells us nothing about Deans's actual experience as a longtime core member of the company even as it positions his persona "Mark" as a potential object for audience sympathy.

*Ganesh* then returns Mark to this questionable position in the end, after he and Scott have reconciled during the physical confrontation with David. In the metatheatrical final scene, David returns to the rehearsal room to pack up his things. Mark is eating lunch there alone and tries with a tear and a hug to keep him from leaving, and David tricks him into a game of hide and seek in order to abandon him alone onstage. David's behavior seems callous and, if one fully accepts these framing scenes as realist, quite sad.

Shameful! Yet Mark is not in fact alone under the rehearsal table at the end of the play any more than Christopher Knowles and Robert Wilson comprised an occult speech community of two in their dialogue performances. In a theater with his audience, Mark looks directly (even winkingly) at them. This moment reminds the audience that they are under surveillance in a different way than David's earlier accusation did, inviting them to look and to see him fully as character and as person. As the character Steve puts it in *small metal objects*, "I want people to see me. I want to be a full human being."[99] To shy away from this invitation in fear of shame would be to deny him full humanity. Bree Hadley points out that disabled persons experience social performativity as a palpable part of daily life, as the spectacle of disability in the public sphere creates a pressure to either conceal the disability or to perform it in the most recognizable form possible.[100] Some autists can pass as neurotypical, which always entails some degree of affective expenditure, whereas others cannot. They may choose to follow a familiar script, in Hadley's terms, or, in Jordynn Jack's, to play a stock character. *Ganesh* pulls its viewers back and forth with two disability stock characters positioned as opposite conceptual poles on a scale of empathic attunement, yet presents only one character as lacking empathy—the neurotypical director. He resembles the theory of mind theorists, experts on autism who dismiss autists' descriptions of their own experience as unreliable.[101] Back to Back challenges its audience to overcome their own presumptions of superior knowledge and to see its performers in their full humanity.

Kuppers observes that the show seems to present this challenge to a normate audience, whereas she as a disabled artist and theorist must "make sense of the success of disabled artists in the nondisabled mainstream" from a different perspective.[102] She expresses approval that

> with companies like Back to Back Theatre, disabled people get training, stimulating work, and gigs, and that's a major infrastructural step forward: disabled people travel, see the world, touch their lives to other disabled people's lives, and we are all enriched by that. The mainstream world can see disabled people as active presences onstage, as able to play in complexly layered scenes, and as people who clearly enjoy their job and have thrown themselves with passion into long-term labor.[103]

She contrasts the skill and complex development evident in this work from Bel's *Disabled Theatre*, which mainstream audiences and critics seem to have received as "some kind of 'authenticity', humanity in the raw." For Kuppers, Bel's use of seemingly improvisational and unskilled performance structures elides the fact that Theater HORA's "experienced professional actors are re-performing, re-enacting complex and memorized scripts,"[104] something that remains more fully visible in Back to Back's performances. She says that "the international art world eats its Others, creates its stars and its modes of re-ception,"[105] which I take to mean that it fattens on them and excretes what it cannot digest. Autists' visual, textual, and musical creations have been more easily digestible than their performances. Anthony Kubiak even asserts im-mediately after noting Knowles's contribution to the libretto for *Einstein on the Beach* that "artistic [sic] savants seem to find vivid expression in all but one art: the art of theatre."[106] In this respect, perhaps *Ganesh* pries further open the stage door that *Queen Victoria* cracked more than three decades earlier. Knowles and Wilson both participate in the international art world as individual geniuses, in spite of other differences in visibility of the two men's support networks. Back to Back brings its collective genius into this world, a genius comprised by its working structures rather than the consid-erable gifts of its individual artists, and its work nourishes a nonmainstream audience as well as the mainstream art world whose menu makes it available. One can more readily savor the political dimension of this work when the seasoning of unique genius becomes less pronounced.

## AUTISTS PERFORMING ADVOCACY

As they claim a shared identity in being perceived to have an intellectual disability, Back to Back's actors perform a right to self-determination and control over representation, both artistic and political. Persons labeled with the less-than-coherent diagnosis of autism similarly claim a shared identity in order to insist upon self-representation as an essential right. The Autistic Self Advocacy Network, for example, adopted the slogan "nothing about us without us," a phrase that disability rights activist Jim Charlton first heard in 1993 from two South African disability rights leaders who in turn reported hearing it from an Eastern European activist. Charlton notes that "the slo-gan's power derives from its location of the source of many types of (disabil-ity) oppression and its simultaneous opposition to such oppression in the context of control and voice."[107] Autistic performance-makers increasingly assert their presence, and autistic actors challenge neurotypical casting for

autistic characters—what we might call Autie-face performance. This issue
came to the fore when the Broadway production of *Curious Incident of the
Dog in the Night-Time* needed to replace the actor in the leading role. In spite
of pressure to consider autistic actors, the production did not seek them for
auditions, and neurotypical actor Tyler Lea took over the role in September
2015.[108] User emmapretzel's response to a blog on the topic addresses concerns similar to those that I discussed in chapter 3:

> i'm not upset about NT [neurotypical] actors playing autistic charac-
> ters because i think only autistic actors should get those roles; i'm upset
> about NT actors playing autistic characters because 1. those characters
> continue to be conform [*sic*] to the same old damaging stereotypes and
> caricatures that have dominated media representation of autistic ppl
> for decades, and 2. because our media/public culture continues to see
> us, and our behavior, as so inherently inhuman and inexplicable and in-
> comprehensible that every time a NT actor really nails a shitty "~AU-
> TISMZ~" caricature-stereotype, the acting world just GUSHES about
> how AMAZING of an acting job it was, how METHOD they must
> have gotten in order to play such a HARD and SPECIAL role, and
> THEN gives them like three oscars for doing such a SERVICE to "peo-
> ple like this character."[109]

This issue intersects with general concerns about diversity in casting, but
autism may differ from other perceived disabilities in its relative potential
to remain invisible. As the original blogger Chavisory pointed out, actors
would have to out themselves in order to be considered for autistic-only
casting. Although some might hesitate to make this move because of its potential to limit their professional opportunities, a few have done just that:
Mickey Rowe specifically addressed the notion that "autism impairs the responsiveness that is a key skill in acting because it lessens the ability to read
others" with a link to photos and video of his own physical theater work
much in the style of *Curious Incident*, evidence of his training and ability
to play such a role.[110] Rowe has also compared the scripting that he must
use in daily interactions to the work he does with a theatrical script.[111] As I
completed final revisions to this chapter, he was in fact cast as Christopher
in a professional coproduction by Indiana Repertory Theatre and Syracuse
Stage of *Curious Incident of the Dog in the Night-Time* opening in fall 2017.[112]
The question of casting brings the category's incoherence into focus: Per-

haps one would not expect a producer to cast a nonverbal classical autist as Christopher; but then what characteristics would be most significant—a fondness for prime numbers?

Rather than hiring autistic actors, productions concerned to move beyond stock characters increasingly employ a "native expert." Alex Plank, who created the *Wrong Planet* Internet forum for Aspies in 2004 at age seventeen, interned as a script consultant for the FX series *The Bridge*,[113] and the National Theatre brought in Cian Binchy to advise Luke Treadaway on playing autistic. Binchy considers himself wrong for the role due to physical type, not due to his autism.[114] He became interested in a theater-related career as a teenager attending a school for autistic pupils but found it difficult to make any inroads as a performer or to pursue professional training. Then in 2014 the London program Access All Areas began to offer a Performance Making Diploma for adults with learning disabilities in collaboration with the Royal Central School of Speech and Drama, University of London.[115] After graduating, Binchy performed his solo work *The Misfit Analysis* at the 2015 Edinburgh Fringe Festival, the 2016 Vault Festival in London, and in ongoing touring engagements.[116] The piece combines performance poetry and video projection to convey his life experience and the repeated frustrations born of people's reliance upon stereotypes and partial knowledge. He recruits audience members to answer a diagnostic questionnaire, to spin various objects, to assist in inflating a blow-up doll, all the while doling out smiley-face stickers such as we see him receive at a sheltered work site in lieu of a paycheck. In this particular video segment, a training manager consistently treats him like a child, gives him the limited and boring task of clicking plastic tags onto clothes hangers, and denies having promised at the outset that this training would lead to paid employment. In another video, Cian and two other men demonstrate autistic behaviors described by a perky voiceover that finishes by assuring viewers that they have now become experts at recognizing autism. Among other behaviors, the three of them read railroad timetables together in dull voices. When addressed as "young men," one of them correctly objects "I'm not young—I'm old!," again highlighting the erasure of adult autism. Binchy observes that "films and books often portray those with the condition as being 'as different as possible' from other characters, when in reality they have the same desires and emotions as those without."[117] He has also been involved in developing *MADHOUSE re-exit* (planned for 2018), and the Autism Arts Festival in April 2017 featured both *Misfit Analysis* and a segment of *MADHOUSE* called *Catch the Baby* in which the six-foot Binchy struggles with the general public expectation that he should remain in his crib. The festival's thirteen performance offerings included puppetry, a participatory audio walk and a participatory environment, standup comedy, and solo performances.[118]

The United Kingdom and Australia are significantly ahead of the United States in producing professional performance by autists and others perceived to be disabled. Graeae Theatre Company, for example, has been active since 1980 and develops a wide range of work with Deaf and disabled artists in London as well as touring internationally, collaborating with and inspiring other companies. In 2015, they launched an Ensemble program for young theater artists, providing them with paid employment during six months of training in collaboration with drama schools and theater companies.[119] Australia's Company AT (which stands for Autistic Theatre) is unusual in its all-autistic membership. This ensemble operates under the auspices of Tutti Arts, an inclusive arts organization that began as a singing group for intellectually disabled people in 1997, quickly grew into the internationally-renowned choir Tutti Ensemble, and in the early 2000s began to branch out into original music-theater works.[120] Company AT premiered the non-musical play *History of Autism* at the State Opera Studio for the Netley Asia Pacific Autism Conference in 2013, with subsequent performances at the Adelaide Fringe Festival in 2014 and the 2015 Come Out Children's Festival.[121] Actors in role as Leo Kanner and Hans Asperger frame *History of Autism* with narration that links a series of vignettes. In the end, they urge the audience to try understanding and respecting every person as a unique individual. This rather straightforward approach counters shame and misconception by making the variety of autism visible and sharing information, ultimately supporting autism pride.[122] In the United States, Tectonic Theater Project members Anushka Paris-Carter and Andy Paris developed *Uncommon Sense* over a five-year period, with a 2017 premiere at the University of Northern Iowa's Gallagher Bluedorn Performing Arts Center. Beginning with the writers' experience as parents of a daughter with Asperger syndrome, the creative team interviewed Iowa residents, developed material through devising workshops with university students, and worked throughout this period with actors "both on and off the spectrum." Rather extensive publicity materials focus on increasing awareness of autism and the experience of autism families.[123]

Differing approaches to autism advocacy and self-advocacy generate fierce debate well summarized by the literature that I have cited here, and entering these debates is outside my purpose except in one respect: I see limited benefit in applying the label "autistic" to any person who does not publicly claim it. Conceivably, Christopher Knowles provides a positive role model for autists in his audience, but this would be true without the diagnostic label. I advocate retiring the use of this adjective in reference to him. Although I conform to other published material about Back to Back including their website and refrain from labeling any of the actors as autistic, I note that Scott Price claims the hashtag #autismpride.[124] Shame and pride would seem to be a opposed pair, both organized in relation to a desire for visibility.[125] Asserting pride reclaims a previously abject label and shifts its valence—a replacement that potentially cuts connection to those before whom one might otherwise be expected to feel shame. As Elspeth Probyn elaborates on Tomkins, "Without interest, there can be no shame; conversely, shame alerts us to things, people, and ideas that we didn't even realize we wanted. It highlights unknown or unappreciated investments."[126] Perhaps more important, though, both asserting pride and performing self-advocacy include a nonnormate audience among a performance's addressees.

CHAPTER 6

# Mimetic Mixing and Technologies
# for Becoming-

As a way to experiment with the "uncompromising sweeping-away of identities, whether human or animal," as Steve Baker puts it, Deleuze and Guattari first propose becoming-animal in *Kafka* as an alternative to the "Oedipal forces of fixity, conservatism, and compliance."[1] They develop the concept most fully a few years later in *A Thousand Plateaus*, taking some pains to distinguish this conceptual scheme from both the Jungian archetype ("a serial organization of the imaginary" based upon resemblance) and the Lévi-Straussian totem ("a symbolic and structural order of understanding" based upon functional homology).[2] If I were to dream of a hawk soaring above the world, for example, I might on the one hand interpret my dream's content as emerging from "instinctual meaning structures (archetypes) common to all human beings"; that is, from what Jung termed the collective unconscious.[3] Examining myths that involve hawks, birds of prey, or even birds in general might then suggest that my dream concerned death, renewal, or transformation. Dana Levin's poem "Augur" offers me a model, using resemblance to link a "hawk perched low on a hedge of vine" to the sun-god Ra and a series of attributes that a human might share: sharp vision, vigilant attention, a hood removed and tether loosed, ascension, and death.[4] Levi-Strauss, on the other hand, might help me understand kinship structures but would be of little use for dream analysis. He examines the relationship between actual hawks and turtles in order to understand something about the structural relationship between a hawk clan and a turtle clan. Resemblance to hawks has no significance in this scheme.[5]

Instead of resemblance or functional homology, Deleuze and Guattari propose "irreducible dynamisms drawing lines of flight and implying . . .

forms of expression" other than those captured by archetypal myth or totemic ritual.[6] These lines of flight escape from known identities as the human enters into alliance with the animal in reciprocal becoming; that is, they affect one another. Consider this concrete example of becoming-predator from Helen MacDonald's memoir of falconry and mourning:

> Hunting with the hawk took me to the very edge of being a human. Then it took me past that place to somewhere I wasn't human at all. The hawk in flight, me running after her, the land and the air a pattern of deep and curving detail, sufficient to block out anything like the past or the future, so that the only thing that mattered were the next thirty seconds. I felt the curt lift of autumn breeze over the hill's round brow, and the need to tack left, to fall over the leeward slope to where the rabbits were. I crept and walked and ran. I crouched. I looked. I saw more than I'd ever seen. The world gathered about me. It made absolute sense. But the only things I knew were hawkish things, and the lines that drew me across the landscape were the lines that drew the hawk: hunger, desire, fascination, the need to find and fly and kill.
>
> Yet every time the hawk caught an animal, it pulled me back from being an animal into being a human again.[7]

She learned to harden her heart, to administer the coup de grace to her hawk Mabel's prey, but found that "hardening the heart was not the same as not caring. The rabbit was always important. Its life was never taken lightly. I was accountable for these deaths."[8] MacDonald became-hawk in relation to the rabbit as prey while remaining human in relation to the death.

Even though MacDonald owned and controlled Mabel, she describes a becoming-hawk that exceeds ownership. For a human to become-animal is to escape categorization (that is, membership in the "Oedipal symbolic community") by entering into "an inhuman connivance with the animal" in relation to some third term. Deleuze and Guattari's prescription bears quoting at length:

> Do not imitate a dog, but make your organism enter into composition with something else in such a way that the particles emitted from the aggregate thus composed will be canine as a function of the relation of movement and rest, or of molecular proximity, into which they enter. Clearly, this something else can be quite varied, and be more or less di-

rectly related to the animal in question: it can be the animal's natural food (dirt and worm), or its exterior relations with other animals (you can become-dog with cats, or become-monkey with a horse), or an apparatus or prosthesis to which a person subjects the animal (muzzle and reindeer, etc.), or something that does not even have a localizable relation to the animal in question.[9]

For MacDonald, rabbit constitutes the third term. Engaged in the hunt, she and Mabel become a woman-hawk rhizome.

Deleuze and Guattari propose the rhizome as an analytical alternative to the tree structure, drawing a number of examples from evolution. As I briefly mentioned in the preface, they map the relationship between baboons, a type-C virus, and cats horizontally; the linkage alters the DNA of all three organisms. Their evolution thus connects rhizomatically but clearly does not proceed in a linear fashion, cat evolving into baboon for instance.[10] Take also the resemblance between certain orchids and wasps: one might trace the orchid's linear descent, with resemblance to a pollinating insect as an adaptive step along the way. Accounts typically characterize this evolution as deceptive mimesis by the naughty female orchid, who tricks the male wasp into fruitlessly mating with her. Deleuze and Guattari instead map the relationship horizontally as an instance of "aparallel evolution" in which two organisms that "have absolutely nothing to do with each other" form a useful linkage:

> The orchid deterritorializes by forming an image, a tracing of a wasp; but the wasp reterritorializes on that image. The wasp is nevertheless deteritorrialized, becoming a piece in the orchid's reproductive apparatus. But it reterritorializes the orchid by transporting its pollen. Wasp and orchid, as heterogeneous elements, form a rhizome. It could be said that the orchid imitates the wasp, reproducing its image in a signifying fashion. . . . But this is true only on the level of the strata—a parallelism between two strata such that a plant organization on one imitates an animal organization on the other. At the same time, something else entirely is going on: . . . a veritable becoming, a becoming-wasp of the orchid and a becoming-orchid of the wasp.[11]

To *deterritorialize* is to undo existing functional limits; to *reterritorialize*, to reinscribe a definite functionality. In another example, perhaps more legible in theatrical terms, marionette strings rhizomatically connect puppet and puppeteer. The pulls go in both directions, through puppet strings and human nerve fibers, affecting every node of this assemblage. There is no set boundary to the connections—they can extend beyond a single puppet and a single puppeteer as indeed the puppets of *War Horse* demonstrate (although they are not marionettes).[12]

The nodes of a rhizome—wasp-orchid, puppet-puppeteer, hawk-woman—affect one another in very real ways even though the woman does not "really" become a hawk, the puppeteer a puppet, or the orchid a wasp. "Becoming produces nothing other than itself" through a process of reciprocal affect or *involution* as opposed to evolution: "To involve is to form a block that runs its own line 'between' the terms in play and beneath assignable relations."[13] Involution folds the relational field in upon itself, bringing new surfaces into contact and thus forming a new in-between layer with the potential to become fixed but always susceptible to further destratification. Becoming- is one of the concepts that Deleuze and Guattari use to discuss immanence; others include the plane of consistency, the body without organs, and deterritorialization—all of which they oppose to processes of organization.[14] Looking back to chapter 4, consider the goose-penis rhizome that *O Sensibility* involved. Otto Muehl organ-ized the headless goose's neck, pulling on a condom and inserting it into a performer's vagina. The becoming-phallus of the goose neck fleetingly dis-organ-ized the penis, no longer bound to strict functionality in relation to sexual intercourse. (Descriptions do not suggest a comparable deterritorialization for the vagina or, indeed, the woman herself.) Recall that Muehl used his own penis to piss on a volunteer performer who wished to use his for vaginal penetration. As the female performer put it, "that wasn't exactly why she was there," and Muehl prevented that particular re-organ-ization.[15] As the decapitation of the goose makes clear, though, to deterritorialize another creature over whom one already has complete control does not have a positive ethical value comparable to a willing flight from power and privilege.

Deleuze and Guattari stipulate that to become-animal does not mean to imitate; indeed, "resemblance . . . would represent an obstacle or stoppage."[16] Yet as Baker observes, "many of contemporary art's becomings-animal still look like an animal."[17] Ann Carlson's *Animals* series, also discussed in chapter 4, mixes mimesis with becoming-animal: she lopes and swings like a gorilla but also becomes-gorilla in relation to the kitten, imitates a whale's song and tail movement but becomes-whale in relation to the voice that simultaneously displays and trivializes her. In performances that I will discuss in this chapter, Paula Josa-Jones's hands tense and extend like a tiger's claws. Jennifer Monson's head reaches forward as her shoulders and arms shrug back, birdlike. Yet these dancers do not represent animals in the way that puppets do in *War Horse* or *The Lion King* or in the way that an actress does when playing the eponymous dog in A. R. Gurney's *Sylvia*.

Insisting upon becoming-animal as an affect, which Deleuze and Guattari define as "the kind of thinking done by art," Laura Cull objects to a binary opposition between mimesis and becoming-:

> The critique of imitation . . . concerns the imitation of the animal as defined as an organism (as a fixed form viewed from a position of subjective detachment) rather than as a set of relations, a field of forces or a complex of powers to affect and be affected. Indeed, Deleuze and Guattari suggest that the artist will be affected and transformed by the encounter with the animal whether or not this is something they intend; we *cannot* simply imitate or repeat, even if we try.[18]

Considering imitation as a starting point for becoming-, she further notes that Butoh dancer Tatsumi Hijikata's childhood imitations of his neighbor's dog "focus[ed] on movement—as a key aspect of what a body can do," thus positioning the animal as a verb rather than a noun.[19] As Deleuze and Guattari put it, "the wolf is not fundamentally a characteristic or a certain number of characteristics; it is a wolfing. The louse is a lousing, and so on."[20] In their affective attunement, the puppeteers who animate Handspring's horses thus become-animal not because they and the puppet so thoroughly resemble a horse—which they do—but because the three humans become-molecular and enter into composition with one another through the cane armature. According to Deleuze and Guattari, "affect is not a personal feeling, nor is it a characteristic; it is the effectuation of a power of the pack that throws the self into upheaval and makes it reel."[21] The human performers escape their individuation and enter into assemblage as a pack, drawing in the audience as they too catch the affect. "Packs form, develop, and are transformed by contagion,"[22] which operates across multisensory channels: Jennifer Parker-Starbuck describes a kind of becoming-pig while hearing Matthew Herbert's composition *One Pig*, drawn into the animal's sonic environment over the course of its brief life. Then the smell of cooking pork brought her back to her human and vegetarian self at some affective distance from the meat-eating audience members.[23]

Unbound by dramatic narrative and linguistic coherence, dance and postdramatic theater offer particularly suitable fields for becoming-, and scholars have drawn productively upon Deleuze and Guattari in analyzing these forms of performance.[24] Both the artists and the theorists shift focus away from the strictly visual and linguistic realms upon which neurotypical humans premise their superiority, paying increased attention to hearing, smell, taste, and touch and exploring divergent sensory capacities. Returning to an example from chapter 5, consider Robert Wilson's work: critics tend to focus upon its visual aspects, and he recommends slowing down to look at his performances as one would look at a painting. Yet the auditory qualities of this work are every bit as distinctive as the visual. Holmberg describes Wilson's typical use of sound, which he has most often created in collaboration with Hans-Peter Kuhn:

> Bizarre noises startle and disturb. Actors may be speaking on stage and standing stock-still, but the sound of their voices jumps around erratically from location to location in the house. Language dissolves into noise. The sense of acoustical space keeps shifting. One soon feels lost, drifting on a sea of sound. Organizing the auditory information flooding our senses suddenly becomes problematic.[25]

Lehmann observes that this "postdramatic 'audio landscape' . . . does not mimetically represent reality but creates a space of association in the mind of the spectator."[26] Wilson thus impels an audience not only to look more slowly but also to listen more deeply or at least differently, because listening for information (plot, discursive meaning) is pointless. He also stresses the importance of listening as a working method. Performing in San Antonio very early in his career, he discovered that an audience would sit and watch something without any perceivable structure or action if the performers relaxed sufficiently: "When we tuned in to listening—just the three of us [performers] being together—in terms of performance—if we could hear that then the audience might hear it, you know, or it was more likely that they would tune in to us."[27] As discussed in chapter 2, the multisensory attunement among the puppeteers for The Lion King and War Horse interacted with the productions' sophisticated sonic space to draw their audiences into complex relation. To varying degrees, performances and their audiences involve across shifting affective fields, the senses folding and refolding in upon one another, bringing points along the sensory surfaces into new proximities.

PAULA JOSA-JONES, BODILY BECOMING-

Performance-makers use specific techniques to facilitate multisensory involution. After thirteen years of making dances primarily with horses, for
example, Paula Josa-Jones returned to solo and duet work in the studio, a
process that felt to her "exhilarating, wild, unhinged" because no horse was
present "to shape things, to create a certain kind of boundary, intention
and necessity for the work."[28] Josa-Jones's work (with or without horses)
begins with two essential practices, Authentic Movement and Deep Listening. Mary Starks Whitehouse created Authentic Movement out of Jungian
depth psychology as a bridge between consciousness and the unconscious,
with "authentic" designating movement that genuinely belongs to the mover
rather than drawing upon a learned dance vocabulary. According to Janet
Adler, who further developed and wrote about the practice, "the core of the
movement experience is the sensation of moving and being moved."[29] In a
typical structure for pairs, a person with eyes closed responds in movement
to inner impulses, while the partner observes. Then the witness might describe what she saw or respond with movement, and the pair might discuss
the experience before switching roles. Authentic Movement foregrounds visual processes but activates multilayered and fully embodied cognition, as
does Deep Listening. Composer Pauline Oliveros developed this practice to
cultivate full attention to the sonic environment—attending to the sounds
that we cannot help but hear and yet habitually tune out as well as those to
which we actively listen. She describes it as "listening in every possible way
to everything possible to hear no matter what one is doing."[30]

Alone in the studio, Josa-Jones lets herself feel called into movement by
"an image, a feeling in the body, a poem, a painting, some music, a dancer's
movement, something observed, something read, something felt, a place, a
journey, a memory, a fragment of gesture that keeps interrupting, demanding. Something quiet, something loud, something big, something small."[31]
She also cultivates and responds through what she calls a "receptive body,"
listening with more than the auditory sense to "the inner and outer landscapes of the body and its relationship to what surrounds us."[32] The work
begun in 2013 coalesced into a trilogy of solo dances, each of which "explores
liminal states of being: ambiguous, disorienting moments when we find ourselves poised on a threshold between one world and another."[33] Reviewing
the trilogy in June 2016, Marcia Siegel observes that *Of This Body* "suggested
floating identities, journeys but not destinations"; for example, in *Mam-*

*mal*, the dancer "could have been channeling anything that walked on four legs, writhed on the ground, crouched and gazed around warily. We heard strangled screams, muted growls and screeches that could have come from a nighttime forest a long way away."[34] Josa-Jones describes *Mammal* as "a cellular, poetic echolocation that viscerally connects male and female, human and non-human, self and other at the porous borderland where they intersect and blend."[35] She told me that although this piece did respond to some animal images, the primary bridge to movement was through her own bodily organs—"taking a movement from the organ but taking it out into space through gesture—lung out through arm, bladder in foot,"[36] and also "fluids, glands, fascia as a way of bridging to the soma of other species."[37] In watching an earlier performance of *Mammal*, I was struck by the equivalence of legs and arms as they participated equally in all types of movements; the alternation between outward flow and containment of the body; the fine-grained articulation of all joints that became most visible in the hands, which for humans are most developed; and finally by Josa-Jones's focused presence as she danced.[38] Christine Joly de Lotbiniere's layered, intricately detailed, humanimal costume for this dance augments the movement and strengthens the impression of tiger claws at some points, and Josa-Jones refers to the tie as simultaneously "trunk, limb, garment."[39] Figure 14 shows her from the knees up, left hand gesturing near her temple, thumb and forefinger touching one another, her gaze directed downward and right hand by her thigh, elbows angled away from her body and from one another. Loose threads extend hair-like from the light-brown embroidery of her dark brown dress and matching above-elbow gloves. Horse and flower tattoos cover her exposed upper arms and shoulders. The bare human fingertips of her gesturing hand contrast with the claw-like points draped along the back of the other glove.

Just as she does not mimic any specific animal for *Mammal*, for *Speak* Josa-Jones does not represent an autist in the way that actors do for *Curious Incident of the Dog in the Night-Time* or *Falling*. The first time I watched the five-minute version, without any knowledge of the movement source, I read it as a female dancer exploring masculinity, street dance, and coolness. Siegel "thought it could have been a gender statement, or possibly a comment on aging."[40] The dancer wears a suit and dark glasses, the music by Organic Grooves keeps repeating the phrase "let your hair down and let yourself go," and the movement resembles robot and other hip-hop dance forms.[41] The full ten-minute version begins with her body closed in on itself and facing away from the viewer, shoulders or hands breaking out and withdrawing

Figure 14. Paula Josa-Jones performing *Mammal*, 2016. Photo by Dariel Sneed. Courtesy of Paula Josa-Jones.

again, the accompaniment solo guitar. The piece's final section brings more tension to the gestures, especially when the hands move near the mouth, and more of the movement reaches toward the viewer, with more ominous music.[42] Josa-Jones writes that "*Speak* springs from questions about language and the absence of language in its usual form. It is about obsession and excavating meaning from the body when words cannot be shaped. *Speak* is inspired by fifteen years of working with my profoundly autistic godson and physical research into aphasia, apraxia and synesthesia."[43] Only with this explanatory statement does the relation to autism emerge; given this context, I can interpret the gestures as providing kinesthetic feedback, releasing energies, and soothing as do hand flapping and other stims.

Josa-Jones takes the gestural repertoire for *Speak* from her godson's movement patterns. At times, she says, his nonverbal communication is "quite clear: 'come here, follow me, do this, join up, get out of my way, stay away, look, don't look.' Because he is so fast, so strong (an adolescent boy!) I have to be hyperalert, because the signalling can change direction, intention, quality so fast." Both Authentic Movement and Deep Listening offer her tools for engaging with him. Josa-Jones uses "the body/effort/shape/space language" of Laban Movement Analysis to interpret "certain repeated gestures that are unreadable for meaning" through the channels available to most people, and Body-Mind Centering at times enables her to "feel an attunement with fluids, other times with a specific organ—via a kind of somatic empathy, or a sense of heaviness, energy, image, sensation from a particular part of [her] body" in responding to him.[44] As she duplicates his gestures—including "a lot of very specific mudra positions of his hands: crossing the third finger over the fourth and touching pinky to thumb, a Chaplin-like mustache action"—they "drop into the soil of [her] body" and then resurface during her work in the dance studio.[45] Josa-Jones shapes this emergent movement for performance, but the choreography maintains its own integrity rather than representing or making a statement about autism.

In spite of nonnarrative contemporary dance's conventions, the narrative impulse tends to intervene and make it difficult for spectator to see anything in *Speak* beyond what they already know. Siegel, for example, observes that "Josa-Jones's movement is so specific you want to assign a meaning to it, even as you realize it has no specific meaning." She describes the opening movement sequence as "gestur[ing] around her body, as if getting dressed," the middle as "swagger[ing]" and "falling into nameless characters," and the conclusion as perhaps "primping before an unforgiving mirror."[46]

Siegel watches *Speak* through social and aesthetic lenses, as I did upon first viewing. And of course I still do—but conversation with Josa-Jones has now added another refraction. The choreography does not aim for legibility but rather to "ignite the audience systemically, to provide an irresistible somatic disturbance; to give the audience a portal for a transformative bodily experience of their own," so that they cease trying to figure out a meaning and instead enter into the shared affective space. Josa-Jones says that "it isn't always comfortable, and that is, in part, the point."[47] This encounter with the unfamiliar can world us in new ways when we accept the aesthetic "shock to thought" that I mentioned in the introduction to this book. As Cull writes, "the body's affective encounters with other bodies are that which forces thought, understood first as an unconscious movement and only subsequently as conscious recognition."[48] Although violent shocks such as the animal deaths that I discuss in chapter 4 can surely precipitate this worlding, more gentle approaches have affective capacity as well. Referring back to the language of categorical affects, I see no evidence that an event must disgust in order to engage an audience's interest. Jennifer Monson's sustained practice of becoming-animal allows me to further elaborate the ethical potential of affective coemergence.

## BECOMING-BIRD WITH JENNIFER MONSON

Choreographer Jennifer Monson's *Bird Brain* and its subsequent development *Live Dancing Archive* have minimal animal resemblance and include no nonhuman animal performers; instead, they become-animal and create maps through new locations. *Bird Brain Dance*, a four-year investigation of possible relations between the dancer's navigational systems and those of migratory species, began in an urban environment. Monson was living in Williamsburg, Brooklyn, regularly watching the flocks of pigeons that neighborhood building superintendents kept on their roofs and walking her dog through the abandoned riverfront industrial site that she described to Nancy Galeota-Wozny as the only natural area easily accessible to her:

> Over the ten or so years that I've been going there, the buildings have been torn down; the river has worn away at the pier. Ailanthus trees, phragmites (reeds), and other wetlands grasses have taken hold. I can find song sparrows, mockingbirds, peregrine falcons; and in the fall and

spring, I see all kinds of migrating water fowl, such as buffleheads, ruddy ducks, mergansers, black ducks, and of course brants and Canada geese.[49]

She grew curious about the birds' "phenomenal navigational abilities, their need for habitat, and how they connect multiple ecosystems throughout their migration."[50] She also wondered about atavistic capacities lurking in the human sensorium:

> What remnants of navigation have been sustained in our human genes? What have they evolved into? Are they part of our calculating mathematical linguistic sense, our intuitive sense of home, of finding comfort, of the need to move, to be a nomad? Has language evolved from our need to navigate, establish place, and communicate location? How does the body continue to orient itself and navigate distance and time in response to the constant and rapidly increasing impositions and transmutations of technology on our human systems?[51]

The first exploration concerned "navigational strategies in the urban environment through the natural and cultural history of pigeons." For *The Pigeon Project* (2000), Alejandra Martorell, Astrud Angarita, and Ermira Gorou danced with Monson on a rooftop in Brooklyn, followed by an indoor performance at Performance Space 122. The same dancers joined her for the *Gray Whale Migration* (2001) from Baja/Mexico to Vancouver. From March to May, they camped and danced for rangers and whale-watching tourists as well as doing prearranged performances and workshops at nature centers, schools, and museums. Some locations offered interpretive events with rangers and panels with scientists who study birds and whales. The *Osprey Tour* (2002) traveled from Maine in August to Venezuela in October, again with Martorell and joined by Javier Cardona and Morgan Thorson. For the spring *Ducks and Geese Migration* (2004), Willa Carroll, Juliette Mapp, and Osmany Tellez traveled with Monson from Texas to Minnesota, with Thorson and Sheldon Smith joining them in Chicago. Monson still hopes to realize a fifth project, intended to follow the migration of northern wheatears from the Arctic down through Europe to West Africa.

*Bird Brain* employed some of the same strategies over its various incarnations. Typical workshop exercises ask participants first to close their eyes and face north, some of them being able to do this intuitively and others relying on landmarks; then to face home, whatever that might mean; to awaken their spatial orientation through activities such as walking with eyes closed toward a partner ten feet away; and finally to expand this awareness to the group as they move, shifting their relative positions as a flock, making turns in unison with eyes closed. Monson explained the "advantage to being located in the center of the flock. You are safe from predators. If birds are on the outside, they want to get to the inside if danger is coming. Generally the way birds change formation is by an outside bird turning towards the center. Relationships in the flock are constantly changing."[52] When pelicans fly together along the surf, for example, several birds take turns leading the formation, working harder in this position because they're providing a wind-break that makes flying easier for the birds behind them.

Like Josa-Jones, Monson works with both Deep Listening and Authentic Movement. Julia Handschuh's discussion of the 2010 project *SIP (Sustained Immersive Process)/Watershed* includes listening scores that Monson provided to participants:

> Walk through the environment. As you are walking, listen. Find a sound that is far away, live with this sound, become accustomed to it. Find a sound that is closest to you, live with this sound, become accustomed to it. Find a sound that is in the middle, live with this sound, become accustomed to it. If a louder sound comes along and covers the sound you chose let it cover it and try to listen to it through the louder sound.[53]

A similar score for seeing instructs the participant to "find a place on the horizon as far away as you can see. Trace a line from this point on the horizon to where you now stand, as if your gaze is a pencil or record needle. Do this three times with three different points."[54] As Nigel Stewart notes, Monson and others have turned the response-ability nurtured by techniques such as Authentic Movement outward to the environment.[55] Thus the version of a paired score for *SIP/Watershed* begins with gazing at the Hudson River, and the first mover responds to the movement of the water.[56]

For *Bird Brain*, some set choreography developed out of earlier improvisations, particularly for segments danced in unison. Bird behavior inspired some of this movement; for example, Martorell described a hop with an upward snatching movement of the arms as an osprey swooping down to grab a fish. Less directly mimetic, a spiraling phrase responded to observation of ospreys as they take off and use the lift provided by thermal columns to soar. More abstractly, the dancers investigated the ways in which different

parts of the human body can develop momentum and then glide. Much of
the performance was improvised, but working together over an extended
period led to a shared vocabulary of form, images, ideas, and movement, and
scores provided a structure by setting a length and a succession of solos, duets, quartets, and so forth.[57] The score for a rehearsal at Boardwalk Beach on
Cape Cod, for example, called for four solos, each of which first responded
to the environment and then built a location. Monson's solo travels slowly
through the sand and beach grass, her arms floating on the air currents,
her fingers sometimes floating as extensions of the arms and at other times
quickly articulating, each transfer of weight extended to explore possibilities of one-legged balance. At one point her entire chest, arms, and head
arch back and seem to rest briefly on the air behind her.[58] Monson's journal
describes her experience:

> Immediately the wind is the strongest influence to me. My arms and fin-
> gers start to ride the air currents. It feels very familiar and a tiny bit trite.
> I try to let that go and send the airy energetic flow down in to my torso
> through my organs and bones. Then there are the waves lapping against
> the rocky shore, a gentle ripple with an internal pulling back. Then there
> is the ever present roar of the ocean waves coming up over the dunes,
> then the feel of rock and sand on my feet, then the searing sun moving
> through my skin and the reflected light off the rippling water. All of this
> is literally [a]ffecting me and I dance it through me at a quick pace. My
> mind lightly moving from sensation to sensation, trying to integrate it
> all in a complex system in my dancing. One arm moves with the wind,
> the other with the lapping waves, my spine rolls with distant sound of
> the ocean, my legs attempt to reflect light, my organs drop into the solid
> small round rocks between my feet. As I transition to building my own
> "location" I feel the relief of this concentrated task with its many dimen-
> sions and layers.[59]

Monson uses the term *location* to designate "something created by our dancing but not necessarily beholden to any kind of geographical or physical
space. This 'location' is something that we can then enter into together as
dancers and arrive and depart from."[60] This usage resonates with Rosi Braidotti's conception of location as a "collectively shared and constructed, jointly
occupied spatio-temporal territory."[61] As conceived in Braidotti's nomadol-
ogy, subjectivity moves through various locations, rather than settling down

in any one clearly defined position. This notion preserves individual agency, since we actively participate in shaping these locations, but at the same time takes into account the degree to which they, in turn, define us. Locations are not places: as Deleuze and Guattari put it, rhizomes have no "points or positions," but instead "only lines."[62]

Martorell explained that during the *Whale Migration* the outdoor environment had tended to overwhelm the dancers, and their movement remained taken up with imitation and expressions of awe. To get beyond this limited pattern during the *Osprey Migration*, they began building locations along with their responsive movement.[63] For a long quartet improvisation at Nags Head Beach in North Carolina, for example, the dancers traveled the length of the beach from north to south, staying fairly close together but shifting positions, reminiscent of birds changing places as they fly in formation.[64] Here, the dancer's movement becomes-bird in relation to the sensory landscape and also in relation to the ever-shifting group as it travels across that landscape. As with Monson's Cape Cod grass phrase, the movement is slow at first, with a focused response to the limbs' relation to the air. The individual dancers respond to one another's movement: one hand might echo another hand or a foot. They roll and crawl through the sand, stand in the wind and slowly lift a foot, revolve while making tight circles around one another, accelerate, leap, and fling themselves through the air and through the sand, share weight and catch one another's momentum, headstand, handstand, cartwheel, fall, and recover. This nineteen-minute improvisation tells no story, creates neither characters nor dramatic tension—fleeting moments of tension arrive and then dissipate without being personalized or contained by narrative impulse.

Monson shifts the authenticity of movement away from an occult inner being and toward cumulative affect as the dancers experience becoming-bird through human rather than avian bodies. They affect the environment, leaving footprints and paths traced in the sand. The environment affects them, and their movement archives that affection. In 2012, Monson took up the challenge of archiving dance in her body by dancing it again. The resulting *Live Dancing Archive* comprises live performances, a video installation, and a digital archive available online that includes eighteen journal entries and sixteen thirty- to forty-second video clips from the *Gray Whale Migration*. The *Osprey Tour* produced longer video clips of higher quality, and this documentation forms the core of the archive and of my analysis as well. Each component captures in its own way what Monson describes as "something about the way in which bodies hold, transmit and convey experiences and understandings of ecological systems as they relate to human movement."[65] The online archive includes still photos, video, and excerpts from the dancers' journals. As part of "Performance Archiving Performance," the New Museum in New York displayed a three-hour video installation by Robin Vachal, edited down from her more than fifty hours of *Bird Brain* documentation.[66]

A chain of solo improvisations at Ocracoke Island, a bit south of Nags Head Beach, generated the bulk of the movement material that *Live Dancing Archive* reactivates (along with the grass phrase). My descriptions of movement often rely upon analogy, which I hope will more effectively suggest its qualities than would a laborious technical account, but I stress that these analogies rely upon imaginative structures that the dancing evokes for me and in no way attempt to capture a symbolic meaning. First Monson moves for three minutes, flinging arms and legs, entire body following the spine through arches and curves as if buffeted by wind or waves; after a brief stillness, glides first upright then lower and lower to and then through the sand; rising again, pauses, spins through a series of hops, twists, squiggles; pauses again to feel the air under arms and leg, then extends the spins through leaping turns that arch and curve as at the beginning; flings herself headlong into the sand, quickly rolls and turns while rising; finally shifts parallel arms side to side as if holding something large that grows smaller as the arms zig-zag up on a diagonal until the hands release into the air above a shoulder. Next, Cardona uses Monson's improvisation as a map, beginning with his own hops; alternating more often and with greater dynamic contrast between stillness and quick movement; extending her glides as discrete arm and leg gestures. Throughout his sideways leaps or running steps, Cardona develops a toe-drag through the sand that appeared in Monson's solo. He falls headlong in a spot near the traces of her fall and spends some time there, wriggling through it on his belly; arcing up from it and then rocking the arc onto its side, holding the pose while his head explores in isolation; following one arm through its trajectory in space, sitting and then rising. Finally he travels across the sand in tiny, stiff-legged, flat-footed steps, hands and head finally bobbing and shaking as the knees begin to bend and the feet to release up from the sand.

Martorell's solo uses the first two maps, and I can discern much movement similar to what I've seen already. She picks up and broadens Cardona's bobbing walk with a wide stance and lifted knees at the beginning of her improvisation and backs up through the sand with tiny steps near the end; the flinging, leaping, arching turns appear more than once; the headlong fall happens in a couple of different places, the first time after a variation on Cardona's fall to his knees, hers an explosive jump landing in a kneel. When Martorell slides onto her belly near the surf, she bisects the line drawn by foot-marks of his final walk. She explores wrist and hand articulations to a greater extent than the earlier solos did, and her arms hug and encircle her torso more often. Thorson dances last, the camera zooming in on her toes tracing sharp curves in the sand as she begins, shoulders and then arms responding to the foot's impetus. She explores the momentum and balance shifts of the leaping turns, letting them throw her off-center through the air, down onto the sand and up again for more. After a few cycles, she rolls over and over then arcs up from her belly following the map of the first three dancers. Like her descent, her recovery goes through several up-and-down cycles including a back walkover. Her explorations of suspension echo Monson's but then interlace the fingers or press the palms together so that the arms begin moving as a single unit. She moves through the kneeling position a couple of times but gets there from the sand rather than landing there from a jump. At the simplest level, each dance traces a similar spatial path away from the three dancers who are watching, then back to a spot more or less even with them. Each roughly three-minute improvisation also moves through a similar dynamic range; through vertical and horizontal planes; through variations and echoes of gestural, locomotive, lyrical, and percussive movement.[67] This accumulated response to place—including the sand underfoot, the sea to the east, the surrounding air, the changing soundscape, and the previous dances—creates an embodied cartography of the space.

Back at the University of Illinois at Urbana-Champaign, Monson worked in the studio with her students and the video documentation of this movement research. Her solo *Live Dancing Archive* premiered at the University of Vermont in 2012 with performances at The Kitchen that same year and the Chicago Humanities Festival in 2013.[68] Monson began the latter performance by explaining to the audience that, in order to transfer the dance from beach to video to stage, she oriented her movement toward them in the ocean's place. I recognize the arching back into the air, the slow weight transfers, the delicate fingers feeling the air, and the quick birdlike head shrug of the Cape Cod grass phrase. From Ocracoke, I recognize the leap-fling turns, toe drags, spinning hops, headlong fall, arced rocking on the belly. Remembering individual dancers, I catch Martorell's torso hugging, double-footed jumps with a wide stance, her particular arching back from the knees with a sweeping arm, her backward walk; the fall to the knees and leg extensions that Cardona introduced and others varied along with the single-legged hops that began his solo and his isolated head movement while lying in a bow shape; Thorson's seal-like drag, her run, her way of pushing up from the ground with an arm behind her.

Wearing flesh-toned fishnet tights and a square of skin-side-out fur held over her chest by wide elastic straps that cross in the back, Monson dances isolated within the proscenium stage's darkened volume. The initially warm light gives her body three-dimensional modeling, and she seems to glow, the only thing present in a vast darkness, herself the source of illumination. As the light cools and its focus widens, the stage floor enters the perceptible field. Around the midpoint the focus warms and contracts again, as she curls into a fetal ball, head down; then slowly a hand reaches along the floor, a foot extends, she moves up into a crouch and then returns to more vigorous movement. As her movement expands, the light cools and expands its range again and before the end of the seventeen minutes includes within the visible—just barely—the stage's black wings and the audience. The space itself creates an atmosphere, as the sound and the light reflect off all its surfaces, including all the bodies present. These elements profoundly affect the dancer's experience, so that she responds to a new and changing sensory environment with each performance regardless of the degree to which the movement itself may be set. Figure 15 shows Monson traveling low to the floor, seeming to be all bare arms and legs as her torso curves down over the left leg upon which she steps forward, crossed in front of a right leg visible only below the knee as she shifts her weight off it. Her arms curve down parallel to one another and scoop the space she's leaving behind, the crown of her head following the angle of her hands. Lighting designer Joe Levasseur shines a handheld lamp on the brick wall behind her, its reflected light pooling toward her feet.

Monson collaborated on *Live Dancing Archive* with Levasseur and composer Jeff Kolar and then expanded her collaboration in 2014 to include dancers Niall Jones and Tatyana Tenenbaum. Kolar's live and improvisational sonic environment became most apparent to me during a work-in-progress showing in unoccupied office space at One Liberty Plaza.[69] I was present at this showing, but because my descriptions depend upon viewing the video archive as well as my notes, I describe the dance in present tense consistent with the materials to which I have access only through the online

Figure 15. Jennifer Monson with Joe Levasseur, *Live Dancing Archive* solo version, 2013. Photo © Ian Douglas.

archive. At a table next to the nearly floor-to-ceiling windows offering slices of skyscrapers, construction, and construction cranes, Kolar manipulates the radio frequencies picked up by a group of hand-built transmitters and receivers. To begin the performance, the dancers first carry his radios to the periphery, then move together and circle one another, activating this very live sonic space twelve stories up in Lower Manhattan's financial district. The dancer bodies, audience bodies, and other electromagnetic phenomena all affect the sound, which in turn affects their movement and our reception. Working from the observation that much of natural light is reflected, Levasseur used a twelve-foot-long, eighteen-inch-high screen and three photo lights to provide different spaces for various sections of the dance. He, stage manager Valerie Oliveiro, and the three dancers frequently move the screen and lights, restricting and reshaping the space, but the ambient light in the office space limits the extent to which these materials affect the dance. They become more active for a subsequent, more fully developed performance at New York Live Arts in November 2014 that also features fur vests designed by Susan Becker such as Monson wore in the solo version.[70] In the theater, the minimal lighting often isolates their bodies and body parts so that they seem to swim in darkness or fly through the night sky. The darkness creates a sense of movement within a void, seen against the horizontal screen nearby. At other points, the screen moves farther away and light washes the entire space, making the flow of impulses between dancers readily visible, their spatial interrelation prominent.

Dancing the archive across all these elements, including three human bodies rather than Monson's alone, makes it easier to see the multiplicity of this becoming-bird. In the office space, for example, the three dancers begin by performing the grass phrase together twice. Their unison movement becomes-flocking on two levels: they resemble three birds moving in orderly formation, but they also become-flock as disparate body parts or even molecules moving together through air and changing their relative positions. Techniques such as Authentic Movement and Deep Listening explicitly serve to dis-organ-ize bodily habits and open up new relational possibilities even as they manifest the kind of perceptible affective attunement that I discussed earlier among the *War Horse* puppeteers. Improvisation reactivates locations from Ocracoke as the dancers respond to the sound, light, air, and other dancers in the present environment as well as to the mental and physical maps provided by the *Live Dancing Archive*'s video archive: leaping-flinging turns, certain kinds of jumping, a gliding lean forward, delicate hand flicks, headlong slides onto the belly that land so differently on the floor than they did on the sand.

The movement has some intrinsic affective temperatures that vary from lyrical and expansive to abrupt and powerful to curled in and vibrating. I watch the flow of impulses throughout, but constricted movement in the later sections of the piece feels much different from the extensions and movement through space with which the dancers begin. Monson curls in a fetal ball close to the audience and hums into the floor as Tenenbaum and Jones vibrate on the floor further away, a disturbing backdrop. Here the bodies' affect, their capacities to affect other bodies of any sort, diminish to such an extent that they seemingly can't uncurl, can't move. Tenenbaum and Jones gradually come together, augmenting one another until they gradually rise while Monson remains curled up at some distance from them. After an interlude during which she repositions the screen and moves through some quiet human-bird steps in front of it as they sing "Bird Gerhl,"[71] Monson falls abruptly back to the floor, then begins a slow curling and uncurling rolling over, tension in hands hugged into her chest. The movement looks difficult, painful, like fighting out of an egg or an oil slick. In sharp contrast, Jones and Tenenbaum are flying through the space with unison Ocracoke movement as Monson continues her slow roll on a diagonal along the line of a power cord stretching away from the audience. The sound grows loud and industrial. They circle her, pass her, slide onto their bellies downstage of her. She stops in the middle of the space, face down, perhaps dead or—if interpreted in conjunction with the recently sung lyrics—failed in her search for wings that she would need to "be born into / soon the sky."

In the version performed at New York Live Arts, the three wear sheer sleeves twice the length of their arms for this section to sing just the vowels and open tones of a fractured "Bird Gerhl," developing the human-bird strut, a simultaneous becoming-bird, becoming-woman destined to fail. The dancers reposition the lights and fall in close proximity to begin Monson's roll-crawl along the power cord, Tenenbaum and Jones vibrating on the floor where they land. Monson's roll is affected by the tension in her hands and arms, by the interruptions to the flow of movement. The vibration resembles a neurological disorder, and the dancers huddle together, support and cling to one another as they slowly rise from the floor, create a sense of involuntariness as if they cannot remain still and yet cannot move freely, shaking and feeble. The fingers remain curled in so that the energy doesn't release out from the arms. The torso repeatedly curls forward and in on itself. As Jones and Tenenbaum gradually regain a more upright and extended style of movement, Monson rises and begins moving the screen, rotating it through an orbit, creating changes in light much as the reflected sun does on the moon or the earth's rotation does in its sky but also chasing Jones with it across the stage. The lights and sounds continue to change through different improvised solos and pairings, and finally the three dance together and then settle to the floor, affective capacity intact to end this version.

In an interview with Zachary Whittenberg after the Chicago solo performance, Monson enumerated the things absent such as the limitless space outdoors and the sand underfoot on the beach, the difference of dancing something that another body had improvised—an otherness that extends not only to the dancers with her on the migration but also to her body twelve years earlier. But something else becomes present, similar to the way ecosystems keep changing—and this implies, for her, a hopefulness in the face of climate change. The *Live Dancing Archive* does not impart a message or directly call its audience to action. Yet the project's temporal dimension generates an activist space that extends onward from *Bird Brain*'s attention to migratory species, their free traverse challenged by political borders and environmental obstacles. Their habitats are necessarily bound to time, since they must live in a series of places. We cannot think of ensuring their continued existence simply by preserving any one local habitat. The spectator is free to think about the implications for human populations, also moving from place to place in a spatial flow.

AFFECTIVE SPACE

What particularly distinguishes Monson's becoming-bird is the sustained complexity of this embodied research across years and geographies. Elucidating the links between different forms of dance, conceptions of audience response, and choreographic space, Susan Leigh Foster's *Choreographing Empathy* invokes for the twenty-first century a "cyborgian synthesis of digital and physical matter."[72] The flow of Monson's work from one archival medium to another certainly fits within this rubric, although the notion "cyborg" conjures a visibly machine- or technology-oriented performance more readily than it does her low-tech engagement with both urban and wild ecosystems.[73] Yet contact improvisation and related practices such as hers conceptualize the body as coextensive with the space of performance, with reciprocal impact. The listening, the looking, and the responsive moving are *spatial practices* in the sense articulated by Henri Lefebvre, who conceives of space as something socially produced rather than being an emptiness waiting to be filled by variable contents. Lefebvre defines space as both a "tool of thought and of action" and "a means of control."[74] Buildings, for example, can take on a controlling function as their "walls, enclosures and façades serve to define both a *scene* (where something takes place) and an *obscene* area to which everything that cannot or may not happen on the scene is relegated: whatever is inadmissible, be it malefic or forbidden, thus has its own hidden space on the near or the far side of a frontier."[75] Various spatial practices produce and reproduce space as a social relation that can be represented and thus read. But space itself also represents. In a city, certain buildings and their relations symbolize their functions: consider the architectural features that make it easy to distinguish spaces for government, business, and commerce from one another and from domestic space; further, cities arrange these various sorts of building in meaningful spatial relation to one another.

One reads these spatial codes, to be sure, but this does not exhaust the city's spatial practice; more important, one internalizes the reading as one goes about the business of living an urban life, following its codes for quotidian existence and, by doing so, producing the urban space.[76] Representation *of* space dominates the overly determined scene of late capitalism, banishing *representational* space to the obscene, which we access only as a space of revolt. As Lefebvre argued in the mid-1970s:

> Within this [abstractly represented] space, and on the subject of this space, everything is openly declared: everything is said or written. . . . History is experienced as nostalgia, and nature as regret—as a horizon fast disappearing behind us. This may explain why affectivity, which, along with the sensory/sensual realm, cannot accede to abstract space and so informs no symbolism, is referred to by a term that denotes both a subject and that subject's denial by the absurd rationality of space: that term is "the unconscious."[77]

To shift the terms of Authentic Movement away from the Jungian discourse of their origin, improvisational practices such as Monson's access this "unconscious" space of sensory and affective experience, of that which civilization brackets with the label "nature," and through movement produce a representational space coextensive with human bodies. The activist potential of this space gains clarity as it extends to encompass the Interdisciplinary Laboratory for Art, Nature and Dance (iLAND), a nonprofit organization that Monson founded in 2005 as "a dance research organization that investigates the power of dance, in collaboration with other fields, to illuminate our kinetic understanding of the world."[78] Her own projects with iLAND have involved scientists as well as other artists and show a particular interest in water sources and wetlands in urban environments. One part of this performative activism involves dancing in specific outdoor locations, a concrete spatial practice with ramifications over time; for example, *iMAP (Interdisciplinary Mobile Architecture and Performance)/Ridgewood Reservoir* (2007) supported ultimately successful efforts by environmental activists to preserve a reservoir in Queens: the New York City Parks Department abandoned plans to remove trees and build roads in this area.[79] The dance itself didn't change anyone's mind, nor did it attempt in agit-prop fashion to do so; rather, it worlded a space of intensity for affective engagement with the location. And beyond the dance itself, iLAND extends practices and methods for nonhierarchical collaboration not only among artists but also among very diverse stakeholders with respect to specific, local issues.

The practices of listening and witnessing that characterize Monson's work readily extend to encounters between autistic and neurotypical humans, such as Josa-Jones's engagement with her godson. Therapists and other helpers use similar techniques to become-with an autist in multisensory space. These practices may help a nonverbal individual to communicate substantively with others, or perhaps to create easier ways of being together. But full engagement transforms all participants, as shown by the ways in which collaboration with Christopher Knowles affected Robert Wilson's work, as discussed in chapter 5; the ways in which Erin Manning has adjusted her participatory art in collaboration with DJ Savarese; or the impact of community-based performance work that Telory Arendell discusses.[80]

Embodied technologies of becoming- and becoming-with resemble but are quite distinct from disability simulation such as blindfolds or wheelchairs used to train occupational therapists and others to understand their patients' challenges. Tobin Siebers argues that such exercises produce an experience of deficit absent any positive aspects of this particular embodiment; furthermore, the exercise is "an act of individual imagination, not an act of cultural imagination."[81] Mapping Monson's dancing exploration of equivalences between avian and human sensoria to the neurotypical-autistic borderlands, moreover, raises the specter of what one might call Autie-face performance, borrowing the term from black-, yellow-, and redface casting. Separating the imaginative effort of acting from the politics of casting, Stan Garner argues for the ethical value of playing the other. Although "kinesthetic empathy is oriented in terms of what we know and have experienced," and imaginative empathy always falls short, training and practice can facilitate a strengthening of connection through both automatic and conscious channels by expanding our kinesthetic and imaginative vocabulary.[82] Garner proposes that we might productively ask "whether actors and spectators take up the kinesthetic invitation that disability offers and whether they accept the ethical responsibilities that empathy entails."[83] One model for accepting this responsibility and engaging in the sort of cultural imagination that Siebers advocates would entail creating clearly legible performances advocating for the others with whom one is empathizing, whatever the basis may be for that otherness. Another model would grant equal access to others, with all the challenges to artistic practice that this might require. Yet the need to address others properly pales in comparison to the imperative to find new ways of listening. As DJ Savarese puts it, "realize that I have lots on my mind and lots to say."[84]

## CONCLUSIONS

Earlier chapters of *Affect, Animals, and Autists* analyze the categorical affects elicited by a particular set of performances that engage with autism or animality, in some cases simulated and in others, actual. This analysis takes up Michael Peterson's question "whether the animal presence stabilizes the identity of the bourgeois human spectator or troubles it. Do we use the animal to become more human, or less so?"[85] Perhaps purposely, he does not specify what it means to become more human—to become better, more humane people, or to further remove ourselves from animality? To formulate a parallel question, whether the autist's presence stabilizes or troubles the identity of the neurotypical spectator, would produce a more disturbing correlative. Quite aside from the potentially interesting implications of asking whether we use the autist to become more neurotypical, or less so, the question presumes a normate "we." Such a presumption directly contravenes the entire purpose and spirit of my inquiry; moreover, these questions leave the categories (mostly) intact even as they trouble identity and responsibility. Yet the questions lead productively to tracing the prosthetic function of autism and animality across these chapters.

Only a few of the performances analyzed here have much to do with the living beings positioned at the edges of the human: *The Unreliable Bestiary* (*ELEPHANT*), *Falling*, and *Ganesh Versus the Third Reich* explicitly address mass extinction, the dearth of viable support systems for autists, and the right to both agency and visibility. More often, the performances put into circulation affective energies that reroute anxieties about or dissatisfaction with the heterosexual nuclear family or bourgeois individualism, often in combination with postindustrial capitalism. I develop the analysis explicitly in relation to the neoliberal happy family and *Curious Incident*, but this sort of narrative prosthesis equally organizes *Body Awareness*, *Chekhov Lizardbrain*, *Curse of the Starving Class*, *Equus*, *The Goat*, *The Lion King*, *Orgies Mystery Theatre* (Nitsch), *O Sensibility* (Muehl), *The Sound and the Fury*, *Two Thousand Years*, and *War Horse*. Some of these works seem to mourn the loss of stable domestic and economic structures; others, to foreground the oppressive force of these structures. Discussing disability in literature, Mitchell and Snyder describe the narrative prosthesis as "a crutch upon which literary narratives lean for their representational power, disruptive potentiality, and analytical insight." In the works that they analyze, disability "recurs as a potent force that challenges cultural ideals of the 'normal' or 'whole' body."[86] Yet the power of this disruption dissipates, because "the artifice of disability binds disabled characters to a programmatic (even deterministic) identity."[87] Considered in narrative terms, then, many of the performances considered here seem to secure existing borders around the human.

Other works that I've discussed, though, explore performative ways of occupying the borderland together or of expanding the boundaries: Ann Carlson's dances with animals, Höller and Trockel's *House for Pigs and People*, Paula Josa-Jones's dances with horses, Miru Kim's *The Pig That Therefore I Am*, Chris Knowles's collaborations with Robert Wilson and his solo *The Sundance Kid is Beautiful*, Kira O'Reilly's *inthewrongplaceness* and *Falling Asleep with a Pig*. For these explorations of becoming-with, animality and autism function as nonnarrative prostheses. As Timothy Murray observes, the *Oxford English Dictionary* gives the familiar definition as compensatory device (such as an artificial limb) only second, first defining prosthesis as "'the addition of a letter or syllable at the beginning of a word.'"[88] Murray writes about prosthetic uses of digital media to catalyze choreographic processes, and I expand this concept to include as prosthesis any element added to start or redirect a line of flight. Grappling with technological mediation has quite logically spurred the growth of posthumanist theory because, as Braidotti points out, digital technologies extend the political and discursive organization of life (*bios*) beyond the borders of discrete human bodies even as genetics and biotechnology render it infrahuman.[89] Yet technologies need not be digital or inorganic, and bodies can be abstract. Braidotti defines a "body-machine" minimally as "an embodied affective and intelligent entity that captures, processes, and transforms energies and forces."[90]

The embodied technologies with which Jennifer Monson and Paula Josa-Jones begin their work, Authentic Movement and Deep Listening (among others), set desiring-machines in motion. So does the presence of a pig, a horse, a sheep, another human in a deterritorialized relational field where one does not yet know what the other is for, in the space of coemergence that Agamben and Haraway call *the open*. I acknowledge that even within a performance that treats disability or animality metaphorically, using the nonhuman or atypical as narrative prosthesis, various elements or moments of affective engagement retain the potential to escape known categories and trigger new lines of flight. In these cases, recapture of intensity is more likely but not inevitable.

If the anthropological machine that produces the human by distinguishing it from the inhuman is premised upon the existence of human language, and that language is understood to have been invented at some point by Homo sapiens, then, as Agamben argues, "the machine necessarily functions by means of an exclusion (which is also always already a capturing) and an inclusion (which is also always already an exclusion)."[91] The first speakers of something that counts as language were either excluded from the category human, which means that nonhuman animals invented language, or they must be categorized as human, which means that humans were already distinguished from other animals before they invented language: "Indeed, precisely because the human is already presupposed every time, the machine actually produces a kind of state of exception, a zone of indeterminacy in which the outside is nothing but the exclusion of an inside and the inside is in turn only the inclusion of an outside."[92] Premising the distinction between human and inhuman upon language requires an impossible Other who is neither. This premise in turn rests upon the internal self-division of the human being into two animals: the fully conscious, socially embedded *bios* and the vegetative, organic *zoë* or bare life. Agamben observes that humanism and human rights make no sense without this internal self-division.[93] The collapse of difference leads him to the concentration and extermination camps as a place of modern collapse, where people are rendered inhuman.

Rejecting this captivation by negativity and death, Braidotti instead recategorizes a perpetually emergent *bios/zoë*. Abandoning the categorical divide makes it possible to move past anthropocentric privileging of the human over the inhuman, normate over anomalous bodies, neurotypical over neurodiverse ways of communicating and being in the world. This is not to say that we can simply decree the end of self-division, or that we can trust power to stop operating on the basis of inclusive exclusion even to the point of annihilating whatever animals and humanimals it classifies as bare life. But the strategic essentialism that makes for effective advocacy need not recapture the intensity at play in a productive zone of indistinction.

# Notes

## Preface

1. Information about Stalking Cat's views and personal history relies upon my interview in April 2007 and subsequent personal communications. See Stalking Cat's website at http://www.stalkingcat.net; for more information about Steve Haworth, see http://www.stevehaworth.com

2. See Anthony Kubiak, "The Sacred Clade and the Rhizomatic Dis-ease of History," *Modern Language Quarterly* 70, no. 1 (2009): 43–66. The study is reported in Daocheng Zhu et al., "A Chimeric Human-Cat Fusion Protein Blocks Cat-Induced Allergy," *Nature Medicine* 11, no. 4 (2005): 446–49.

3. Gilles Deleuze and Félix Guattari, *A Thousand Plateaus: Capitalism and Schizophrenia*, trans. Brian Massumi (Minneapolis: University of Minnesota Press, 1987), 10, originally published as *Mille Plateaux* (Paris: Les éditions de Minuit, 1980).

4. For the fruits of his questioning, see Anthony Kubiak, "Cave Mentem: Disease and the Performance of Mind," *TDR* 59, no. 2 (2015): 114–28.

5. Marla Carlson, "Furry Cartography: Performing Species," *Theatre Journal* 63, no. 2 (2011): 191–208.

6. Visitor impressions and history of the Anchorage from *Mirage* program notes, 1994.

7. Nicholas Gane, "When We Have Never Been Human, What Is to Be Done? Interview with Donna Haraway," *Theory, Culture & Society* 23, nos. 7–8 (2006): 138, 147. Haraway takes the concept of torque from Susan Leigh Star and Geoffrey C. Bowker's discussion of racial categorization and pass laws in South Africa. *Sorting Things Out: Classification and Its Consequences* (Cambridge: MIT Press, 1999), 196–225.

*Chapter 1*

1. Rosemarie Garland-Thomson, *Extraordinary Bodies: Figuring Physical Disability in American Culture and Literature* (New York: Columbia University Press, 1997), 8.

2. Judith Butler, "Performative Acts and Gender Constitution," in *Performing Feminisms*, ed. Sue-Ellen Case (Baltimore: Johns Hopkins University Press, 1990), 271. "Autist" has been in colloquial use for some time. Most definitions offered by Urban Dictionary characterize it as an insult, and I certainly do not intend it in this way. For a debate on grammatical correctness without derogatory valence, see "'Autist' or 'Autistic' Correct Term?" *Wrong Planet,* 2014, http://wrongplanet.net/forums/viewtopic.php?t=245825

3. See, e.g., Katherine Runswick-Cole, "'Us' and 'Them': The Limits and Possibilities of a 'Politics of Neurodiversity' in Neoliberal Times," *Disability & Society* 29, no. 7 (2014): 1117–29, doi:10.1080/09687599.2014.910107.

4. Tobin Siebers, *Disability Aesthetics* (Ann Arbor: University of Michigan Press, 2010), 23, citing Harriet McBryde Johnson, "Should I Have Been Killed at Birth? The Case for My Life," *New York Times Magazine,* 16 February 2003; Martha C. Nussbaum, *Frontiers of Justice: Disability, Nationality, Species Membership* (Cambridge: Harvard University Press, 2006), 181.

5. Tobin Siebers, *Disability Theory* (Ann Arbor: University of Michigan Press, 2008), 48.

6. Sunaura Taylor, "Vegans, Freaks, and Animals: Toward a New Table Fellowship," *American Quarterly* 65, no. 3 (2013): 761, doi:10.1353/aq.2013.0042.

7. Ibid., 762.

8. René Descartes, "Discourse on the Method of Rightly Conducting One's Reason and Seeking Truth in the Sciences" (1637), ed. and trans. Jonathan Bennett, *Some Texts from Early Modern Philosophy,* November 2007, http://www.earlymoderntexts.com/assets/pdfs/descartes1637.pdf, part 5, 22–23.

9. Giorgio Agamben, *The Open: Man and Animal,* trans. Kevin Attell (Stanford: Stanford University Press, 2004), 30.

10. Adriana S. Benzaquén, *Encounters with Wild Children: Temptation and Disappointment in the Study of Human Nature* (Montreal: McGill-Queen's University Press, 2006), 55–56. Also see Michael Newton, *Savage Girls and Wild Boys: A History of Feral Children* (New York: Thomas Dunne Books/St. Martin's Press, 2003); Kalpana Seshadri, *Humanimal: Race, Law, Language* (Minneapolis: University of Minnesota Press, 2011).

11. Roy Richard Grinker, *Unstrange Minds* (New York: Basic Books, 2007), 51–54.

12. Patrick McDonagh, *Idiocy: A Cultural History* (Liverpool: University of Liverpool Press, 2008), 6.

13. Gil Eyal, Brendan Hart, Emine Onculer, Neta Oren, and Natasha Rossi, *The Autism Matrix: The Social Origins of the Autism Epidemic* (Cambridge: Polity Press, 2010), 89.

14. Karen Gainer Sirota, "Narratives of Distinction: Personal Life Narrative as a Technology of the Self in the Everyday Lives and Relational Worlds of Children with Autism," *Ethos* 38, no.1 (2010): 93, doi:10.1111/j.1548–1352.2009.01083.x.

15. Leo Kanner, "Autistic Disturbances of Affective Contact," *Nervous Child* 2 (1943): 236, 241.

16. John Duffy and Rebecca Dorner, "The Pathos of 'Mindblindness': Autism, Science, and Sadness in 'Theory of Mind' Narratives," *Journal of Literary & Cultural Disability Studies* 5, no. 2 (2011): 203, 207, doi:10.1353/jlc.2011.0015.

17. Siebers, *Disability Theory*, 3.

18. Irene Rose, "Autistic Autobiography: Introducing the Field," *Autism and Representation: Writing, Cognition, Disability Conference*, 2005, http://case.edu/affil/sce/Texts_2005/Autism%20and%20Representation%20Rose.htm; cited by Melanie Yergeau, "Clinically Significant Disturbance: On Theorists Who Theorize Theory of Mind," *Disability Studies Quarterly* 33, no. 4 (2013): n.p., doi:10.18061/dsq.v33i4.3876.

19. Temple Grandin, *Thinking in Pictures: And Other Reports from My Life with Autism* (New York: Doubleday, 1995). Also see Grandin and Catherine Johnson, *Animals in Translation: Using the Mysteries of Autism to Decode Animal Behavior* (New York: Scribner, 2005).

20. Dawn Prince-Hughes, *Songs of the Gorilla Nation: My Journey through Autism* (New York: Harmony Books, 2004), 104. Because later publications use the surname name Prince alone, I refer to her in this way for consistency.

21. Olga Solomon, "What a Dog Can Do: Children with Autism and Therapy Dogs in Social Interaction," *Ethos* 38, no. 1 (2010): 162 n2, doi:10.1111/j.1548–1352.2009.01085.x.

22. See "Romancing the Meat," chapter 14 in Sunaura Taylor, *Beasts of Burden: Animal and Disability Liberation* (New York: New Press, 2017), for an extended critique of Grandin.

23. *The Horse Boy*, directed by Michel Orion Scott, DVD (New York: Zeitgeist Films, 2009); also see the websites linked to http://www.horseboyfoundation.org. For further discussion, see Carlson, "Furry Cartography."

24. Solomon, "What a Dog Can Do," 144. Like Grinker, Solomon accepts the suggestion that these children very likely became feral because they were abandoned due to disability.

25. Ibid., 157.

26. Cary Wolfe, *What Is Posthumanism?* (Minneapolis: University of Minnesota Press, 2009), 141, emphasis in original.

27. Nathan H. Lents, *Not So Different: Finding Human Nature in Animals* (New York: Columbia University Press, 2016), 1–2; Debra Herrmann, *Avian Cognition: Exploring the Intelligence, Behavior, and Individuality of Birds* (Boca Raton, FL: CRC Press, 2016), viii, emphasis in original; Michael Garstang, *Elephant Sense and Sensibility: Behavior and Cognition* (London: Academic Press/Elsevier, 2015), 3.

28. Julianne Kaminski, Joseph Call, and Julia Fisher, "Word Learning in a Domestic Dog:

Evidence for 'Fast Mapping,'" *Science* 304 (2004): 1682–83; Wolfe, *What Is Posthumanism?*, 31–47, 312 n33; Donna Haraway, *When Species Meet* (Minneapolis: University of Minnesota Press, 2008), 373 n43, 44. Wolfe traces the persistence of human exceptionalism in much of post-Cartesian philosophy on this topic, including Martin Heidegger and Jacques Lacan but focusing on Daniel Dennett. Wolfe and Haraway discuss one another's work and also provide references to the extensive literature on animal communication.

29. Dawn Prince, "The Silence Between: An Autoethnographic Examination of the Language Prejudice and Its Impact on the Assessment of Autistic and Animal Intelligence," *Disability Studies Quarterly* 30, no. 1 (2010): n.p., http://dsq-sds.org/article/view/1055/1242. For an extended discussion, see Erin Manning, *Always More Than One: Individuation's Dance* (Durham: Duke University Press, 2013), 204–21.

30. Erica Fudge, *Animal* (London: Reaktion, 2002), 127.

31. See Sirota, "Narratives of Distinction," 93.

32. See, e.g., Temple Grandin and Margaret M. Scariano, *Emergence: Labeled Autistic* (Novato, CA: Arena Press, 1986); Donna Williams, *Nobody Nowhere: The Extraordinary Autobiography of an Autistic* (New York: Times Books, 1992); Prince-Hughes, *Songs of the Gorilla Nation*; Daniel Tammet, *Born on a Blue Day: Inside the Extraordinary Mind of an Autistic Savant—a Memoir* (New York: Free Press, 2007); Tito Rajarshi Mukhopadhyay, *How Can I Talk if My Lips Don't Move? Inside My Autistic Mind* (New York: Arcade Publishing, 2008). Also see Olga Bogdashina, *Communication Issues in Autism and Asperger Syndrome: Do We Speak the Same Language?* (London: Jessica Kingsley Publishers, 2005), 219–43, 107.

33. For further discussion, see Bogdashina, *Communication Issues*; Olga Solomon and Nancy Bagatell, "Introduction: Autism: Rethinking the Possibilities," *Ethos* 38, no.1 (2010): 1–7; Victoria McGeer, "Autistic Self-Awareness," *Philosophy, Psychiatry, & Psychology* 11, no. 3 (2004): 235–51.

34. See the discussion at Yergeau, "Clinically Significant Disturbance," section II.

35. For measured advocacy and references to relevant literature, see Donald N. Cardinal and Mary A. Falvey, "The Maturing of Facilitated Communication: A Means toward Independent Communication," *Research and Practice for Persons with Severe Disabilities* 39, no. 3 (2014): 189–94, doi:10.1177/1540796914555581. Mark Sherry, "Facilitated Communication, Anna Stubblefield and Disability Studies," *Disability & Society* 31, no. 7 (2016): 974–82, doi:10.1080/09687599.2016.1218152, summarizes the evidence discrediting facilitated communication and discusses the 2016 conviction of a disability studies scholar found to have sexually exploited a nonverbal man. Also see Manning, *Always More Than One*, 244–45 n8 (on facilitated communication) and 149–71 ("An Ethics of Language in the Making").

36. Lauren Berlant, *Cruel Optimism* (Durham: Duke University Press, 2011), 70 (affectsphere), 66 (shared nervous system).

37. Peter Goldie, *The Emotions: A Philosophical Exploration* (Oxford: Clarendon Press, 2000), 178–79, emphasis in original.

38. Martha Craven Nussbaum, *Upheavals of Thought: The Intelligence of Emotions* (Cambridge: Cambridge University Press, 2001), 327.

39. Goldie, *Emotions*, 178.

40. See, e.g., Stephanie D. Preston and Frans B. M. de Waal, "Empathy: Its Ultimate and Proximate Bases," *Behavioral and Brain Sciences* 25 (2002): 18.

41. See, e.g., Frans B. M. de Waal, *The Age of Empathy: Nature's Lessons for a Kinder Society* (New York: Harmony Books, 2009).

42. For a clear and concise overview, see C. Daniel Batson, "These Things Called Empathy: Eight Related but Distinct Phenomena," in *The Social Neuroscience of Empathy*, ed. Jean Decety and William John Ickes (Cambridge: MIT Press, 2009), 3–15.

43. See Erin Hurley and Sara Warner, introduction to special section on "Affect/Performance/Politics," *Journal of Dramatic Theory and Criticism* 26, no. 2 (2012): 99.

44. For a treatment of the term "cognitive" that begins with the observation that cognitive science fails to provide adequate clarification, see Jesse Prinz, *Gut Reactions: A Perceptual Theory of Emotions* (New York: Oxford University Press, 2004), 41–45. For a reassessment of the relation between consciousness and cognition, see N. Katherine Hayles, "The Cognitive Nonconscious: Enlarging the Mind of the Humanities," *Critical Inquiry* 42, no. 4 (2016): 783–808.

45. Teresa Brennan, *The Transmission of Affect* (Ithaca: Cornell University Press, 2004), 5.

46. Martin Welton, *Feeling Theatre* (Houndmills, Basingstoke, Hampshire: Palgrave Macmillan, 2012), 9–10.

47. Brennan, *Transmission of Affect*, 5–6.

48. Silvan Tomkins, "What Are Affects?," in *Shame and Its Sisters: A Silvan Tomkins Reader*, ed. Eve Kosofsky Sedgwick, Adam Frank, and Irving E. Alexander (Durham: Duke University Press, 1995), 36, 33–34. As art historian Susan Best notes, *affect* functions within psychoanalytic theory as an umbrella term encompassing both expressible, conscious feeling and its unconscious emotional substrate. *Visualizing Feeling* (New York: I. B. Tauris, 2011), 5–6.

49. Tomkins, "What Are Affects?," in Sedgwick, Frank, and Alexander, *Shame and Its Sisters*, 60–61.

50. Paul Ekman, "Basic Emotions," in *Handbook of Cognition and Emotion*, ed. Tim Dalgleish and Michael J. Power (Chichester, England: Wiley, NetLibrary, 1999), 55–56.

51. Ibid., 54.

52. Paul Ekman, "Facial Expressions," in Dalgleish and Power, *Handbook of Cognition and Emotion*, 304–5.

53. Ibid., 318.

54. Sianne Ngai, *Our Aesthetic Categories: Zany, Cute, Interesting* (Cambridge: Harvard University Press, 2012).

55. Brian Massumi, "Notes on the Translation and Acknowledgments," in Gilles

Deleuze and Félix Guattari, *A Thousand Plateaus: Capitalism and Schizophrenia*, trans. Massumi (Minneapolis: University of Minnesota Press, 1987), xvi.

56. Deleuze and Guattari, *Thousand Plateaus*, 257.

57. Patricia Ticineto Clough, "The Affective Turn: Political Economy, Biomedia, and Bodies," in *The Affect Theory Reader*, ed. Melissa Gregg and Gregory J. Seigworth (Durham: Duke University Press, 2010), 209, citing Brian Massumi, *Parables for the Virtual: Movement, Affect, Sensation* (Durham: Duke University Press, 2002), 25, 29, 30.

58. Elizabeth Grosz, *Volatile Bodies: Toward a Corporeal Feminism* (Bloomington: Indiana University Press, 1994), 165.

59. Massumi, *Parables for the Virtual*, 14.

60. Ibid., 35–36.

61. Gilles Deleuze and Félix Guattari, *Anti-Oedipus: Capitalism and Schizophrenia*, trans. Robert Hurley, Mark Seem, and Helen R. Lane (Minneapolis: University of Minnesota Press, 1983), 5, originally published as *L'Anti-Oedipe* (Paris: Les éditions de Minuit, 1972).

62. James Thompson, *Performance Affects: Applied Theatre and the End of Effect* (Houndmills, Basingstoke, Hampshire: Palgrave Macmillan, 2009), 119.

63. Brennan, *Transmission of Affect*, 7.

64. See, e.g., Thompson, *Performance Affects*, 124–5; Laura Cull, *Theatres of Immanence: Deleuze and the Ethics of Performance* (Houndmills, Basingstoke, Hampshire: Palgrave Macmillan, 2012), 87–88.

65. Massumi, *Parables for the Virtual*, 28.

66. Laura Cull, "Affect in Deleuze, Hijikata, and Coates: The Politics of Becoming-Animal in Performance," *Journal of Dramatic Theory and Criticism* 26, no. 2 (2012): 192.

67. Anna Gibbs, "After Affect: Sympathy, Synchrony, and Mimetic Communication," in *The Affect Theory Reader*, ed. Gregg and Seigworth, 188.

68. Berlant, *Cruel Optimism*, 158.

69. Also see Marla Carlson, "Mapping Abramović: From Affect to Emotion," in *Performance, Feminism, Affect and Activism in Neoliberal Times*, ed. Elin Diamond, Denise Varney, and Candice Amich (Houndmills, Basingstoke, Hampshire: Palgrave Macmillan, 2017), 133–45.

70. Joe Kelleher, "Sentimental Education at the National Theatre," *PAJ: A Journal of Performance and Art* 27, no. 3 (2005): 47.

71. I viewed the *NTLive* production video at the National Theatre archives.

72. For recent work on therapeutic performance, see, e.g., Nicola Shaughnessy, "Imagining Otherwise: Autism, Neuroaesthetics and Contemporary Performance," *Interdisciplinary Science Reviews* 38, no. 4 (2013): 321–34; Melissa Trimingham and Nicola Shaughnessy, "Material Voices: Intermediality and Autism," *Research in Drama Education* 21, no. 3 (2016): 293–308.

73. See, e.g., Laura Cull's discussion of clarinetist David Rothenberg making music not only with but also for birds and whales. "From *Homo Performans* to Interspecies

Collaboration," in *Performing Animality: Animals in Performance Practices*, ed. Lourdes Orozco and Jennifer Parker-Starbuck (Houndmills, Basingstoke, Hampshire: Palgrave Macmillan, 2015), 25–29.

## Chapter 2

1. Nicholas Hytner and Nick Starr, "Arts Are Economic Gold for Britain," *Telegraph*, 24 April 2013, http://www.telegraph.co.uk/culture/theatre/10015356/Sir-Nicholas-Hytner-Arts-are-economic-gold-for-Britain.html

2. The National initiated this programming shift in 2003 with an adaptation of Phillip Pullman's trilogy *His Dark Materials* (1995–2000) directed by Hytner, an experiment successful enough for a return engagement the next holiday season followed by *Coram Boy* for the next two years. See Susannah Clapp, "A Grand National Treasure: Transcendent Puppeteering Turns Michael Morpurgo's War Novel into the Ultimate Horse Play," *Observer*, 21 October 2007, 15; Kate Kellaway, "Pullman Class," *Observer Review*, 2 November 2003, 5. Thanks also to the National's archivist, Gavin Clarke, for discussion of this programming history.

3. Quoted in Doug Strassler, "Building a Better Horse Puppet," *Show Business*, April/May 2011, 34.

4. *War Horse* by Nick Stafford, adapted for the stage from the novel by Michael Morpurgo in association with Handspring Puppet Company, directed by Marianne Elliott and Tom Morris, produced by National Theatre of Great Britain, Lincoln Center Theater at the Vivian Beaumont, New York, 18 May, 29 September 2012; *The Lion King*, music and lyrics by Elton John and Tim Rice, book by Roger Allers and Irene Mecchi, directed by Julie Taymor, produced by Disney, Minskoff Theatre, New York, 29, 30 September 2012.

5. *ELEPHANT* by Deke Weaver, directed by Weaver and Jennifer Allen, Stock Pavilion, University of Illinois Urbana-Champaign, recorded September 2010, UnreliableBestiary.org, DVD.

6. Originally published by Frederick Warne, the books are freely available online from Project Gutenberg.

7. See, e.g., Marion C. Hodge, "The Sane, the Mad, the Good, the Bad: T. S. Eliot's *Old Possum's Book of Practical Cats*," *Children's Literature* 7 (1978): 129–46, doi:10.1353/chl.0.0381; Paul Douglass, "Cats: Serious Play behind the Playful Seriousness," *Children's Literature* 11 (1983): 109–24, doi:10.1353/chl.0.0030.

8. Vagelis Siropoulos, "*Cats*, Postdramatic Blockbuster Aesthetics and the Triumph of the Megamusical," *Image & Narrative* 11, no. 3 (2010): 130, https://doaj.org/article/b053d2aba7bc4ccfbc29356ed0a9af30

9. Jessica Sternfeld, *The Megamusical* (Bloomington: Indiana University Press, 2006), 2–5.

10. Alan Filewod, "Theatrical Capitalism, Imagined Theatres and the Reclaimed Au-

thenticities of the Spectacular," in *Crucible of Cultures: Anglophone Drama at the Dawn of a New Millennium*, ed. Marc Maufort and Franca Bellarsi (Brussels: Peter Lang, 2002), 224–25.

11. Ibid., 219.

12. Richard Schechner, "Julie Taymor: From Jacques Lecoq to 'The Lion King': An Interview," *TDR* 43, no. 3 (1999): 39, http://www.jstor.org/stable/1146767

13. Ibid., 42.

14. Ibid., 51.

15. See, e.g., Henry A. Giroux and Grace Pollock, *The Mouse That Roared: Disney and the End of Innocence*, updated and expanded edition (Lanham, MD.: Rowman and Littlefield, 2010).

16. Nick Stafford, *War Horse*, adapted for the stage from the novel by Michael Morpurgo (London: Faber and Faber, 2007), 5 (for the breed specification). Further page references to this script are given parenthetically.

17. For a comparison of the film and theatrical versions, see Jennifer Parker-Starbuck, "Animal Ontologies and Media Representations: Robotics, Puppets, and the Real of *War Horse*," *Theatre Journal* 65, no. 3 (2013): 373–93, doi:10.1353/tj.2013.0080.

18. Susannah Clapp, for example, identifies *War Horse* as part of a recent series of productions at the National that have together worked to "heave children's theatre—for years, at least in the subsidised sector, a place of Edwardian and Victorian moralising, of pinafores and simpering—into the 21st century. The stage is waking up to the notion that it should take advantage of the great blossoming of children's literature in the last few decades—and in doing so lure in a new generation of theatre-goers." "A Grand National Treasure: Transcendent Puppeteering Turns Michael Morpurgo's War Novel into the Ultimate Horse Play," *Observer*, 21 October 2007, 15.

19. Una Chaudhuri calls the process of discovery through which *Equus* leads its spectator a "valorizing and mobilizing of clichés," but she argues that these unsatisfactory rational structures keep the audience occupied and draw them into the drama, where its theatrical structures can affect them. "The Spectator in Drama/Drama in the Spectator: Peter Shaffer's *Equus*," in *Contemporary British Drama, 1970–90: Essays from Modern Drama*, ed. Hersh Zeifman and Cynthia Zimmerman (Houndmills, Hampshire: Macmillan, 1993), 51, 57–59; orig. pub. in *Modern Drama* 27 (1984): 281–98.

20. In the 1970s, Barry Witham compared the play to *Look Back in Anger*, twenty years earlier, considering *Equus* to be "still infused with the same philosophical outlook which was so popular and controversial in 1956"; that is, the notion that "being truly alive is synonymous with suffering an intensity of experience which frequently borders on the abnormal and which is repeatedly glamorized as 'passion.'" "The Anger in *Equus*," *Modern Drama* 22, no. 1 (1979): 62.

21. Peter Hammond Schwartz, "Equestrian Imagery in European and American Political Thought: Toward an Understanding of Symbols as Political Texts," *Western Political Quarterly* 41, no. 4 (1988): 662, http://www.jstor.org/stable/448488

22. Georgina K. Crossman and Rita Walsh, "The Changing Role of the Horse: From Beast of Burden to Partner in Sport and Recreation," *International Journal of Sport and Society* 2, no. 2 (2011): 96–97, http://sportandsociety.com/journal/

23. Ibid., 104–6; also see Kim Marra, "Massive Bodies in Mortal Performance: *War Horse* and the Staging of Anglo-American Equine Experience in Combat," in *Performing Animality*, ed. Orozco and Parker-Starbuck, 117–34.

24. *Making War Horse*, dir. David Bickerstaff and Phil Grabsky, UK: More4, 2009.

25. "War Horse Platform #1: A Talk with Basil Jones and Adrian Kohler," moderated by Anne Cattaneo, *Lincoln Center Theater*, 5 April 2011; no longer available online.

26. Ibid.

27. Paul Solman, "The Lion King's Queen," *News Hour with Jim Lehrer*, 5 June 1998, quoted in Alan Woods, "'Bringing Together Man and Nature': The Theater of Julie Taymor," in *American Puppetry: Collections, History and Performance*, ed. Phyllis T. Dircks (Jefferson, NC: McFarland and Co., 2004), 236.

28. Schechner, "Julie Taymor," 52, emphasis in original.

29. Dacher Keltner and John Haidt, "Approaching Awe, a Moral, Spiritual, and Aesthetic Emotion," *Cognition and Emotion* 17, no. 2 (2003): 303, doi:10.1080/02699930244000318, citing Edmund Burke, *A Philosophical Inquiry into the Origin of Our Ideas of the Sublime and Beautiful* (1757) (Oxford: Oxford University Press, 1990), 61, 103.

30. Emily Brady, *The Sublime in Modern Philosophy* (Cambridge: Cambridge University Press, 2013), 36, 58–62.

31. Ibid., 117–65.

32. Keltner and Haidt, "Approaching Awe," 309.

33. Ibid., 304.

34. Schechner, "Julie Taymor," 42, emphasis in original.

35. Maurya Wickstrom, *Performing Consumers: Global Capital and Its Theatrical Seductions* (New York: Routledge, 2006), 86.

36. Ibid., 87.

37. Ibid., 86.

38. Filewod, "Theatrical Capitalism," 228.

39. Rebecca Coyle and Jon Fitzgerald, "Disney Does Broadway: Musical Storytelling in *The Little Mermaid* and *The Lion King*," in *Drawn to Sound: Animation Film Music and Sonicity*, ed. Rebecca Coyle (London: Equinox, 2010), 236. Coyle and Fitzgerald note that Lebo M's singing the chant on the movie soundtrack enabled the president of Walt Disney Music, Chris Montan, to claim that "at that point it wasn't a bunch of Hollywood people trying to do what we thought Africa should be. It was somebody from that place able to express his feelings about that place," an expressiveness that "immediately took you to Africa." Interview included in *The Making of "The Lion King*," documentary directed by Dan Boothe (1994), first broadcast on the Disney Channel and included on the Walt Disney Platinum Edition of *The Lion King* (2003).

40. Ibid., 237–29. The extensive collaboration between Zimmer and Lebo M makes

it overly simplistic to read this as a simple progression from South African to European sounds, yet persons involved in making and marketing the animated film consistently elide the European contributions and stress African authenticity.

41. Ngai, *Our Aesthetic Categories*, 53.

42. Ibid., 65.

43. Ibid., 59–60, citing for the cute commodity always seeking its mother Lori Merish, *Sentimental Materialism: Gender, Commodity Culture, and Nineteenth-Century American Literature* (Durham: Duke University Press, 2000). Merish makes further connections to disgust, freakishness, and the "containment of child sexuality" (186).

44. Sara Ahmed, "Happy Objects," in *The Affect Theory Reader*, ed. Melissa Gregg and Gregory J. Seigworth (Durham: Duke University Press, 2010), 31.

45. Ibid., 37.

46. In *Making War Horse*, lighting designer Paule Constable and sound designer Christopher Shutt both discuss their work in creating this sense of security and the later atmospheres of chaos and danger.

47. John Tams, "War Horse Songbook," in Nick Stafford, *War Horse*, adapted for the stage from the novel by Michael Morpurgo (London: Faber and Faber, 2007), 91–92.

48. *Making War Horse*. A performer designated as Song Man leads the songs.

49. Ahmed, "Happy Objects," 29, 33, 35.

50. Ngai, *Our Aesthetic Categories*, 60.

51. Quoted in Strassler, "Building a Better Horse Puppet."

52. Pia Catton, "A Harmony of the Head, Heart—and Haunch," *Wall Street Journal*, 8 April 2011, A20. Because the horse's actual breathing pattern (expansion to the sides) "wouldn't register onstage," the puppeteers create a vertical breath by crouching and straightening up. Their "custom-made shoulder packs" are connected "to a metal bar where the spine would be." For further discussion of the puppetry, see Marra, "Massive Bodies in Mortal Performance," 122–26.

53. Rae Smith, "War Horse Sketchbook," *Rae Smith*, 2007, http://www.raesmith. co.uk/selected_warhorse.html; no longer available, but see *Making War Horse*.

54. 59 Productions, "The Making of *War Horse*—Projection and Animation," *Vimeo*, 2011, http://vimeo.com/22145320

55. Filewod, "Theatrical Capitalism," 226.

56. Siropoulos, "*Cats*, Postdramatic Blockbuster Aesthetics," 131.

57. Walter Kerr, "Off Broadway Fades Victoriously," *New York Times*, 17 August 1975, sec. 2.1.

58. Basil Jones, "Financing Handspring Puppet Company: A South African Experience," in *African Theatre: Companies*, ed. James Gibbs (Woodbridge, Suffolk: James Currey, 2008), 94–108.

59. "Handspring Productions," *Handspring Puppet Company*, 2016, http://www. handspringpuppet.co.za

60. "War Horse Platform #1."

61. Schechner's interview with Taymor provides a handy chronology, 36–55. See also Woods, "Bringing Together Man and Nature."

62. Schechner, "Julie Taymor," 44.

63. Deke Weaver, *The Unreliable Bestiary*, 2009–16, http://www.unreliablebestiary. org. Information about the project not otherwise attributed is taken from this website, and performance descriptions are based on the DVDs available for purchase here.

64. Interview with Matthew Green, "Art in WOLF's Clothing," *Smile Politely*, 11 September 2013, http://www.smilepolitely.com/arts/art_in_wolfs_clothing/

65. Deke Weaver, "Excerpts from *ELEPHANT* (2010)," in *Animal Acts: Performing Species Today*, ed. Una Chaudhuri and Holly Hughes (Ann Arbor: University of Michigan Press, 2014), 166. Unless otherwise indicated, citations to the script will refer to this source and be included parenthetically within the text.

66. Marissa Perel, "'ELEPHANT,' or Why I Love Performance Art", *Art 21*, 9 December 2010, http://blog.art21.org/2010/12/09/elephant-or-why-i-love-performance-art/

67. Ibid.

68. Anonymous e-mail dated 29 September 2010, *Unreliable Bestiary Blog*, 13 October 2011.

69. I found this story a bit hard to follow and consulted the source listed on *The Unreliable Bestiary* website bibliography: John Kistler, *War Elephants* (Westport, CT: Praeger, 2006), 14–18. Accompanying the voiceover narrative, Jennifer Allen embodies the queen, wielding a rubber snake and a rubber bat.

70. Chris Peck, "Why Did You Go (for the Elephant)?" *YouTube*, 30 September 2010, http://youtu.be/cv-Yv4qQcaU

71. Interview with Matthew Green, "Art in WOLF's Clothing," *Smile Politely*, 11 September 2013, http://www.smilepolitely.com/arts/art_in_wolfs_clothing/

72. Anonymous e-mail dated 24 September 2010, *Unreliable Bestiary Blog*, 13 October 2011.

73. Bob Ferris, "Going Wolfy on the Weekend," *Cascadia Wildlands*, 2 May 2014, http://www.cascwild.org/?s=Deke+Weaver

74. *WOLF* by Deke Weaver (solo version), Goat Farm Arts Center, Atlanta, 10 November 2014. Solo excerpts and video from *WOLF, ELEPHANT,* and other installments of *Unreliable Bestiary* are also included in Weaver's TED talk and his presentation for the Chicago Humanities Festival, *YouTube*, 10 February 2014, http://youtu.be/kJwlB7CHLxQ

## Chapter 3

1. Ahmed, "Happy Objects," 38; for a slightly different development of the same argument, see Ahmed, *The Promise of Happiness* (Durham: Duke University Press, 2010), 44–46.

2. See Berlant, *Cruel Optimism*.

3. Bleuler identified autistic withdrawal as one of the four As characterizing schizophrenia, the others being "association loosening, ambivalence, affect inappropriateness." Majia Holmer Nadesan, *Constructing Autism: Unraveling the "Truth" and Understanding the Social* (London: Routledge, 2005), 39. For the fraught history and ambiguity of schizophrenia as a diagnosis, see Kieran McNally, *Critical History of Schizophrenia* (New York: Palgrave Macmillan, 2016). Also see Ian Hacking, *Mad Travelers: Reflections on the Reality of Transient Mental Illnesses* (Charlottesville: University Press of Virginia, 1998). With specific reference to schizophrenia, Anne Wilson and Peter Beresford discuss the continuum of distress that diagnostic categories carve up into illnesses, and the history of psychiatry's reification of these fractured diagnoses as a persistent identity. "Madness, Distress and Postmodernity: Putting the Record Straight," in *Disability/Postmodernity: Embodying Disability Theory*, ed. Mairian Corker and Tom Shakespeare (London: Continuum, 2002), 143–58.

4. For doubts about this independence, see Steven Silberman, *Neurotribes: The Legacy of Autism and the Future of Neurodiversity* (New York: Avery, 2015), 167–68: Georg Frankl and Anni Weiss worked closely with Asperger and then, after fleeing the Third Reich, with Kanner at Johns Hopkins. For evidence that came to light in 2010 of Asperger's complicity with the Nazi regime, see John Donvan and Caren Zucker, *In a Different Key: The Story of Autism* (New York: Crown Publishers, 2016), 327–41. Both of these journalistic accounts give clear and thorough histories of autism and the arguments surrounding etiology and diagnostic criteria. For more scholarly versions, see Nadesan, *Constructing Autism*; Eyal, et al., *Autism Matrix*.

5. Silberman, *Neurotribes*, 195–96, citing Loretta Bender, "Childhood Schizophrenia: Clinical Study of One Hundred Schizophrenic Children," *American Journal of Orthopsychiatry* 17, no. 1 (1947): 40–56; "Theory and Treatment of Childhood Schizophrenia," *Acta Paedopsychiatrica* 34 (1968): 298–307.

6. This idea originated with Kanner, although he later rejected it in favor of a conception of autism as an inborn condition, whereas Bettelheim continued to blame the mothers. See Donvan and Zucker, *In a Different Key*, 74–94; Silberman, *Neurotribes*, 188–92.

7. The DSM is a specifically American manual for psychiatric diagnoses only, and most of my research focuses upon U.S. audiences as well as medical and educational context. The World Health Organization publishes another manual, the International Classification of Diseases, which includes medical as well as psychiatric diagnoses and is more widely used in other countries. In spite of reciprocal influence, the history is not uniform.

8. See Donvan and Zucker, *In a Different Key*, 310–15.

9. "Data and Statistics," *Autism Spectrum Disorders (ASD)*, Centers for Disease Control, 10 March 2017, http://www.cdc.gov/ncbddd/autism/data.html. Also see Roy

Richard Grinker, "Diagnostic Criteria for Autism through the Years," *Unstrange Minds*, 2007, http://www.unstrange.com/dsm1.html

10. "Autism Spectrum Disorder," "Clinician-Rated Severity of Autism Spectrum and Social Communication Disorders," *American Psychiatric Association*, 2013, https://www.psychiatry.org/File%20Library/Psychiatrists/Practice/DSM/APA_DSM-5-Autism-Spectrum-Disorder.pdf; https://www.psychiatry.org/File%20Library/Psychiatrists/Practice/DSM/APA_DSM5_Clinician-Rated-Severity-of-Autism-Spectrum-and-Social-Communication-Disorders.pdf

11. Stuart Murray, "Autism and the Contemporary Sentimental: Fiction and the Narrative Fascination of the Present," *Literature and Medicine* 25, no. 1 (2006): 26, doi:10.1353/lm.2006.0025; Ian Hacking, "Autism Fiction: A Mirror of an Internet Decade?" *University of Toronto Quarterly* 79, no. 2 (2010): 632–33, doi:10.1353/utq.2010.0225.

12. Murray, "Autism and the Contemporary Sentimental," 27–31.

13. David T. Mitchell and Sharon L. Snyder, *Narrative Prosthesis: Disability and the Dependencies of Discourse* (Ann Arbor: University of Michigan Press, 2000), 53–54.

14. Ibid., 48.

15. Murray, "Autism and the Contemporary Sentimental," 28.

16. Mark Haddon, *The Curious Incident of the Dog in the Night-Time* (New York: Doubleday, 2003).

17. Mark Osteen, "Autism and Representation: A Comprehensive Introduction," in *Autism and Representation*, ed. Osteen (New York: Routledge, 2008), 38–39.

18. See, e.g., Gyasi Burks-Abbott, "Mark Haddon's Popularity and Other Curious Incidents in My Life as an Autistic," in Osteen, *Autism and Representation*, for the argument that Haddon's "singular portrayal of autism, a portrayal that fails to capture the nuances and complexities of the autism spectrum, serves to perpetuate stereotypes" and that "the author's conclusions and the book's reception actually militate against autistic self-representation" (291). Osteen, in contrast, says that "*Curious Incident* is by far the best novel with an autistic character yet published, and though it promulgates certain stereotypes, it presents autism as just another way of being human" (40).

19. Katy Rudd, "Diagnosing Christopher Boone," *National Theatre Background Pack*, March 2013, 13, nationaltheatre.org.uk. According to his program notes, Haddon "drew upon a long list of beliefs, habits, quirks and behaviours which [he] borrowed from friends and acquaintances and members of [his] own family." The essay to which he refers is published in Oliver Sacks, *An Anthropologist on Mars: Seven Paradoxical Tales* (New York: Knopf, 1995).

20. Katy Rudd, "Workshop Diary: Planes, Trains, and Automobiles," *National Theatre Background Pack*, March 2013, 11; "'The Curious Incident of the Dog in the Night-Time': Working on the Spectrum," *National Theatre Live*, accessed 25 June 2013, http://ntlive.nationaltheatre.org.uk/behind-the-scenes

21. *The Curious Incident of the Dog in the Night-Time* by Simon Stephens, directed by Marianne Elliott, with Luke Treadaway, National Theatre, Apollo Theatre, London, 17 and 22 May 2013. In addition to seeing two performances, I was able to watch the video recording of the initial Cottesloe production made for *NTLive* at the NT Archive and rely primarily upon this resource in my description. The West End staging differed in ways not particularly significant for my analysis. Treadaway stayed with the production, with Ed Ritter and Nicola Walker as Ed and Judy at the Cottesloe replaced by Seán Gleeson and Holly Aird at the Apollo. The New York production initially featured Alexander Sharp in the leading role.

22. James Berger, "Mark Haddon's *Curious Incident* in the Neurological Spectrum," in Osteen, *Autism and Representation*, 280.

23. For these concepts and terminology, see Louis Althusser, "Ideology and Ideological State Apparatuses (Notes toward an Investigation)," in *Lenin and Philosophy* (New York: Monthly Review Press, 2001), 85–126.

24. Ahmed, "Happy Objects," 30, citing Darrin McMahon, *Happiness: A History* (New York: Atlantic Monthly Press, 2006). Ahmed says elsewhere, "One history of happiness could be described as the removal of the hap from happiness" (*Promise of Happiness*, 207).

25. Eyal, et al., *Autism Matrix*, 85.

26. Ibid. On psychiatric institutionalization, see 76–97; on deinstitutionalization, 98–110.

27. Ahmed, "Happy Objects," 30–31, with further reference to Mihály Csíkszentmihályi, *Flow: The Psychology of Optimal Experience* (London: Rider, 1992), 2.

28. Wendy Brown, "Neoliberalism and the End of Liberal Democracy," *Edgework: Critical Essays on Knowledge and Politics* (Princeton: Princeton University Press, 2009), 42–43.

29. Osteen, "Conclusion: Toward an Empathetic Scholarship," in Osteen, *Autism and Representation*, 298.

30. Ahmed, "Happy Objects," 33; Ahmed, *Promise of Happiness*, 25–26.

31. Catherine Chaput, "Rhetorical Circulation in Late Capitalism: Neoliberalism and the Overdetermination of Affective Energy," *Philosophy and Rhetoric* 43, no. 1 (2010): 14, doi:10.1353/par.0.0047, citing Sara Ahmed, *The Cultural Politics of Emotion* (New York: Routledge, 2004), 45.

32. Jordynn Jack, *Autism and Gender: From Refrigerator Mothers to Computer Geeks* (Champaign: University of Illinois Press, 2014), 2–4.

33. Ibid., 107.

34. My list comes from McGeer, "Autistic Self-Awareness," 236. The language has shifted somewhat in DSM-V to emphasize difficulties in communication, but the other points of the triad remain: "People with ASD tend to have communication deficits, such as responding inappropriately in conversations, misreading nonverbal interactions, or having difficulty building friendships appropriate to their age. In addition, people with

ASD may be overly dependent on routines, highly sensitive to changes in their environ-ment, or intensely focused on inappropriate items." "Autism Spectrum Disorder," *APA*.

35. Annie Baker, *Body Awareness* (New York: Samuel French, 2009), 27, 25 (further page references to this script given parenthetically); *Body Awareness* by Annie Baker, directed by Karen Kohlhaas, Atlantic Theater Company, New York, 1 June 2008.

36. See McGeer, "Autistic Self-Awareness," 236.

37. Mike Leigh, *Two Thousand Years* (London: Faber and Faber, 2006), 17–18 (further page references to this script given parenthetically); *Two Thousand Years* by Mike Leigh, directed by Scott Elliott, The New Group, Acorn Theatre, New York, 24 January 2008. Leigh developed *Two Thousand Years* for the National Theatre, and it opened at the Cottesloe in 2005, then transferred to the larger Lyttelton.

38. Leigh says that Kwame Kwei-Armah's portrayal of a black community in *Elmina's Kitchen* at the National Theatre inspired him to write what he refers to as his "Jewish play" on commission for the same venue. Aleks Sierz, "'All My Work Has a Certain Jewishness in It,'" *Telegraph*, 17 April 2006, http://www.telegraph.co.uk. The play takes as its theme the ongoing struggle in the Middle East and the difficulty that Israel's history and present policies create for liberals—including but not limited to Jewish people. This family's cultural connection to Israel and their rejection of any religious connec-tion highlight the troubled position of religion in the Middle Eastern struggle, at a time (now) when militant religious identity politics enflame both sides in the conflict and make resolution seem impossible. Grandfather Dave participated in the early Zionist movement, when Israel was building itself after World War II and the whole enterprise was an optimistic new beginning after the devastation of the Holocaust. Then, it seemed easy to support Israel, especially for Jews. This feeling carried through for his daughter's generation, and the obligatory experience of living on a kibbutz was culturally and per-sonally important for Rachel. The political issues have become more and more heated, though, and harder to ignore. Josh's disruption of the family identity raises the ques-tion whether neutrality is possible, given one's allegiances and background. His atypi-cal behaviors call into question the appeal of a return to religious tradition, suggesting that it compensates for Josh's social isolation. Early in the play he prays, alone on stage, binding his bare arm with a phylactery in a manner explicitly meant to resemble drug paraphernalia—one might think he's about to shoot up, suggesting a Marxist equation of religion with opiates.

39. Josh's aunt Michelle presents all the negative stereotypes of Jewish worldly striving and success—it's no accident that she's a banker. She shows up late in the play, entirely self-involved and estranged from her family. Tammy is well adjusted, bright and shiny. She works as a freelance translator, cares about world politics, and in the second act brings her new Israeli boyfriend, Tzachi, home to meet the family. The only character not all tied up in knots about his heritage and world politics and religion, Tzachi finally shouts at the family, ending their ever-accelerating arguments and beginning the play's denouement.

40. Simon Baron-Cohen, "Christopher and Asperger Syndrome," program for *The Curious Incident of the Dog in the Night-Time*, Apollo Theatre, London, May 2013, 20–21.

41. Simon Baron-Cohen, *Mindblindness: An Essay on Autism and Theory of Mind* (Cambridge: MIT Press, 1995), esp. 51–55, 69–83.

42. Uta Frith and Francesca Happé, "Theory of Mind and Self-Consciousness: What Is It Like to Be Autistic?," *Mind and Language* 14, no. 1 (1999): 10–11.

43. As reported by Burks-Abbott, "Mark Haddon's Popularity," 291, citing Dania Jekel, director of the Asperger/Autism Network.

44. Jon Baio, "Prevalence of Autism Spectrum Disorder among Children Aged 8 Years—Autism and Developmental Disabilities Monitoring Network, 11 Sites, United States, 2010," *Morbidity and Mortality Weekly Report*, CDC, 28 March 2014, http://www.cdc.gov/mmwr/preview/mmwrhtml/ss6302a1.htm?s_cid=ss6302a1_w, citing Donna M. Werling and Daniel H. Geschwind, "Sex Differences in Autism Spectrum Disorders," *Current Opinion in Neurology* 26, no. 2 (2013): 146–53.

45. Simon Baron-Cohen, *The Essential Difference: The Truth about the Male and Female Brain* (New York: Basic Books, 2003).

46. Jack, *Autism and Gender*, 121–33. She further notes that psychologists initially developed theory of mind tests in order to measure animal cognition and reinforce human exceptionalism (133, citing David Premack and Guy Woodruff, "Does the Chimpanzee Have a Theory of Mind?," *Behavioral and Brain Sciences* 1, no. 4 [1978]: 515–26).

47. Stuart Murray, *Representing Autism: Culture, Narrative, Fascination* (Liverpool: Liverpool University Press, 2008), 155–56.

48. Jack, *Autism and Gender*, 107–11.

49. Angela Willey, Banu Subramaniam, Jennifer A. Hamilton, and Jane Couperus, "The Mating Life of Geeks: Love, Neuroscience, and the New Autistic Subject," *Signs* 40, no. 2 (2015): 370.

50. Ibid., 378, citing Meredith Melnick, "Could the Way We Mate and Marry Boost Rates of Autism?," *Time*, 9 August 2011; Lizzie Buchen, "Scientists and Autism: When Geeks Meet," *Nature* 479, no. 7371 (2011): 25–27; Steve Silberman, "The Geek Syndrome," *Wired* 9, no. 12 (2001), http://archive.wired.com/wired/archive/9.12/aspergers.html. Also see Jack, *Autism and Gender*, 116; Gayle C. Windham, Karen Fessel, and Judith K. Grether, "Autism Spectrum Disorders in Relation to Parental Occupation in Technical Fields," *Autism Research* 2, no. 4 (2009): 183–91; Rosa A. Hoekstra, Meike Bartels, Catharina J. H. Verweij, and Dorret I. Bomsma, "Heritability of Autistic Traits in the General Population," *Archives of Pediatric and Adolescent Medicine* 161, no. 4 (2007): 372–77.

51. Willey, et al., "Mating Life of Geeks," 371.

52. Jack, *Autism and Gender*, 6.

53. McGeer, "Autistic Self-Awareness," 239. Also see Bogdashina, *Communication Issues in Autism and Asperger Syndrome*.

54. McGeer, "Autistic Self-Awareness," 249.

55. As Stuart Murray observes, the appearance of rationality and scientific inquiry in discourse around autism (and other disabilities) continues to depend upon "the selective use of wonder." *Representing Autism*, 99.

56. Deanna Jent, *Falling* (New York: Dramatist's Play Service, 2013), 37 (further citations to this source included parenthetically); *Falling* by Deanna Jent, directed by Lori Adams, Minetta Lane Theatre, New York, 20 November 2012.

57. Jim Sinclair, "Don't Mourn for Us," *Our Voice* 1, no. 3 (1993), http://www.autreat.com/dont_mourn.html

58. Telory Davies Arendell, *The Autistic Stage: How Cognitive Disability Changed 20th-Century Performance* (Rotterdam: Sense Publishers, 2015), 16. In Arendell's assessment, the production's connections "have somehow let the motif of autistic behavior decode Chekhov" (17). Also see her detailed analysis of *Chekhov Lizardbrain*, 15–23.

59. See Grandin and Johnson, *Animals in Translation*. Also see Arendell, *Autistic Stage*, 17–18.

60. Pig Iron Theatre Company (conception and creation) and Robert Quillen Camp (text), *Chekhov Lizardbrain*, in *Pig Iron: Three Plays* (Chicago: 53rd State Press, 2012), 76. Further citations to this source will be included parenthetically within the text. I also thank Pig Iron managing director John Frisbee for providing a performance DVD.

61. R. Glenn Northcutt, "Evolution of the Telencephalon in Nonmammals," *Annual Review of Neuroscience* 4 (1981): 303. Some homologous brain features have developed from a common evolutionary predecessor. Other homoplastic features have evolved separately, either through parallel evolution from a recently common feature and involving similar parts of the genome or a convergence of features for which common ancestry is quite distant and involving different parts of the genome (306). Also see Georg F. Streidter, et al., "Précis of *Principles of Brain Evolution*," *Behavioral and Brain Sciences* 29 (2006): 1–36.

62. For critique, also see Joseph E. LeDoux and Elizabeth A. Phelps, "Emotional Networks in the Brain," in Lewis, Haviland-Jones, and Barrett, *Handbook of Emotions*, ed. Michael Lewis, Jeannette M. Haviland-Jones and Lisa Feldman Barrett (New York: Guilford Press, 2008), 161; supporting some portions of MacLean, see Jaak Panksepp, "The Affective Brain and Core Consciousness: How Does Neural Activity Generate Emotional Feelings?" in Lewis, Haviland-Jones, and Barrett, *Handbook of Emotions*, 47–67.

63. Ngai, *Our Aesthetic Categories*, 7–9.

64. Ibid., 11.

65. Ibid., 8.

66. Ibid., 16.

67. Nicholas and Peter use the Russian names Nikolai and Pyotr when they occupy the long-underwear version of the past. Dmitri and Sascha keep the same names.

68. *The Sound and the Fury: April Seventh, 1928* by Elevator Repair Service, directed

by John Collins, New York Theatre Workshop, 17 May 2008; Public Theater, 13 June 2015. I also thank ERS producing director Ariana Smart Truman for giving me access to video of the 2008 version.

69. John B. Cullen, *Old Times in the Faulkner Country*, in collaboration with Floyd C. Watkins (Baton Rouge: Louisiana State University Press, 1975), vii, quoted in Maria Truchan-Tataryn, "Textual Abuse: Faulkner's Benjy," *Journal of Medical Humanities* 26, nos. 2/3 (2005): 160.

70. William Faulkner, *The Sound and the Fury* (New York: Random House, [1929] 1956), 40.

71. Eyal, et al., *Autism Matrix*, 79.

72. Ibid., 78.

73. On the eugenics movement and Kanner's opposition to "mercy killing," also see Donvan and Zucker, *In a Different Key*, 20–24.

74. Eyal, et al., *Autism Matrix*, 90.

75. Stuart Murray mentions Benjy as a proto-autistic character. *Representing Autism*, 80.

76. Truchan-Tataryn, "Textual Abuse," 161–62, quoting James B. Meriwether and Michael Millgate, eds., *Lion in the Garden: Interviews with William Faulkner, 1926–1962* (New York: Random House, 1968), 245.

77. Peggy Back, "A Serious Damn: William Faulkner and Evelyn Scott," *Southern Literary Journal* 28 (1995): 128–43, quoted in Truchan-Tataryn, "Textual Abuse, 163.

78. Truchan-Tataryn, "Textual Abuse," 162.

79. For a related analysis focused on the production's open ending as opposed to the chapter's absent ending, see Olga Muratova, "Dionysian Symphony of Distorted Reality: Elevator Repair Service's Eisegesis of *The Sound and the Fury*," *Contemporary Theatre Review* 19, no. 4 (2009): 453, doi:10.1080/10486800903209752. Muratova goes on to argue that ERS makes Benjy's thought patterns comprehensible by translating the novel's abstraction into sound: "Benjy's aural universe is filled with rigid leitmotifs, i.e.[,] unbreakable connections between life phenomena and their sound representations. A certain sound triggers a certain image that, in turn, may trigger a certain memory" (455). Muratova provides evocative descriptions of Matt Tierney's sound score and a detailed description of the production's opening.

80. See Claire Epstein, "Nothing but Novel: Elevator Repair Service Does Faulkner," *Brooklyn Rail*, 4 April 2008, http://brooklynrail.org

81. Sara Jane Bailes, "Dislocations of Practice: Elevator Repair Service," in her *Performance Theatre and the Poetics of Failure: Forced Entertainment, Goat Island, Elevator Repair Service* (London: Routledge, 2011), 148–98.

82. Ibid., 171–72.

83. Coco Fusco, "Elevator Repair Service" (interview), *Bomb* 67, 1999, http://bombmagazine.org/article/2231/elevator-repair-service

84. Bailes, "Dislocations of Practice," in *Performance Theatre and the Poetics of Failure*,

184. She uses "reterritorializing" in a Deleuzian sense that I will discuss more fully in chapter 6.

85. Muratova, "Dionysian Symphony," 458–59, 456. See *Talking Feet: Solo Southern Dance: Buck, Flatfoot, and Tap*, directed by Mike Seeger, Smithsonian Folkways Recordings, (1987) 2005; http://www.folkstreams.net/film,121

86. Muratova, "Dionysian Symphony," 456.

87. Ben Brantley, "Faulkner's Haunted Family, Moving in and out of Time," *New York Times*, 30 April 2008, 1.

88. Hilton Als, "Intruder in the Wings," *New Yorker*, 26 May 2008, 82–83.

89. Truchan-Tataryn, "Textual Abuse," 163.

90. Yergeau, "Clinically Significant Disturbance," section IV, par. 18.

## Chapter 4

1. Corey Kilgannon, "A White Rat Finds Fame on the Great White Way," *New York Times*, 11 November 2014, A22. A replacement rat proved even more newsworthy, rescued from the West Side highway and seeming born for the boards; sadly, an accident during play abruptly ended her life. Andy Newman, "Enter Rose, a Rat with a Past," *New York Times*, 24 January 2016, MB2; "Rat Who Escaped Peril and Made It on Broadway Dies in a Fall," *New York Times*, 27 January 2016, A22.

2. Martin McDonagh, *The Lieutenant of Inishmore* (London: Methuen, 2001), 3. Further page references parenthetical.

3. *The Lieutenant of Inishmore* by Martin McDonagh, directed by Wilson Milam, New York: Atlantic Theatre Company, 10 March 2006.

4. Paul Rozin, Johnathan Haidt, and Clark R. McCauley, "Disgust," in Lewis, Haviland-Jones, and Barrett, *Handbook of Emotions*, 757–62. In another article, the authors distinguish disgust from other food rejections: "*distaste* is motivated by undesirable sensory properties, *danger* by undesirable consequences of ingestions, and *disgust* by offensive properties having to do with the nature or origin of the potential food." Paul Rozin, Jonathan Haidt, and Clark R. McCauley, "Disgust: The Body and Soul Emotion," in Dalgleish and Power, *Handbook of Cognition and Emotion*, 432, emphasis in original. Valerie Curtis observes a current "mini-boom" of interest in disgust, noting that the number of books on the topic has doubled since 2011 but that most of this literature is highly speculative. *Don't Look, Don't Touch, Don't Eat: The Science behind Revulsion* (Chicago: University of Chicago Press, 2013), viii. Her field research spreads across the Indian subcontinent along with Africa and Europe.

5. Rozin, Haidt, and McCauley, "Disgust," in Dalgleish and Power, *Handbook of Cognition and Emotion*, 429.

6. "Futz!," *Time*, 21 June 1968, 79. Also see Clive Barnes, "'Futz!' Opens at the de Lys: Rochelle Owens Play Staged by O'Horgan, Bakos in Title Role with La Mama Troupe," *New York Times*, 14 June 1968, Billy Rose Theatre Collection, New York Public Library (hereafter NYPL).

7. Ben Brantley, "A Secret Paramour Who Nibbles Tin Cans," *New York Times*, 11 March 2002, E1. For an illuminating analysis of Albee's repurposing of structures familiar from popular entertainment, see Linda Ben-Zvi, "'Playing the Cloud Circuit': Albee's Vaudeville Show," in *Cambridge Companion to Edward Albee*, ed. Stephen Bottoms (Cambridge: Cambridge University Press, 2005), 178–98. For further treatment of the humor, also see John Kuhn, "Getting Albee's Goat: 'Notes toward a Definition of Tragedy,'" *American Drama* 13, no. 2 (2004): 8; J. Ellen Gainor, "Albee's *The Goat*: Rethinking Tragedy for the 21st Century," in *Cambridge Companion to Edward Albee*, 204.

8. Una Chaudhuri, "(De)Facing the Animals: Zooësis and Performance," *TDR* 51, no. 1 (2007): 16, http://www.jstor.org/stable/4492732; also see Chaudhuri, *The Stage Lives of Animals: Zooësis and Performance* (London: Routledge, 2017), which includes this and related essays but was published too late to be consulted for this project.

9. Peta Tait, "Confronting Corpses and Theatre Animals," in *Animal Death*, ed. Jay Johnston and Fiona Probyn-Rapsey (Sydney: Sydney University Press, 2013), 76.

10. *The Goat, or Who is Sylvia?* by Edward Albee, directed by David Esbjornson, with Bill Pullman and Mercedes Ruehl, New York: John Golden Theatre, 16 May 2002, Theatre on Film and Tape (hereafter TOFT) Archive, NYPL.

11. Rozin, Haidt, and McCauley, "Disgust," in Dalgleish and Power, *Handbook of Cognition and Emotion*, 440.

12. Carolyn Korsmeyer, *Savoring Disgust: The Foul and the Fair in Aesthetics* (Oxford: Oxford University Press, 2011), 37.

13. Aurel Kolnai, *On Disgust* (1929), ed. Barry Smith and Carolyn Korsmeyer (Chicago: Open Court, 2004), 39.

14. Ibid.

15. Ibid., 43; also see Korsmeyer, *Savoring Disgust*, 37.

16. McDonagh also blurs the line between humans and other species by butchering human bodies (replicas, of course) on stage during *Lieutenant's* final scene.

17. William E. Kleb, "*Curse of the Starving Class* and the Logic of Destruction," *Contemporary Theatre Review* 8, no. 4 (1998): 6.

18. Sheila Rabillard, "Sam Shepard: Theatrical Power and American Dreams," *Modern Drama* 30, no. 1 (1987): 65, doi:10.1353/mdr.1987.0035.

19. Stephen J. Bottoms, *The Theatre of Sam Shepard: States of Crisis* (Cambridge: Cambridge University Press, 1998), 166.

20. Anita Gates, "Longing to Escape from the Debt and the Dirt: A Review of 'Curse of the Starving Class' at the Long Wharf Theatre," *New York Times*, 3 March 2013, CT9.

21. Sam Shepard, *Curse of the Starving Class* in *Seven Plays* (New York: Dial Press, 1984), 154. Taylor is Ella's lawyer, and the children suspect a more intimate relationship. Further references to this source are cited parenthetically.

22. David J. DeRose reports that "both the productions of *Curse* that [he has] seen have had the actor turn away from the audience in order to 'urinate' on the charts" although the stage directions call for full frontal exposure and real rather than faked urina-

tion. "A Kind of Cavorting: Superpresence and Shepard's Family Dramas," in *Rereading Shepard: Contemporary Critical Essays on the Plays of Sam Shepard*, ed. Leonard Wilcox (New York: St. Martin's Press, 1993), 148 n31.

23. Nicholas Ridout, *Stage Fright, Animals, and Other Theatrical Problems* (Cambridge: Cambridge University Press, 2006), 97–98. Ridout argues that animal and child performers make visible the normally (and neurotically) elided "alienation of the actor and . . . the economic conditions of her presence on the stage" (101).

24. Stanton B. Garner, Jr., "Sensing Realism: Illusionism, Actuality, and the Theatrical Sensorium," in *The Senses in Performance*, ed. Sally Banes and André Lepecki (New York: Routledge, 2007), 121.

25. Bottoms, *Theatre of Sam Shepard*, 173. Some critics equate the eagle with Weston and the cat with Ella, but the dialogue specifies that the cat is male.

26. See, e.g., Leanne Maxwell, "Sam Shepard's *Curse of the Starving Class* at A.C.T." *Gothamist*, San Francisco, 2 May 2008, http://sfist.com/2008/05/02/sam_shepards_cu.php; Margaret Gray, "Theater Review: 'Curse of the Starving Class' at Open Fist Theatre Company," *Los Angeles Times*, 11 April 2011, http://latimesblogs.latimes.com/culturemonster/2011/04/theater-review-curse-of-the-starving-class-at-open-fist-theatre-company.html; "Meet Edie, the Newest Cast Member of Curse of the Starving Class," *Loading Dock*, Long Wharf Theatre, 2 February 2013, https://www.longwharf.org/blog/?p=386

27. Bottoms, *Theatre of Sam Shepard*, 168–69.

28. Joseph Roach, *Cities of the Dead: Circum-Atlantic Performance* (New York: Columbia University Press, 1996), 36.

29. Ibid.

30. For a typical action, see the description of *The Death of Sharon Tate* in Brus, Muehl, Nitsch, Schwarzkogler: *Writings of the Vienna Actionists*, ed. and trans. by Malcolm Green in collaboration with the artists (London: Atlas Press, 1999), 113.

31. Otto Muehl, "Material Action Manifesto 1968," in Green, *Writings of the Vienna Actionists*, 110, capitalization in original; orig. pub. *Burgtheater Ausgestopft* (Vienna: Zock Press, 1968). This publication for the Vienna Festival Week included the "Zock Manifesto."

32. Otto Muehl, "Film Action," *Mama & Papa* (Frankfurt-am-Main: Kohlkunstverlag, 1969), excerpt in Green, *Writings of the Vienna Actionists*, 112.

33. *O Tannenbaum*, 17 December 1969, Art College, Brunswick; scenario in Green, *Writings of the Vienna Actionists*, 114; film available on *UbuWeb*, accessed 25 April 2017, http://www.ubu.com/film/vienna_actionists.html

34. Green, *Writings of the Vienna Actionists*, 113–14.

35. *O Sensibility*, 20 August 1970, Ostheimer Gallery, Frankfurt; film available on *UbuWeb*. Kurt Kren filmed *Leda and the Swan*, cutting rapidly from one single frame of the action to another, and the swan appears to be inflatable. *O Sensibility* gives better evidence of the live action, because Muehl himself controlled its filming.

36. Malcolm Green in *Writings of the Vienna Actionists*, 113.

37. Muehl, correspondence, 3 September 1970, in Green, *Writings of the Vienna Actionists*, 117; orig. pub. by Günter Brus, *Die Schastrommel*, no. 3.

38. Green in *Writings of the Vienna Actionists*, 119.

39. Various articles in *Oznews*, International Film Festival Supplement OZ30, October 1970, reproduced in Green, *Writings of the Vienna Actionists*, 120.

40. Cecilia Novero, "Painful Painting and Brutal Ecstasy: The Material Actions of Günter Brus and Otto Muehl," *Seminar—A Journal of Germanic Studies* 43, no. 4 (2007): 460.

41. Ibid., 466, citing Herbert Marcuse, *Eros and Civilization* (1955) (Boston: Beacon Hill Press, 1966), 49–52.

42. Muehl correspondence in Green, *Writings of the Vienna Actionists*, 117.

43. Muehl, "Catastrophe Measurement," in Green, *Writings of the Vienna Actionists*, 123; orig. pub. by Brus, *Die Drossel*, no. 13 (1975).

44. Beth Hinderliter, "Citizen Brus Examines His Body: Actionism and Activism in Vienna, 1968," *October* 147 (2014): 86. Hinderliter groups Muehl's action with those of Günter Brus, the central focus of her analysis, and distinguishes them from Nitsch.

45. Hermann Nitsch, "O.M. Theatre Manifesto," *Die Blutorgel* (Vienna: Self-published, 1962), unpaginated; in Green, *Writings of the Vienna Actionists*, 132–34.

46. Susan Jarosi, "Traumatic Memory and the Continuum of History: Hermann Nitsch's Orgies Mysteries Theater," *Art History* 36, no. 4 (2013): 852, doi:10.1111/1467-8365.12001. I thank Aaron Kelly for bringing this article to my attention.

47. Ibid., 835, citing Nitsch, "Programm zum 6-Tage-Spiel," http://www.nitsch.org/ien/6tage_e.htm#materialien; no longer available.

48. Ibid., 850, 858.

49. Ibid., 854.

50. "Hermann Nitsch—6 Tage Spiel—Das Orgien Mysterien Theater. Day 3: Day of Dionysus (Excerpt)," 1998; video on *YouTube*, 18 Jul 2015, https://youtu.be/xDQLO-9QYgtI; no longer available.

51. Jarosi, "Traumatic Memory," 858.

52. Ibid., 856.

53. Ibid., 841.

54. Giorgio Agamben, *Homo Sacer: Sovereign Power and Bare Life*, trans. Daniel Heller-Roazen (Stanford, : Stanford University Press, 1998), 104–11. For discussion of animals classified as pets and thus not eaten, see Cary Wolfe, "Before the Law: Animals in a Biopolitical Context," *Law, Culture and the Humanities* 6, no. 1 (2010): 8–23, doi:10.1177/1743872109348986; Ron Broglio, "After Animality, before the Law: Interview with Cary Wolfe," *Angelaki* 18, no. 1 (2013): 181–89, doi:10.1080/096972 5X.2013.783438; Nicole Shukin, *Animal Capital: Rendering Life in Biopolitical Times* (Minneapolis: University of Minnesota Press, 2009).

55. Jarosi, "Traumatic Memory," 851.

56. Romeo Castellucci, "The Animal Being on Stage," *Performance Research* 5, no. 2 (2000): 24, doi:10.1080/13528165.2000.10871727. For an exegesis of this assertion based on Marx and Engels's *The German Ideology*, see Ridout, *Stage Fright*, 110–19.

57. Suzana Marjanić, "The Zoostage as Another Ethical Misfiring: The Spectacle of the Animal Victim in the Name of Art," *Performance Research* 15, no. 2 (2010): 74, doi :10.1080/13528165.2010.490434, emphasis added. Marjanić discusses animal death in Croatian theater and performance art, 1995–2007.

58. Martin Puchner, "Performing the Open: Actors, Animals, Philosophers," *TDR* 51, no.1 (2007): 28, http://www.jstor.org/stable/4492733. Puchner offers a useful explanation of Agamben's *Homo Sacer* supplemented by *The Open* (2004) and *The State of Exception* (2005).

59. Daniel Birnbaum, "Mice and Man: The Art of Carsten Höller and Rosemarie Trockel," *Artforum* 39, no. 6 (2001): 114.

60. Giovanni Aloi, "In Conversation with Carsten Höller," *Antennae*, no. 12 (2010): 15, http://www.antennae.org.uk/back-issues/4583697895

61. Birnbaum, "Mice and Man," 115.

62. Ibid. Another work staged in 1997, *Addina*, reversed the arrangement: human visitors could smell and hear the egg-laying chickens but could not see them, whereas the chickens could look down through one-way glass upon people eating their eggs.

63. Aloi, "In Conversation with Carsten Höller," 16.

64. Ibid., 15. Apart from one piglet "sacrificed" for the breeder's birthday dinner, the porcine participants all went to breeding programs after Documenta, and the previously rare breed became quite popular as a result of images in the tabloid press (16).

65. Birnbaum, "Mice and Man," 114.

66. Christine Ross, *The Aesthetics of Disengagement: Contemporary Art and Depression* (Minneapolis: University of Minnesota Press, 2006), 172.

67. Jean Baudrillard, *Impossible Exchange*, trans. Chris Turner (London: Verso, 2001), 107.

68. Rozin, Haidt, and McCauley, "Disgust," in Dalgleish and Power, *Handbook of Cognition and Emotion*, 434.

69. William Ian Miller, *The Anatomy of Disgust* (Cambridge: Harvard University Press, 1997), 204; also see Rozin, Haidt, and McCauley, "Disgust," in Lewis, Haviland-Jones, and Barrett, *Handbook of Emotions*, 766.

70. Jennifer Parker-Starbuck, "Chasing Its Tail: Sensorial Circulations of *One Pig*," *Antennae*, no. 27 (2013): 110.

71. Susan Guettel Cole, *Landscapes, Gender, and Ritual Space: The Ancient Greek Experience* (Berkeley: University of California Press, 2004), 140.

72. Mark Essig, *Lesser Beasts: A Snout-to-Tail History of the Humble Pig* (New York: Basic Books, 2015), 60; for a summary of evidence, see 43–60.

73. Marvin Harris, "The Abominable Pig," in *Food and Culture: A Reader*, ed. Carole Counihan and Penny Van Esterik (New York: Routledge, 2013), 70, 72.

74. Peter Stallybrass and Allon White, *The Politics and Poetics of Transgression* (Ithaca: Cornell University Press, 1986), 45.

75. Brett Mizelle, *Pig* (London: Reaktion Books, 2011), 16, quoting Lyall Watson, *The Whole Hog: Exploring the Extraordinary Potential of Pigs* (Washington, DC: Smithsonian Books, 2004), 99, 92.

76. Anton Ervynck, An Lentacker, Gundula Müldner, Mike Richards, and Keith Dobney, "An Investigation into the Transition from Forest Dwelling Pigs to Farm Animals in Medieval Flanders, Belgium," in *Pigs and Humans: 10,000 Years of Interaction*, ed. Umberto Albarella, Keith Dobney, Anton Ervynck, and Peter Rowley-Conwy (Oxford: Oxford University Press, 2007), 171–73.

77. Sarah Phillips, "The Pig in Medieval Iconography," in *Pigs and Humans*, 384–87.

78. Stallybrass and White, *Politics and Poetics of Transgression*, 44–59.

79. Mizelle, *Pig*, 167.

80. See, e.g., Monica Mattfeld, "'Genus Porcus Sophisticus': The Learned Pig and the Theatrics of National Identity in Late Eighteenth-Century London," in *Performing Animality*, ed. Orozco and Parker-Starbuck, 57–76.

81. Kira O'Reilly, "Pigginess Fantasies" (interview), *Hybrid Reflections*, 26 April 2017, http://www.ibmc.up.pt/hybrid/content.php?menu=6&submenu=43

82. Commissioned by HOME, London, for the *One to One Salon* series (2005); subsequent performances include *Tract*, Newlyn Art Gallery/Art Surgery, Penzance, 2006.

83. "*Inthewrongplaceness* archive," *Tract Live Art*, 18 August 2006, no longer available; some portions reproduced in *Antennae*, no. 12 (2010): 87.

84. Kira O'Reilly, "Marsyas—Beside Myself," *sk-interfaces*, ed. Jens Hauser (Liverpool: Liverpool University Press, 2008), 101.

85. Gianna Bouchard, "Skin Deep: Female Flesh in UK Live Art since 1999," *Contemporary Theatre Review* 22, no. 1 (2012): 102 n43, doi:10.1080/10486801.2011.645230. For the continuity from O'Reilly's earlier work with archaic medical procedures such as leeching and wet cupping to the pig performances, see 101–5.

86. Giovanni Aloi, *Art and Animals* (London: I. B. Tauris, 2012), 18.

87. Jennifer Parker-Starbuck, "Pig Bodies and Vegetative States: Diagnosing the Symptoms of a Culture of Excess," *Women & Performance* 18, no. 2 (2008): 143–46, doi:10.1080/07407700802107044. This article, my first acquaintance with the performance, connects pig bodies in art to Terri Schiavo's body in a persistent vegetative state, kept alive by her parents for fifteen years. Interestingly enough, Schiavo entered that state as the result of bulimia; that is, a surfeit of vomiting rather than incorporating what she ate, which one might consider a fatal disgust with the world.

88. Ibid., 139. Parker-Starbuck's inquiry into art that explores the similarities between pigs and people includes, more recently, a discussion of Doo Sung Yoo's "Robotic Pig Heart Jellyfish" in "Animals Dissenting: Re-directing the Anthropocene," paper presented to the Animals Perform working group of the American Society for Theatre Research, 2015.

89. Korsmeyer, *Savoring Disgust*, 105.

90. See Jenny Saville, "Torso 2," *Saatchi Gallery*, accessed 25 April 2017, http://www.saatchi-gallery.co.uk/imgs/artists/saville_jenny/20091202035412_jenny_saville_torso.jpg

91. O'Reilly, *Marsyas*, 101.

92. Miru Kim, "The Pig That Therefore I Am," *Miru Kim*, accessed 25 April 2017, series of twenty-five photos and artist's statement at http://www.mirukim.com

93. Jacques Derrida, "The Animal That Therefore I am (More to Follow)," trans. David Wills, *Critical Inquiry* 28, no. 2 (2002): 384, 390.

94. Carsten Höller and Rosemarie Trockel, "Introduction," *Antennae*, no. 12 (2010): 6–7; orig. publ. in *A House for Pigs and People* (Cologne: W. König, 1997).

95. Kim, "The Pig That Therefore I Am."

96. Ibid.

97. Joy Dietrich, "High on the Hog: Miru Kim's 'The Pig That Therefore I Am,'" *New York Times Style Magazine*, 22 March 2011.

98. Elizabeth Cherry, "'The Pig That Therefore I Am': Visual Art and Animal Activism," *Humanity & Society* 40, no. 1 (2016): 67, doi:10.1177/0160597615586620.

99. Korsmeyer, *Savouring Disgust*, 37.

100. Marina Galperina, "10 Controversial Works of Art Using Live Animals," *Flavorwire*, 18 April 2012, http://flavorwire.com/279255/art-with-live-animals; Galperina and Diana Frame, "Is Miru Kim's Nude Pig Performance Too Weird for Art Basel?," *ANIMALNewYork*, 3 December 2011, http://animalnewyork.com/2011/is-miru-kims-nude-pig-performance-too-weird-for-art-basel/

101. Rozin, Haidt, and McCauley, "Disgust," in Lewis, Haviland-Jones, and Barrett, *Handbook of Emotions*, 761; also see Paul Rozin and April E. Fallon, "A Perspective on Disgust," *Psychological Review* 94, no. 1 (1987): 23–41.

102. Rosemary Deller, "The Animated Aesthetics of Cultured Steak," in *Corporeality and Culture: Bodies in Movement*, ed. Karin Sellberg, Lena Wånggren, and Kamillea Aghtan (Farnham, Surrey: Ashgate, 2015), 72–79.

103. Paul Rae, "Xeno-," *Contemporary Theatre Review* 23, no. 1 (2013): 86 n8, doi:10.1080/10486801.2013.765129.

104. Johanna Linsley, "Kira O'Reilly Playing in the Lab," *Contemporary Theatre Review* 25, no. 4 (2015): 518, doi:10.1080/10486801.2015.1078323.

105. Ngai, *Our Aesthetic Categories*, 112.

106. Snæbjörnsdottír/Wilson, "Falling Asleep with a Pig" (interview), *Antennae*, no. 13 (2010): 43.

107. Silvan Tomkins, with the editorial assistance of Bertram P. Karon, *Affect, Imagery, Consciousness*, complete edition (vol. 1: *The Positive Affects*, 1962) (New York: Springer, 2008), 191.

108. Ngai, *Our Aesthetic Categories*, 134.

109. Ibid., 132.

110. Ibid., 114–15.

111. See Nigel Rothfels, "Immersed with Animals," in *Representing Animals*, ed. Rothfels (Bloomington: Indiana University Press, 2002), 199–223.

112. John Berger, "Why Look at Animals?" in *About Looking* (New York: Pantheon, 1980), 5, 28.

113. Haraway, *When Species Meet*, 3.

114. Ibid., 16–17, 32. I've added the hyphen between becoming and with to demarcate this as a particular meaning of the combination.

115. Ibid., 226.

116. Agamben, *Open*, 83.

117. Rosi Braidotti, *Transpositions: On Nomadic Ethics* (Cambridge: Polity Press, 2006), 37.

118. Haraway, *When Species Meet*, 34.

119. Holly Hughes, "The Dog and Pony Act (Bring Your Own Pony)," with commentary by Donna Haraway, "Agility Is Performance Art," in *Animal Acts: Performing Species Today*, ed. Una Chaudhuri and Holly Hughes (Ann Arbor: University of Michigan Press, 2014), 13–35.

120. Ann Carlson, *Animals*, New York: Dance Theatre Workshop, 13 February 1988; video documentation of this full performance and other versions of individual pieces available from the Performing Arts Research Collection of the NYPL. Also see Jon Erickson, "*Animals* by Ann Carlson (Review)," *Theatre Journal* 43, no. 1 (1991): 116–18, http://www.jstor.org/stable/3207956

121. Janice Ross, "The Solo That Isn't a Solo: Ann Carlson's Dances with Animals," in *On Stage Alone: Soloists and the Modern Dance Canon*, ed. Claudia Gitelman and Barbara Palfy (Gainesville: University Press of Florida, 2012), 60, citing Dance Theatre Workshop documentary, February 2002.

122. Ibid., 57, quoting interview by Irene Borger, in *Force of Curiosity* (Los Angeles: California Institute of the Arts, 1999), 61.

123. *Madame 710* by Ann Carlson and Mary Ellen Strom, *Vimeo*, 2010, https://vimeo.com/18611308

124. "Ann Carlson & Mary-Ellen Strom," *DeAnnaPellechia.com*, 2009, http://www.deannapellecchia.com/pastprojects/anncarlson.html

125. "About: The Equus Projects," *The Equus Projects + Onsite NYC*, accessed 25 April 2017, http://www.equus-onsite.org/#!about_us/cjg9

126. "About: The Long Bio," *Paula Josa-Jones Performance Works*, accessed 25 April 2017, http://www.paulajosajones.org/about/pjj_the_long_bio.html

127. Paula Josa-Jones, *Ride*, 2002, Paula Josa Jones Performance Works, DVD, including interviews as well as performance documentation. This is my primary source of information about *Ride*.

128. Kim Marra, "Riding, Scarring, Knowing: A Queerly Embodied Performance Historiography," *Theatre Journal* 64, no. 4 (2012): 491, http://muse.jhu.edu/journals/tj/

summary/v064/64.4.marra.html. Also see Marra, "Horseback Views: A Queer Hippological Performance," with commentary by Jane C. Desmond, "Kinesthetic Intimacy," in Chaudhuri and Hughes, *Animal Acts*, 111–40.

129. For a multispecies ethnography based on more than sixty interviews with riders, see Anita Maurstad, Dona Davis, and Sarah Cowles, "Co-Being and Intra-Action in Horse-Human Relationships: A Multi-Species Ethnography of Be(com)ing Human and Be(com)ing Horse," *Social Anthropology* 21, no. 3 (2013): 322–35, doi:10.1111/1469-8676.12029.

130. See Karen Barad, "Posthumanist Performativity: Toward an Understanding of How Matter Comes to Matter," *Signs* 28, no. 3 (2003): 801–31.

131. Paula Josa-Jones, "Common Body: The Dancer, the Horse," *Contact Quarterly* 36, no. 1 (2011): 14.

132. Ibid., 15–16. Escorial also has the nickname Pony.

133. Ibid., 17–18.

134. Carol Dine, comment on *Ride*, accessed 25 April 2017, http://paulajosajones.org/the_horse_dances/ride.html

135. Paula Josa-Jones, *Ride*, 2014, https://vimeo.com/93314269, with duet at 2:04–2:35. This compilation is taken from the forty-seven-minute documentary available at the NYPL Performing Arts Research Collection and also on DVD from http://www.paulajosajones.org

136. Press kit available from http://www.paulajosajones.org

137. Telephone interview with Paula Josa-Jones, 22 January 2016, source for all quotations about *All the Pretty Horses*. Bartabas, the renowned European director of equestrian theater, also tends to work with discarded or difficult horses; see David Williams, "The Right Horse, the Animal Eye—Bartabas and Théâtre Zingaro," *Performance Research* 5, no. 2 (2000): 36–37, doi:10.1080/13528165.2000.10871728.

138. For video documentation, see Paula Josa-Jones, *All the Pretty Horses*, 6 October 2012, https://vimeo.com/52434754. Also see the video compilation of stills, primarily beautiful close-up shots of these horses, sometimes embraced by a dancer or showing her in motion and touching the horse, at https://vimeo.com/45542819. They are quite moving—more so than the performance video, in fact, drawing the viewer into relation with the horse in a manner quite similar to Miru Kim's close-up photos of her body right up against a pig.

139. For exemplary discussions of this point, see Ridout, *Stage Fright*, 100–110; Lourdes Orozco, *Theatre and Animals* (New York: Palgrave Macmillan, 2013), 67–68; Michael Peterson, "The Animal Apparatus: From a Theory of Animal Acting to an Ethics of Animal Acts," *TDR* 51, no. 1 (2007): 33–48, esp. 34–35.

140. Nicholas Gane, "When We Have Never Been Human, What Is to Be Done? Interview with Donna Haraway," *Theory, Culture & Society* 23, nos. 7–8 (2006): 144, doi:10.1177/0263276406069228.

141. Carlson choreographed an early sketch during residencies at Alfred University

and UC Riverside in 2015. See *Doggie Hamlet, excerpts,* by Ann Carlson, March 2017, https://vimeo.com/208547446; "2016 Lab Artist: Ann Carlson," *VPL,* 2017, http://www.vermontperformancelab.org/current-artists/85-ann-carlson

142. Gia Kourlas, "But Is It Art? In the Case of 'Doggie Hamlet,' Yes," *New York Times,* 7 April 2017, AR11. The oblique connection to *Hamlet* came from the structure of this novel, David Wroblewski's *The Story of Edgar Sawtelle.*

143. Elizabeth Harrington, "Taxpayers Foot Bill for 'Doggie Hamlet,'" *Washington Free Beacon,* 20 December 2016, http://freebeacon.com/politics/taxpayers-foot-bill-doggie-hamlet/

144. Gia Kourlas, "But Is It Art? In the Case of 'Doggie Hamlet,' Yes," *New York Times,* 7 April 2017, AR11.

## Chapter 5

1. John Donvan and Caren Zucker, "Autism's First Child," *Atlantic,* October 2010, http://www.theatlantic.com/magazine/archive/2010/10/autisms-first-child/3082 27/. For more about Triplett, see Donvan and Zucker, *In a Different Key,* 3–69, 534–46. Also see Lindsay Borthwick, "Life Lessons," *Nature,* 1 November 2012, S10–11.

2. Kanner, "Autistic Disturbances of Affective Contact," 219.

3. Stuart Murray, *Autism* (New York: Routledge, 2012), 52–53.

4. Donvan and Zucker, *In a Different Key,* 67–68.

5. Donvan and Zucker, "Autism's First Child."

6. Personal interview with Christopher Knowles, 17 February 2016. On calendar calculation, see Darold A. Treffert, *Extraordinary People: Understanding "Idiot Savants"* (New York: Harper and Row, 1989), 36–54; Michael J. A. Howe, *Fragments of Genius: The Strange Feats of Idiots Savants* (London: Routledge, 1989), 93–133.

7. Hilton Als and Anthony Elms, "Christopher Knowles: *In a Word* Gallery Guide," *Institute of Contemporary Art,* University of Pennsylvania, 16 September–27 December 2015, http://icaphila.org/exhibitions/7472/christopher-knowles-in-a-word

8. Nadesan, *Constructing Autism,* 9, emphasis in original.

9. For a brief and accessible summary recent findings related to research on the genetics of autism spectrum disorders, see Martin Raff, "Open Questions: What Has Genetics Told Us about Autism Spectrum Disorders?," *BMC Biology* 12, no. 45 (2014): http://www.biomedcentral.com/1741–7007/12/45

10. Laurence Shyer, *Robert Wilson and His Collaborators* (New York: Theatre Communications Group, 1989), 72.

11. Based upon the tape of a 1991 lecture at a gallery in Santa Fe, as seen in Seth Goldstein and Paul Kaiser, "Interview with Christopher Knowles," 15 September 1992, New York, courtesy of the NYPL TOFT Archive. Also see the report of a 2013 lecture, Lian Chikako Chang, "Live Blog—Robert Wilson, Sensory Media Platform," *Harvard*

*GSD M.Arch.l*, 18 October 2013, http://archinect.com/lian/live-blog-robert-wilson-sensory-media-platform

12. Quoted in Katharina Otto-Bernstein, *Absolute Wilson: The Biography* (Munich: Prestel, 2006), 123.

13. Bill Simmer, "Robert Wilson and Therapy," *TDR* 20, no. 1 (1976): 103, 100, http://www.jstor.org/stable/1145044

14. Quoted in the introduction to *A Letter for Queen Victoria* in *The Theatre of Images*, ed. Bonnie Marranca (New York: Drama Book Specialists, 1977), 48. References to the script as printed in this volume will be included parenthetically in the body of the text.

15. Quoted in Shyer, *Robert Wilson*, 79–80.

16. The script refers to a "break drop painted as a dam," which would connect with references to "Sequachee dam" in acts 2 and 4 (59). Stefan Brecht says this was planned but not actualized. *The Theatre of Visions: Robert Wilson* (Frankfurt: Suhrkamp Verlag, 1978), 292.

17. Descriptions unless otherwise attributed refer to *A Letter for Queen Victoria: An Opera in Four Acts*, written and directed by Robert Wilson, music by Alan Lloyd, videorecorded in performance during the Festival d'Automne à Paris, at the Théatre des Variétés, 16 December 1974, NYPL TOFT Archive.

18. Arendell, *Autistic Stage*, 12.

19. Brecht, *Theatre of Visions*, 289.

20. Quoted in the introduction to *A Letter for Queen Victoria*, 48.

21. Mrs. Edward Knowles, letter to Peter Moran, director of the Institute for Neurological Organization of the Philadelphia Institute for Achievement of Human Potential, 1 November 1964; Christopher Knowles Collection; MSS 414; box 6; folder 40; Fales Library and Special Collections, New York University Libraries. Also see Alan M. Aron, MD, director of Child Neurology at the Mount Sinai Hospital, letter, 23 February 1978; Barbara Knowles, letter to Dr. Yale Fisher, 1 May 1990.

22. Handwritten parent's "Progress Report," April 1962; ibid. Visual analysis five years later indicates good acuity for near vision but an inability to measure distance vision "due to lack of fixation at greater than 5 feet," a right eye that turns in and up, "aware of simultaneous perception using red-green lights," but "when using finer materials there is a right eye suppression." Harold N. Friedman, O.D., director of Perceptual Training at Adams School in Brooklyn, letter to Arthur Sandler at the Institute for Human Potential in Philadelphia, 25 December 1967; Knowles Collection 6:40.

23. Otto-Bernstein, *Absolute Wilson*, 39.

24. Quoted in ibid., 20–21. This diagnosis was not available at the time.

25. Ibid., 22.

26. Ibid., 26.

27. Peter Moran, R.P.T., Institute for Neurological Organization, letter to Charles Weymuller, M.D., 14 April 1965, Knowles Collection 6:40.

28. Reports of functional neurological status between July 1965 and September 1970, signed by Evan Thomas, M.D. (initial report); Peter Moran, R.P.T (2–4); Charles Burhns (5); Arthur Sandler, R.P.T. (6–11, with name change to Institute for Learning Disability); and Leland Green, M.D. (13; #12 not present), Knowles Collection 6:41.

29. American Psychiatric Association, *DSM History*, 2017, https://www.psychiatry. org/psychiatrists/practice/dsm/history-of-the-dsm. DSM-I adopted the list of disorders from the sixth edition of the World Health Organization's *International Classification of Diseases*, the first to include mental disorders. DSM-II differed little from the first edition.

30. Eyal, et al., *Autism Matrix*, 18–19. Emphasis added.

31. Otto-Bernstein, *Absolute Wilson*, 29; Hilton Als, "Slow Man: Robert Wilson and His First Masterpiece," *New Yorker* 88, no. 28, 17 September 2012, 78–83.

32. Otto-Bernstein, *Absolute Wilson*, 46–47.

33. Interview with C. Knowles; telephone interview with Barbara Knowles, 29 April 2016; Knowles Collection 6:42.

34. Many accounts credit Wilson with liberating him from either past or impending institutionalization. One of the most egregious says that he had been "institutionalized as brain-damaged for 11 of his 13 years." Cynthia Haven, "Avant-garde Director Robert Wilson: 'What We See Can Be as Important as What We Hear,'" *Stanford Report*, 8 October 2008, http://news.stanford.edu/news/2008/october8/wilsontwo-100808.html

35. "The Closing of Willowbrook," *Disability Justice*, 2017, http://disabilityjustice. org/the-closing-of-willowbrook/

36. A lawsuit that settled for $2.25 million in 2015 alleged that aides at the school starved, beat, and gagged a twenty-two-year-old man whose movements they restricted to a small gym mat. He died of malnutrition and pneumonia in 2011. In 2007, thirteen-year-old Jonathan Carey was crushed to death by an aide who was restraining him in the back of a van, and his family received a $5-million settlement. Anemona Hartecollis, "Settlement in Suit Saying Disabled Man Was Beaten," *New York Times*, 16 April 2015, A22. Chris told me that he does not recall mistreatment but didn't like being away from home.

37. Eyal, et al., *Autism Matrix*, 3–4. For normalization generally, see 111–26.

38. Ibid., 167–72.

39. Ibid., 115. As the result of lobbying by the National Association for Retarded Children, Congress in 1970 officially recognized "developmentally disabled" as a category of handicap requiring "habilitation" rather than cure—unlike a disease, a disability is understood to be chronic.

40. Nadesan, *Constructing Autism*, 9.

41. Amanda Baggs, "In My Language," *YouTube*, 14 January 2007, https://youtu.be/JnylM1hI2jc

42. Amanda Baggs, "Cultural Commentary: Up in the Clouds and Down in the Valley: My Richness and Yours," *Disability Studies Quarterly* 30, no. 1 (2010): par. 3, http://dsq-sds.org/article/view/1052/238

43. Mukhopadhyay, *How Can I Talk if My Lips Don't Move?*, 27–8.

44. Mel Y. Chen, *Animacies: Biopolitics, Racial Mattering, and Queer Affect* (Durham: Duke University Press, 2012), 213. On expanded agency and sociality, also see Wolfe, *What Is Posthumanism?*, 141.

45. Allan M. Kriegsman, "Mad Man Mad Dog Mad Art," *Washington Post*, 31 May 1974, B6 (in Knowles Collection 3:5).

46. Marranca, *Theatre of Images*, 43, emphasis added.

47. Arthur Holmberg, *The Theatre of Robert Wilson* (Cambridge: Cambridge University Press, 1996), 46.

48. *DiaLog-Network* by Christopher Knowles and Robert Wilson, videorecorded at the Mickery Theater Amsterdam, June 1978, NYPL TOFT Archive. Also see *DiaLog/ Curious George*, videorecorded at the Rotterdamse Schouwburg, Rotterdam, during the Holland Festival, 4 June 1980, NYPL TOFT Archive.

49. Christopher Knowles, "Popular Songs A" (1984), audiotape with introductory essay and interview by Lauren DiGiulio, *Lateral Edition* 27, 14 February 2016, http:// www.lateraladdition.org/

50. *Absolute Wilson*, New Yorker Video, 2007, DVD.

51. Philip Fisher, *Wonder, the Rainbow, and the Aesthetics of Rare Experiences* (Cambridge: Harvard University Press, 1998), 11.

52. Ibid., 21.

53. Ibid., 22.

54. Hans-Thies Lehmann, *Postdramatic Theatre*, trans. Karen Jürs-Munby (London: Routledge, 2006), 78–79, emphasis in original. Also see 148 on Wilson's audio landscapes, 156–57 on his "durational aesthetic" and the "aesthetics of repetition" in postdramatic theater more generally.

55. Ibid., 79–80, emphasis in original.

56. Brecht wrote the letter, mimicking the style of actual nineteenth-century letters but destroying their sense. *Theatre of Visions*, 288–89.

57. Brecht, *Theatre of Visions*, 299.

58. John Gruen, "Is It a Play? An Opera? No, It's a Wilson," *New York Times*, 16 March 1975, X1.

59. They met while working on *Queen Victoria* and lived and worked together from 1975 (when he was fifteen) through the early 1980s. Their performances include *This is the One* (1976), *Emily Likes the TV* (1976), and *The Network Play* (1977) in New York, Portland, Seattle, and Toronto. Reviewing the benefit performance *Everyday Business* (1978), Wendy Perron said that "the best part was the way Knowles said the word 'bullshit'—BOOL-SHIT—which he had to say about 50 times." Wendy Perron, "Reading for Fun and Art's Profit," *Soho Weekly News*, 23 February 1978, 22. This was a benefit at Paula Cooper Gallery for the 112 Workshop; see https://whitecolumns.org/archive

60. Interview with Frank Hentschker, 25 March 2016.

61. Interview with C. Knowles; "Christopher Knowles Bio," *Gavin Brown's Enterprise*,

2017, https://www.gavinbrown.biz/artists/christopher_knowles/works. I first saw *The Sundance Kid is Beautiful* at White Box as part of PERFORMA13, 24 November 2013, but my discussion largely relies upon video of the performance 11 November 2015, courtesy Institute of Contemporary Art Philadelphia. Some rehearsal footage from the Segal Center performance is available on *Vimeo*, https://vimeo.com/74430596. Also see Lauren DiGiulio, "'The Sundance Kid is Beautiful with Christopher Knowles' at the University of Rochester," *InVisible Culture*, 22 December 2015, https://ivc.lib.roches-ter.edu/the-sundance-kid-is-beautiful-with-christopher-knowles-at-the-university-of-rochester/

62. Skype interview with Lauren DiGiulio, 30 March 2016.

63. Ibid.

64. For related discussions of outsider art, see Roger Cardinal, "Outsider Art and the Autistic Creator," *Philosophical Transactions: Biological Sciences* 364, no. 1522 (2009): 1459–66, http://www.jstor.org/stable/40485920; David Davies, "On the Very Idea of 'Outsider Art,'" *British Journal of Aesthetics* 49, no. 1 (2009): 25–41, doi:10.1093/aesthj/ayn056; Amanda Cachia, "From Outsider to Participant: Developmentally Disabled Dialogue in Socially Engaged Art," *Museums and Social Issues* 9, no. 2 (2014): 109–23, doi:10.1179/1559689314Z.00000000022.

65. As quoted by Valerie Alhart, "Visual Artist Christopher Knowles to Give Solo Performance," University of Rochester, 16 October 2015, http://www.rochester.edu/newscenter/visual-artist-christopher-knowles-to-give-solo-performance-at-university-of-rochester/

66. As quoted by David Ehrenstein, "The Key to Robert Wilson," *Advocate*, 27 January 2007, http://www.advocate.com/politics/commentary/2007/01/29/key-robert-wilson

67. Mukhopadhyay, *How Can I Talk if My Lips Don't Move?*, 215–16.

68. *Krapp's Last Tape* by Samuel Beckett, directed and performed by Robert Wilson, Peak Performances at Montclair State University, 20 March 2016.

69. Tomkins, *Affect, Imagery, Consciousness*, 352.

70. Ahmed, *Cultural Politics of Emotion*, 104–5.

71. Tomkins, *Affect, Imagery, Consciousness*, 353–54.

72. Ibid., 185–86. Barbara L. Fredrickson and Michael A. Cohn discusses the preponderance of research on negative emotions and argue for the value of studying the positive ones. "Positive Emotions," in Lewis, Haviland-Jones, and Barrett, *Handbook of Emotions*, 778.

73. Arendell, *Autistic Stage*, 4.

74. Some scientific studies following a theory of mind paradigm conclude that he does not; see, e.g., Erin A. Heerey, Dacher Keltner, and Lisa M. Capps, "Making Sense of Self-Conscious Emotion: Linking Theory of Mind and Emotion in Children with Autism," *Emotion* 3, no. 4 (2003): 394–400, doi:10.1037/1528–3542.3.4.394; Tiziana Zallaa, et al., "Feelings of Regret and Disappointment in Adults with High-Functioning

Autism," *Cortex* 58 (2014): 112–22, doi:10.1016/j.cortex.2014.05.008. For a first-person account that contradicts this position, see John Elder Robison, *Look Me in the Eye: My Life with Asperger's* (New York: Crown Publishers, 2007).

75. Tobin Siebers, "Sex, Shame, and Disability Identity: With Reference to Mark O'Brien," in *Gay Shame*, ed. David M. Halperin and Valerie Traub (Chicago: University of Chicago Press, 2009), 202–4. For an analysis of performances that explore the ways in which "particular disabled bodies both feel and prompt feelings of shame, esteem, awkwardness, and desire," including a concise summary of Siebers's related argument in *Disability Theory*, see Kirsty Johnston, "Whose Awkward Moments? Affect, Disability, and Sex in *The Book of Judith, Time to Put My Socks On,* and *the Glass Box,*" in *Theatres of Affect*, ed. Erin Hurley (Toronto: Playwrights Canada Press, 2014), 154–70.

76. Michael Lewis, "Self-Conscious Emotions: Embarrassment, Pride, Shame, and Guilt," in Lewis, Haviland-Jones, and Barrett, *Handbook of Emotions*, 742–56.

77. Ridout, *Stage Fright*, 70–95, especially 90–91. Ridout analyzes Agamben's discussion of this incident in *Remnants of Auschwitz: The Witness and the Archive*, trans. Daniel Heller-Roazen (New York: Zone Books, 1999), 103; Agamben takes the incident from Robert Antelme's 1947 memoir, *The Human Race* (Evanston: Northwestern University Press, 1998), 231–32. Also see Robin Bernstein, "Toward the Integration of Theatre History and Affect Studies: Shame and the Rude Mechs's *The Method Gun,*" *Theatre Journal* 64, no. 2 (2012): 213–30, doi:10.1353/tj.2012.0037.

78. Michael Warner, "Pleasures and Dangers of Shame," in Halperin and Traub, *Gay Shame*, 290.

79. Eve Kosofsky Sedgwick, "Shame, Theatricality, and Queer Performativity: Henry James's *The Art of the Novel,*" in Halperin and Traub, *Gay Shame*, 50, citing Michael Franz Basch, "The Concept of Affect: A Re-Examination," *Journal of the American Psychoanalytic Association* 24 (1975): 765–66.

80. Douglas Crimp, *"Our Kind of Movie": The Films of Andy Warhol* (Cambridge: MIT Press, 2012), 34. I thank Lauren DiGiulio for mentioning this text in connection with *Sundance Kid*.

81. Theater HORA of Zürich commissioned the French choreographer Jérôme Bel to collaborate with them on this work, and he gave the actors six tasks to perform. This chapter does not discuss *Disabled Theatre* in detail because none of the originating ensemble identify as autistic, although some autistic performers have stepped in as the piece continues in their repertoire. Theater HORA typically employs a neurotypical director who shapes and manages work by intellectually disabled actors. In 2014, they began working on a new piece with no director at all, and then autist Remo Zarantanello took on that role. Company director Michael Elber functioned as an assistant to the performers on this project. Yvonne Schmidt, "After *Disabled Theater*: Authorship, Creative Responsibility, and Autonomy in *Freie Republik HORA,*" in *Disabled Theater*, ed. Sandra Umathum and Benjamin Wihstutz (Zürich-Berlin: diaphanes, 2015), 227–28. For discussion of related issues, see essays by Gerald Siegmund, Scott Wallin, and

Benjamin Wihstutz in the same volume; also see Petra Kuppers, "Outsider Histories, Insider Artists, Cross-Cultural Ensembles: Visiting with Disability Presences in Contemporary Art Environments," *TDR* 58, no. 2 (2014): 35.

82. *Ganesh Versus the Third Reich*, devised by Mark Deans, Marcia Ferguson, Bruce Gladwin, Nicki Holland, Simon Laherty, Sarah Mainwaring, Scott Price, Kate Sulan, Brian Tilley, and David Woods, in *"We're People Who Do Shows": Back to Back Theatre*, ed. Helena Grehan and Peter Eckersall (Aberystwyth, Wales: Performance Research Books, 2013), 192. Further page references parenthetical. Performance descriptions refer to a DVD performance recording generously provided by the company.

83. Cas Anderson, Peter Eckersall, Robin Gador, Bruce Gladwin, Helena Grehan, Noel Hart, Barry Kay, and Ian Pidd, "In Conversation," in Grehan and Eckersall, *Back to Back Theatre*, 30–33.

84. Peter Eckersall and Helena Grehan, "The Existential Antagonists: Back to Back, Dramaturgy, and Spectatorship," in Grehan and Eckersall, *Back to Back Theatre*, 15.

85. Kuppers, "Outsider Histories, Insider Artists," 36.

86. Lalita McHenry, "Is There a Gene Responsible for Our Obsession with Perfection?," in Grehan and Eckersall, *Back to Back Theatre*, 46, quoting Back to Back's website, 2008; this statement no longer features on the site but recurs in descriptions.

87. Alice Nash, statement in Grehan and Eckersall, *Back to Back Theatre*, 27.

88. Analyzing the poster iconography, Kuppers notes the link to Joseph Merrick, the so-called elephant man. "Outsider Histories, Insider Artists," 37.

89. See Bruce Gladwin in Conversation with Richard Gough, "Making Room for Elephants," in Grehan and Eckersall, *Back to Back Theatre*, 245 (for Tilley's "incredible knowledge" and the company's "obsession" with popular culture), 255 (for the scene from *Von Ryan's Express*).

90. Ibid., 250; Anderson, et al., "In Conversation," 39–40.

91. Gabriella Coslovich, "The Elephant in the Room," *Age*, 24 September 2011, 20. Also see Gladwin and Gough, "Making Room," 246; Yoni Prior, "'Scott's Aired a Couple of Things': Back to Back Theatre Rehearse *Ganesh Versus the Third Reich*," in Grehan and Eckersall, *Back to Back Theatre*, 211.

92. For financial arrangements, see Gladwin and Gough, "Making Room," 248.

93. Ibid., 247.

94. Prior, "'Scott's Aired a Couple of Things,'" 211.

95. For the connection to freak shows, see Anna Teresa Scheer, "The Impossible Fairytale, or Resistance to the Real," in Grehan and Eckersall, *Back to Back Theatre*, 223.

96. Helena Grehan, "Irony, Parody and Satire in *Ganesh Versus the Third Reich*," in Grehan and Eckersall, *Back to Back Theatre*, 205.

97. Eckersall and Grehan, "The Existential Antagonists," in Grehan and Eckersall, *Back to Back Theatre*, 17–18.

98. Kuppers, "Outsider Histories, Insider Artists," 39.

99. *small metal objects*, devised by Bruce Gladwin, Simon Laherty, Genevieve Morris, Jim Russell, and Sona Teuben, in Grehan and Eckersall, *Back to Back Theatre*, 66.

100. Bree Hadley, *Disability, Public Space Performance and Spectatorship: Unconscious Performers* (Houndmills, Basingstoke, Hampshire: Palgrave Macmillan, 2014), 2.

101. For an angry dissent directed against the purveyors of the theory of mind paradigm and foregrounding its denial of embodiment, see Yergeau, "Clinically Significant Disturbance."

102. Kuppers, "Outsider Histories, Insider Artists," 49.

103. Ibid.

104. Ibid., 35.

105. Ibid., 49.

106. Kubiak, "Cave Mentem," 122.

107. James I. Charlton, *Nothing about Us without Us: Disability Oppression and Empowerment* (Berkeley: University of California Press, 1998), 3.

108. Justin Kaiser, "Inclusivity and *The Curious Incident of the Dog in the Night-Time*," *Howlround*, 24 September 2015, http://howlround.com/inclusivity-and-the-curious-incident-of-the-dog-in-the-night-time

109. emmapretzl, "Achieving Better Autistic Representation on Stage," *Chavisory's Notebook*, 13 October 2015, https://chavisory.wordpress.com/2015/10/13/achieving-better-autistic-representation-on-stage/

110. See Stiofán MacAmhalghaidh Âû, "Casting a Non-Autistic Christopher in *The Curious Incident of the Dog in the Night-Time* on Broadway," *Howlround*, 4 April 2015, http://howlround.com/casting-a-non-autistic-christopher-in-the-curious-incident-of-the-dog-in-the-night-time-on-broadway#sthash.e1dHqHcD.dpuf. Mickey Rowe responded to a comment from user miamifella; see https://mickeyrowe.me

111. Mickey Rowe, "Our Differences Are Our Strengths: Neurodiversity in Theatre," *Howlround*, 2 May 2015, http://howlround.com/our-differences-are-our-strengths-neurodiversity-in-theatre#sthash.afg8bPFe.dpuf. For a related perspective, see the blog of actor/college student Daniel Au Valencia, *Acting NT*, accessed 20 April 2017, http://actingnt.blogspot.com/2014/04/introduction.html

112. Priscilla Frank, "Finally, An Actor with Autism Is Starring in 'Curious Incident,'" *Huffington Post*, 10 May 2017, http://www.huffingtonpost.com/entry/mickey-rowe-autism_us_59130afde4b050bdca6112d7?ncid=APPLENEWS00001

113. Donvan and Zucker, *In a Different Key*, 497. Plank had a small onscreen role in one episode. He had already performed in *West Side Story* at his high school and "found that he loved this sort of structured collaboration, as well as the spotlight" (502). He made a documentary, *autism reality*, available on YouTube, and a series of videos, *Autism Talk TV*, available on *Wrong Planet* and also on the *Autism Speaks* site (504–5). Plank's website identifies him as a filmmaker and lists extensive speaking engagements: accessed 20 April 2017, http://www.alexplank.com

114. Nick Clark, "We Need Autistic Actors Playing Autistic Roles on Stage, Says *Curious Incident* Adviser," *Independent*, 13 August 1015, http://www.independent.co.uk/arts-entertainment/theatre-dance/news/we-need-autistic-actors-playing-autistic-roles-on-stage-says-curious-incident-adviser-10454728.html

115. "I Am Glad There's a Name for My Condition: In the Past We Would Have Been Called Freaks," *Daily Mail*, 27 April 2010, 42. The organization began in 1976 with the name Rainbow Drama Group, becoming Access All Areas in 2009. Gareth Edwards, "Interlude: *Eye Queue Hear*," in *Applied Theatre Aesthetics*, ed. Edwards (London: Bloomsbury Methuen, 2015), 263 n1.

116. Binchy began to develop the piece while doing a 2014 tour with the Access All Areas participatory audio walk *Eye Queue Hear* (2013). "Cian Binchy—A Younger Theatre," *Access All Areas*, 27 July 2015, http://www.accessallareastheatre.org/news/2015/7/27/cian-binchy-a-younger-theatre-1. I thank Alex Covell for making video documentation of the Edinburgh performance available to me. For more on *Eye Queue Hear*, see the promotional video on YouTube, https://youtu.be/6wRop65bstE; Edwards, "Interlude." Binchy was not a member of the ensemble that initially devised that work.

117. Miranda Bryant, "Performer Hopes Show Will Send a Message on Autism," *Evening Standard*, 6 January 2016, 22.

118. See "What's On," *Access All Areas*, April 2017, http://www.accessallareastheatre.org/whats-on/; *Autism Arts Festival*, April 2017, https://autismartsfestival.org

119. *Graeae Theatre Company*, accessed 20 April 2017, http://www.graeae.org/about-us/

120. The company previously operated under the auspices of Autism SA, whose visual and performing arts programs ran in close relationship with Minda, a support organization for people with intellectual disabilities. John Williams, "President Report," 6, and Dorothy O'Brien, "Disability and Quality Manager Report," 7, in "Annual Report 2014," *Tutti Arts*, accessed 20 April 2017, http://tutti.org.au/about/annual-report/

121. "History, Choir and Performing Arts," *Tutti Arts*, accessed 20 April 2017, http://tutti.org.au/about/history-choir-performing-arts/

122. Julian Jaensch and the Company AT Performance Ensemble, *History of Autism*, 2015 Come Out Festival Version, typescript.

123. "Tectonic Theater Project Presents *Uncommon Sense*," *University of Northern Iowa*, 2017, https://uncommon-sense.uni.edu. Actor Andrew Duff, part of the project throughout its development, earlier created a solo performance about his experience as an autist who benefited from early intervention. Andrew Duff, "Actor on the Spectrum Brings Awareness to the Stage," *Uncommon Sense Blog*, 6 December 2016, https://uncommon-sense.uni.edu/blog; with embedded video of 2012 solo performance, "Where Are We Now?" December 2012, https://youtu.be/6Kyp7l5hJaQ. Duff was diagnosed early, participated in Applied Behavior Analysis, graduated from Bennington College, and now works in media production for Autism Speaks. The organization's website, https://www.autismspeaks.org/, has an extensive list of interviews with Duff; e.g., "Fox

5 Interview with Autism Speaks' Andrew Duff," *YouTube*, 23 February 2016, https://youtu.be/W7f7ENwri_A

124. "About: People," *Back to Back Theatre*, 2014–17, http://backtobacktheatre.com/about/people/

125. As I mentioned in chapter 1, Tomkins includes shame-humiliation on his list of categorical affects. He does not list pride but, rather, defines shame in relation to interest. Ekman likewise identifies shame as a basic emotion. He does list pride, but with a qualifier: pride in achievement. Their schemata, then, construe pride as a more complicated phenomenon eliciting a variety of affects/emotions.

126. Elspeth Probyn, *Blush: Faces of Shame* (Minneapolis: University of Minnesota Press, 2005), 14. Probyn cautions that substituting pride for shame "can suffocate other attempts to come up with new politics" (176 n23). Warner summarizes the contention around pairing gay pride/queer shame, the crux being that the pride movement depoliticizes the queer community ("Pleasures and Dangers of Shame," 287).

## Chapter 6

1. Steve Baker, "What Does Becoming-Animal Look Like?," in *Representing Animals*, ed. Nigel Rothfels (Bloomington: Indiana University Press, 2002), 68, citing Deleuze and Guattari, *Kafka: Toward a Minor Literature*, trans. Dana Polan (Minneapolis: University of Minnesota Press, 1986), 7, 13, originally published as *Kafka: Pour une littérature mineure* (Paris: Les éditions de Minuit, 1975); Deleuze and Guattari, *Thousand Plateaus*, 253.

2. Deleuze and Guattari, *Thousand Plateaus*, 234.

3. Christopher M. Moreman, "On the Relationship between Birds and Spirits of the Dead," *Society & Animals* 22 (2014): 483, doi:10.1163/15685306–12341328.

4. Dana Levin, "Augur," *Gulf Coast* 12, no. 1 (2008): 222–24.

5. Claude Lévi-Strauss, "The Logic of Totemic Classifications," in *The Savage Mind* (Chicago: University of Chicago Press, 1966), 35–74.

6. Deleuze and Guattari, *Thousand Plateaus*, 237.

7. Helen MacDonald, *H Is for Hawk* (New York: Grove Press, 2014), 193.

8. Ibid., 195.

9. Deleuze and Guattari, *Thousand Plateaus*, 274.

10. Ibid., 10.

11. Ibid.

12. Ibid., 8.

13. Ibid., 238–39.

14. Ibid., 270. Also see Cull, *Theatres of Immanence*, 6–7, 25–26, 69.

15. Muehl, correspondence 3 September 1970, in Green, *Writings of the Vienna Actionists*, 117.

16. Deleuze and Guattari, *Thousand Plateaus*, 233.

17. Baker, "What Does Becoming-Animal Look Like?," 85. He draws examples primarily from visual art, although he briefly discusses Joseph Beuys's performance with a coyote (whom he did not come to resemble in any very direct manner).

18. Cull, *Theatres of Immanence*, 124, emphasis in original.

19. Cull, "Affect in Deleuze, Hijikata, and Coates," 194–95.

20. Deleuze and Guattari, *Thousand Plateaus*, 239.

21. Ibid., 240.

22. Ibid., 242.

23. Parker-Starbuck, "Chasing Its Tail."

24. In addition to sources cited directly, see Petra Kuppers, *Disability Culture and Community Performance: Find a Strange and Twisted Shape* (Houndmills, Basingstoke, Hampshire: Palgrave Macmillan, 2011); Derek P. McCormack, *Refrains for Moving Bodies: Experience and Experiment in Affective Spaces* (Durham: Duke University Press, 2014).

25. Holmberg, *Theatre of Robert Wilson*, 175–76.

26. Lehman, *Postdramatic Theatre*, 148.

27. Robert Wilson, interview with Stefan Brecht, 1970, quoted in Holmberg, *Theatre of Visions*, 29.

28. Paula Josa-Jones, "Stepping into the Void," *Ride Dance Write*, 23 October 2013, http://www.paulajosajones.org/RideDanceWrite/2013/10/23/stepping-into-the-void/. Prior to the work with horses, she "directed a company of dancers in theatrical work for over 13 years" (e-mail communication, 20 July 2016).

29. Janet Adler, *Offering from the Conscious Body: The Discipline of Authentic Movement* (Rochester: Inner Traditions, 2002), xii.

30. "Mission Statement: Across Boundaries, Across Abilities," *Deep Listening Institute*, accessed 23 April 2017, http://deeplistening.org/site/content/about

31. Josa-Jones, "Stepping into the Void."

32. Josa-Jones, "The Receptive Body," *Ride Dance Write*, 13 October 2014, http://www.paulajosajones.org/RideDanceWrite/2014/10/13/the-receptive-body/

33. Paula Josa-Jones, "Of This Body," *Paula Josa-Jones Performance Works*, accessed 27 April 2017, http://www.paulajosajones.org/pdfs/OF%20THIS%20BODY.pdf

34. Marcia Siegel, "Paula Josa-Jones—Shape Shifter," *Arts Fuse*, 7 June 2016, http://artsfuse.org/146242/fuse-dance-review-paula-josa-jones-shape-shifter/

35. Josa-Jones, "Of This Body."

36. Telephone interview with Paula Josa-Jones, 22 January 2016.

37. Josa-Jones, e-mail communication, 20 July 2016. This approach is common not only to Body-Mind Centering but to various forms of yoga. See "About BMC," *Body-Mind Centering: An Embodied Approach to Movement, Body, and Consciousness*, 2001–17, http://www.bodymindcentering.com/about; Josa-Jones, "The Receptive Body." Many yoga practices integrate principles and practices from Body-Mind Centering, such

as moving from the organs. For the effects of yoga on internal organs, see Ann Pizer, "Yoga Anatomy Myth Busting with Amy Matthews" (Interview), *VeryWell*, 16 March 2017, https://www.verywell.com/yoga-anatomy-myths-with-amy-matthews-3566694

38. *Mammal* by Paula Josa-Jones, Booking Dance Festival, Allen Room, Jazz at Lincoln Center, New York, 17 January 2016.

39. Interview with Josa-Jones.

40. Marcia Siegel, "Paula Josa-Jones—Shape Shifter," *Arts Fuse*, 7 June 2016.

41. *Speak* by Paula-Josa Jones, five-minute version for Booking Dance Festival, 2013, https://vimeo.com/59702496

42. *Speak* by Paula-Josa Jones, full version, 2014, https://vimeo.com/99582135

43. Paula Josa-Jones, "The Solos: Of This Body," *Paula Josa-Jones Performance Works*, accessed 27 April 2017, http://paulajosajones.org/the_human_dances/the_solos.html.

44. Josa-Jones, e-mail communication, 20 July 2016. Josa-Jones also mentions the sort of mirroring that Phoebe Caldwell and Jane Horwood recommend; see *From Isolation to Intimacy: Making Friends without Words* (London: Jessica Kingsley Publishers, 2007).

45. Interview with Josa-Jones.

46. Marcia Siegel, "Paula Josa-Jones—Shape Shifter," *Arts Fuse*, 7 June 2016.

47. Josa-Jones, e-mail communication, 20 July 2016.

48. Cull, *Theatres of Immanence*, 93–94.

49. Nancy Galeota-Wozny, "Following Jennifer Following the Birds," *Contact Quarterly* 29 (2005): 16.

50. Ibid.

51. Artist's statement, "About Bird Brain," *Bird Brain Dance: A Navigational Dance Project by Jennifer Monson*, 2013, http://www.birdbraindance.org. Unless otherwise indicated, information and descriptions related to *Bird Brain* refer to this website.

52. Galeota-Wozny, "Following," 23. Monson describes the exercises at 22–23.

53. Julia Handschuh, "'On Finding Ways of Being': Kinesthetic Empathy in Dance and Ecology," in *Performance on Behalf of the Environment*, ed. Richard D. Besel and Jnan A. Blau (Lanham, MD: Lexington Books, 2011), 149–50.

54. Ibid., 149.

55. Nigel Stewart, "Dancing the Face of Place: Environmental Dance and Eco-Phenomenology," *Performance Research* 15, no. 4 (2010): 36, doi:10.1080/13528165.20 10.539877.

56. Handschuh, "On Finding Ways of Being," 148.

57. "Spatial Awareness Exercises with Hawk Mountain Educators (2)," *Live Dancing Archive*, cf94042510_0068, 22 September 2002, https://vimeo.com/49699387

58. Robin Vachal, "Jennifer Solo—Cape Code," *Vimeo*, 30 August 2002, https://vimeo.com/32323733

59. Rehearsal Diary, 31 August 2002, Boardwalk Beach, Sandwich, MA, http://www.birdbraindance.org/projects.cfm?id=3&sel=4

60. Galeota-Wozny, "Following," 21.

61. Rosi Braidotti, *Metamorphoses: Towards a Materialist Theory of Becoming* (Cambridge: Polity Press, 2002), 12.

62. Deleuze and Guattari, *Thousand Plateaus*, 8.

63. "Spatial Awareness Exercises."

64. "Day of Dancing at the Beach—Long Form Improvisation," *Live Dancing Archive*, cf94042510_0068, 28 September 2002, https://vimeo.com/49919805. For the first portion of this day's work including warm up and Authentic Movement, see cf94042510_0073, with video at https://vimeo.com/49699727

65. "About the Archive," *Live Dancing Archive*, 2013, http://www.livedancingarchive. org/providence/pawtucket/index.php/About/Index

66. "Performance Archiving Performance," *New Museum Exhibitions*, 6 November 2013–12 January 2014, http://www.newmuseum.org/exhibitions/view/performance-archiving-performance

67. "Compilation of Solos," *Live Dancing Archive* cf94042510_0074, 29 September 2002, https://vimeo.com/49699729

68. "Jennifer Monson: Live Dancing Archive," *YouTube*, performance and interview with Zachary Whittenberg recorded at Chicago Humanities Festival, 7 November 2013, http://www.youtube.com/watch?v=QiYDJgCTwnQ. She explained to the audience that the *Live Dancing Archive* has three additional sections not performed at the Chicago Humanities Festival: wearing a wig and lipstick, she sings Antony and the Jonsons' "Bird Gerhl"; wearing a dress, she performs her version of an early expressive modern dance reminiscent of Mary Wigman; and naked, she sweeps coffee-cup lids across the floor.

69. "LDAJuly19," 1 Liberty Plaza, New York, 19 July 2014, https://vimeo. com/101813004. The performance culminated a residency sponsored by the Lower Manhattan Cultural Council.

70. "Live Dancing Archive Volume II," New York Live Arts, 15–18 October 2014, video by Ryutaro Mishima at https://vimeo.com/121317141

71. Antony and the Johnsons, "Bird Gerhl," 2005.

72. Susan Leigh Foster, *Choreographing Empathy: Kinesthesia in Performance* (London: Routledge, 2011), 178.

73. See, e.g., Jennifer Parker-Starbuck, *Cyborg Theatre: Corporeal/Technological Intersections in Multimedia Performance* (Houndmills, Basingstoke, Hampshire: Palgrave Macmillan, 2011).

74. Henri Lefebvre, *The Production of Space* (1974), trans. Donald Nicholson-Smith (Malden, MA: Blackwell, 1991), 26.

75. Ibid., 36, emphasis in original.

76. Ibid., 33, 47–48.

77. Ibid., 51.

78. See http://www.ilandart.org

79. "New Hope for Ridgewood Reservoir," *iLAND*, 9 September 2014, http://www.ilandart.org/new-hope-for-ridgewood-reservoir/

80. Manning, *Always More Than One*, 124–32; Arendell, *Autistic Stage*, 27–47.

81. Siebers, *Disability Theory*, 29.

82. Stanton B. Garner, Jr., "In Search of Merrick: Kinesthetic Empathy, Able-Bodiedness, and Disability Representation," *Journal of Dramatic Theory and Criticism* 29, no. 2 (2015): 90. Also see Wanda Strukus, "Miming the Gap: Physically Integrated Performance and Kinesthetic Empathy," *Journal of Dramatic Theory and Criticism* 25, no. 2 (Spring 2011): 103.

83. Garner Jr., "In Search of Merrick," 91.

84. DJ Savarese, "Cultural Commentary: Communicate with Me," *Disability Studies Quarterly* 30, no. 1 (2010); http://dsq-sds.org/article/view/1051/1237; see discussion in Manning, *Always More Than One*, 163.

85. Peterson, "Animal Apparatus," 45.

86. Mitchell and Snyder, *Narrative Prosthesis*, 49–50.

87. Ibid., 50.

88. Timothy Murray, "Like a Prosthesis: Critical Performance à Digital Deleuze," in *Deleuze and Performance*, ed. Laura Cull (Edinburgh: Edinburgh University Press, 2009), 218–19.

89. Braidotti, *Transpositions*, 37–38.

90. Ibid., 267.

91. Agamben, *Open*, 37.

92. Ibid.

93. Ibid., 14–16.

# Bibliography

Agamben, Giorgio. *Homo Sacer: Sovereign Power and Bare Life.* Translated by Daniel Heller-Roazen. Stanford: Stanford University Press, 1998.

Agamben, Giorgio. *The Open: Man and Animal.* Translated by Kevin Attell. Stanford: Stanford University Press, 2004.

Ahmed, Sara. *The Cultural Politics of Emotion.* New York: Routledge, 2004.

Ahmed, Sara. "Happy Objects." In *The Affect Theory Reader,* edited by Melissa Gregg and Gregory J. Seigworth, 29–51. Durham: Duke University Press, 2010.

Ahmed, Sara. *The Promise of Happiness.* Durham: Duke University Press, 2010.

Aloi, Giovanni. *Art and Animals.* London: I.B. Tauris, 2012.

Aloi, Giovanni. "Ein Haus—A House for Pigs and People." *Antennae,* no. 12 (2010): 9–13.

Aloi, Giovanni. "In Conversation with Carsten Höller." *Antennae,* no. 12 (2010): 14–17.

Althusser, Louis. "Ideology and Ideological State Apparatuses (Notes toward an Investigation)." 1970. Translated by Ben Brewster. In *Lenin and Philosophy and Other Essays,* 85-126. New York: Monthly Review Press, 2001.

Arendell, Telory Davies. *The Autistic Stage: How Cognitive Disability Changed 20th-Century Performance.* Rotterdam: Sense Publishers, 2015.

Baggs, Amanda. "Cultural Commentary: Up in the Clouds and Down in the Valley: My Richness and Yours." *Disability Studies Quarterly* 30, no. 1 (2010): http://dsq-sds.org/article/view/1052/238#top

Bailes, Sara Jane. *Performance Theatre and the Poetics of Failure: Forced Entertainment, Goat Island, Elevator Repair Service.* London: Routledge, 2011.

Baker, Steve. "What Does Becoming-Animal Look Like?" In *Representing Animals,* edited by Nigel Rothfels. Bloomington: Indiana University Press, 2002.

Barad, Karen. "Posthumanist Performativity: Toward an Understanding of How Matter Comes to Matter." *Signs* 28, no. 3 (2003): 801–31.

Baron-Cohen, Simon. *The Essential Difference: The Truth about the Male and Female Brain.* New York: Basic Books, 2003.

Baron-Cohen, Simon. *Mindblindness: An Essay on Autism and Theory of Mind*. Cambridge: MIT Press, 1995.

Batson, C. Daniel. "These Things Called Empathy: Eight Related but Distinct Phenomena." In *The Social Neuroscience of Empathy*, edited by Jean Decety and William John Ickes, 3–15. Cambridge: MIT Press, 2009.

Baudrillard, Jean. *Impossible Exchange*. Translated by Chris Turner. London: Verso, 2001.

Benzaquén, Adriana S. *Encounters with Wild Children: Temptation and Disappointment in the Study of Human Nature*. Montreal: McGill-Queen's University Press, 2006.

Ben-Zvi, Linda. "'Playing the Cloud Circuit': Albee's Vaudeville Show." In *Cambridge Companion to Edward Albee*, edited by Stephen Bottoms, 178–98. Cambridge: Cambridge University Press, 2005.

Berger, James. "Alterity and Autism: Mark Haddon's *Curious Incident* in the Neurological Spectrum." In *Autism and Representation*, edited by Mark Osteen, 271–88. New York: Routledge, 2008.

Berger, John. "Why Look at Animals?" 1977. In *About Looking*, 3–28. New York: Pantheon, 1980.

Berlant, Lauren. *Cruel Optimism*. Durham: Duke University Press, 2011.

Bernstein, Robin. "Toward the Integration of Theatre History and Affect Studies: Shame and the Rude Mechs's *The Method Gun*." *Theatre Journal* 64, no. 2 (2012): 213–30.

Best, Susan. *Visualizing Feeling*. New York: I. B. Tauris, 2011.

Birnbaum, Daniel. "Mice and Man: The Art of Carsten Höller and Rosemarie Trockel." *Artforum* 39, no. 6 (2001): 114–19.

Bogdashina, Olga. *Communication Issues in Autism and Asperger Syndrome: Do We Speak the Same Language?* London: Jessica Kingsley Publishers, 2005.

Bottoms, Stephen J. *The Theatre of Sam Shepard: States of Crisis*. Cambridge: Cambridge University Press, 1998.

Bouchard, Gianna. "Skin Deep: Female Flesh in UK Live Art since 1999." *Contemporary Theatre Review* 22, no. 1 (2012): 94–105.

Brady, Emily. *The Sublime in Modern Philosophy*. Cambridge: Cambridge University Press, 2013.

Braidotti, Rosi. *Metamorphoses: Towards a Materialist Theory of Becoming*. Cambridge: Polity Press, 2002.

Braidotti, Rosi. *Transpositions: On Nomadic Ethics*. Cambridge: Polity Press, 2006.

Brecht, Stefan. *The Theatre of Visions: Robert Wilson*. Frankfurt: Suhrkamp Verlag, 1978.

Brennan, Teresa. *The Transmission of Affect*. Ithaca: Cornell University Press, 2004.

Broglio, Ron. "After Animality, before the Law: Interview with Cary Wolfe." *Angelaki* 18, no. 1 (2013): 181–89.

Brown, Wendy. "Neoliberalism and the End of Liberal Democracy." In *Edgework: Critical Essays on Knowledge and Politics*, 37–59. Princeton: Princeton University Press, 2009.

Burks-Abbott, Gyasi. "Mark Haddon's Popularity and Other Curious Incidents in My

Life as an Autistic." In *Autism and Representation*, edited by Mark Osteen, 289–96. New York: Routledge, 2008.

Butler, Judith. "Performative Acts and Gender Constitution." In *Performing Feminisms*, edited by Sue-Ellen Case, 270–82. Baltimore: Johns Hopkins University Press, 1990.

Cachia, Amanda. "From Outsider to Participant: Developmentally Disabled Dialogue in Socially Engaged Art." *Museums and Social Issues* 9, no. 2 (2014): 109–23.

Cardinal, Roger. "Outsider Art and the Autistic Creator." *Philosophical Transactions: Biological Sciences* 364, no. 1522 (2009): 1459–66.

Carlson, Marla. "Furry Cartography: Performing Species." *Theatre Journal* 63, no. 2 (2011): 191–208.

Castellucci, Romeo. "The Animal Being on Stage." *Performance Research* 5, no. 2 (2000): 23–28.

Chaput, Catherine. "Rhetorical Circulation in Late Capitalism: Neoliberalism and the Overdetermination of Affective Energy." *Philosophy and Rhetoric* 43, no. 1 (2010): 1–25.

Charlton, James I. *Nothing about Us without Us: Disability Oppression and Empowerment.* Berkeley: University of California Press, 1998.

Chaudhuri, Una. "(De)Facing the Animals: Zooësis and Performance." *TDR* 51, no. 1 (2007): 8–20.

Chaudhuri, Una. "The Spectator in Drama/Drama in the Spectator: Peter Shaffer's *Equus*." In *Contemporary British Drama, 1970–90: Essays from Modern Drama*, edited by Hersh Zeifman and Cynthia Zimmerman, 41–61. Houndmills, Hampshire: Macmillan, 1993; orig. pub. in *Modern Drama* 27 (1984): 281–98.

Chaudhuri, Una, and Holly Hughes, eds. *Animal Acts: Performing Species Today*. Ann Arbor: University of Michigan Press, 2014.

Chen, Mel Y. *Animacies: Biopolitics, Racial Mattering, and Queer Affect*. Durham: Duke University Press, 2012.

Cherry, Elizabeth. "'The Pig That Therefore I Am': Visual Art and Animal Activism." *Humanity & Society* 40, no. 1 (2016): 64–85.

Clough, Patricia Ticineto. "The Affective Turn: Political Economy, Biomedia, and Bodies." In *The Affect Theory Reader*, edited by Melissa Gregg and Gregory J. Seigworth, 206–25. Durham: Duke University Press, 2010.

Cole, Susan Guettel. *Landscapes, Gender, and Ritual Space: The Ancient Greek Experience*. Berkeley: University of California Press, 2004.

Coyle, Rebecca, and Jon Fitzgerald. "Disney Does Broadway: Musical Storytelling in *The Little Mermaid* and *The Lion King*." In *Drawn to Sound: Animation Film Music and Sonicity*, edited by Rebecca Coyle, 223–48. London: Equinox, 2010.

Crimp, Douglas. *"Our Kind of Movie": The Films of Andy Warhol*. Cambridge: MIT Press, 2012.

Crossman, Georgina K., and Rita Walsh. "The Changing Role of the Horse: From Beast of Burden to Partner in Sport and Recreation." *International Journal of Sport and Society* 2, no. 2 (2011): 95–110.

Cull, Laura. "Affect in Deleuze, Hijikata, and Coates: The Politics of Becoming-Animal in Performance." *Journal of Dramatic Theory and Criticism* 26, no. 2 (2012): 189–203.

Cull, Laura. "From *Homo Performans* to Interspecies Collaboration." In *Performing Animality: Animals in Performance Practices*, edited by Lourdes Orozco and Jennifer Parker-Starbuck, 19–36. Houndmills, Basingstoke, Hampshire: Palgrave Macmillan, 2015.

Cull, Laura. *Theatres of Immanence: Deleuze and the Ethics of Performance.* Houndmills, Basingstoke, Hampshire: Palgrave Macmillan, 2012.

Curtis, Valerie. *Don't Look, Don't Touch, Don't Eat: The Science behind Revulsion.* Chicago: University of Chicago Press, 2013.

Davies, David. "On the Very Idea of 'Outsider Art.'" *British Journal of Aesthetics* 49, no. 1 (2009): 25–41.

Deleuze, Gilles, and Félix Guattari. *A Thousand Plateaus: Capitalism and Schizophrenia.* Translated by Brian Massumi. Minneapolis: University of Minnesota Press, 1987.

Deller, Rosemary. "The Animated Aesthetics of Cultured Steak." In *Corporeality and Culture: Bodies in Movement*, edited by Karin Sellberg, Lena Wånggren, and Kamillea Aghtan, 67–79. Farnham, Surrey: Ashgate, 2015.

Derrida, Jacques. "The Animal That Therefore I Am (More to Follow)." *Critical Inquiry* 28, no. 2 (2002): 369–418.

Donvan, John, and Caren Zucker. "Autism's First Child." *Atlantic*, October 2010.

Donvan, John, and Caren Zucker. *In a Different Key: The Story of Autism.* New York: Crown Publishers, 2016.

Duffy, John, and Rebecca Dorner. "The Pathos of 'Mindblindness': Autism, Science, and Sadness in 'Theory of Mind' Narratives." *Journal of Literary & Cultural Disability Studies* 5, no. 2 (2011): 201–15.

Ekman, Paul. "Basic Emotions." In *Handbook of Cognition and Emotion*, edited by Tim Dalgleish and Michael J. Power, 45–60. Chichester: Wiley, NetLibrary, 1999.

Ekman, Paul. "Facial Expressions." In *Handbook of Cognition and Emotion*, edited by Tim Dalgleish and Michael J. Power, 301–20. Chichester: Wiley, NetLibrary, 1999.

Erickson, Jon. "*Animals by Ann Carlson* (Review)." *Theatre Journal* 43, no. 1 (1991): 116–18.

Ervynck, Anton, An Lentacker, Gundula Müldner, Mike Richards, and Keith Dobney. "An Investigation into the Transition from Forest Dwelling Pigs to Farm Animals in Medieval Flanders, Belgium." In *Pigs and Humans: 10,000 Years of Interaction*, edited by Umberto Albarella, Keith Dobney, Anton Ervynck, and Peter Rowley-Conwy, 171–93. Oxford: Oxford University Press, 2007.

Essig, Mark. *Lesser Beasts: A Snout-to-Tail History of the Humble Pig.* New York: Basic Books, 2015.

Eyal, Gil, Brendan Hart, Emine Onculer, Neta Oren, and Natasha Rossi. *The Autism Matrix: The Social Origins of the Autism Epidemic.* Cambridge: Polity Press, 2010.

Filewod, Alan. "Theatrical Capitalism, Imagined Theatres and the Reclaimed Authenticities of the Spectacular." In *Crucible of Cultures: Anglophone Drama at the Dawn of a New Millennium*, edited by Marc Maufort and Franca Bellarsi, 219–30. Brussels: Peter Lang, 2002.

Fisher, Philip. *Wonder, the Rainbow, and the Aesthetics of Rare Experiences*. Cambridge: Harvard University Press, 1998.

Foster, Susan Leigh. *Choreographing Empathy: Kinesthesia in Performance*. London: Routledge, 2011.

Fredrickson, Barbara L., and Michael A. Cohn. "Positive Emotions." In *Handbook of Emotions*, edited by Michael Lewis, Jeannette M. Haviland-Jones, and Lisa Feldman Barrett, 777–96. New York: Guilford Press, 2008.

Frith, Uta, and Francesca Happé. "Theory of Mind and Self-Consciousness: What Is It Like to Be Autistic?" *Mind and Language* 14, no. 1 (1999): 1–22.

Fudge, Erica. "Intelligence and Instinct: Questions of Power." In *Animal*, 112–58. London: Reaktion, 2002.

Gainor, J. Ellen. "Albee's *the Goat*: Rethinking Tragedy for the 21st Century." In *Cambridge Companion to Edward Albee*, edited by Stephen Bottoms, 199–216. Cambridge: Cambridge University Press, 2005.

Galeota-Wozny, Nancy. "Following Jennifer Following the Birds." *Contact Quarterly* 29 (2005): 12–24.

Gane, Nicholas. "When We Have Never Been Human, What Is to Be Done? Interview with Donna Haraway." *Theory, Culture & Society* 23, nos. 7–8 (2006): 135–58.

Garland-Thomson, Rosemarie. *Extraordinary Bodies: Figuring Physical Disability in American Culture and Literature*. New York: Columbia University Press, 1997.

Garner, Stanton B., Jr. "In Search of Merrick: Kinesthetic Empathy, Able-Bodiedness, and Disability Representation." *Journal of Dramatic Theory and Criticism* 29, no. 2 (2015): 81–103.

Garner, Stanton B., Jr. "Sensing Realism: Illusionism, Actuality, and the Theatrical Sensorium." In *The Senses in Performance*, edited by Sally Banes and André Lepecki, 115–22. New York: Routledge, 2007.

Gibbs, Anna. "After Affect: Sympathy, Synchrony, and Mimetic Communication." In *The Affect Theory Reader*, edited by Melissa Gregg and Gregory J. Seigworth, 186–205. Durham: Duke University Press, 2010.

Giroux, Henry A., and Grace Pollock. *The Mouse That Roared: Disney and the End of Innocence*. Updated and expanded ed. Lanham, MD: Rowman and Littlefield, 2010.

Goldie, Peter. *The Emotions: A Philosophical Exploration*. Oxford: Clarendon Press, 2000.

Grandin, Temple. *Thinking in Pictures: And Other Reports from My Life with Autism*. New York: Doubleday, 1995.

Grandin, Temple, and Catherine Johnson. *Animals in Translation: Using the Mysteries of Autism to Decode Animal Behavior*. New York: Scribner, 2005.

Green, Malcolm, in collaboration with the artists. *Brus, Muehl, Nitsch, Schwarzkogler: Writings of the Vienna Actionists*. edited and translated by Green. London: Atlas Press, 1999.

Grehan, Helena, and Peter Eckersall, eds. *"We're People Who Do Shows": Back to Back Theatre*. Aberystwyth, Wales: Performance Research Books, 2013.

Grinker, Roy Richard. *Unstrange Minds*. New York: Basic Books, 2007.

Grosz, Elizabeth. *Volatile Bodies: Toward a Corporeal Feminism*. Bloomington: Indiana University Press, 1994.

Hacking, Ian. "Autism Fiction: A Mirror of an Internet Decade?" *University of Toronto Quarterly* 79, no. 2 (2010): 632–55.

Hacking, Ian. *Mad Travelers: Reflections on the Reality of Transient Mental Illnesses*. Charlottesville: University Press of Virginia, 1998.

Hacking, Ian. *The Social Construction of What?* Cambridge: Harvard University Press, 1999.

Hadley, Bree. *Disability, Public Space Performance and Spectatorship: Unconscious Performers*. Houndmills, Basingstoke, Hampshire: Palgrave Macmillan, 2014.

Handschuh, Julia. "'On Finding Ways of Being': Kinesthetic Empathy in Dance and Ecology." In *Performance on Behalf of the Environment*, edited by Richard D. Besel and Jnan A. Blau, 147–74. Lanham, MD: Lexington Books, 2011.

Haraway, Donna. *When Species Meet*. Minneapolis: University of Minnesota Press, 2008.

Harris, Marvin. "The Abominable Pig." In *Food and Culture: A Reader*, edited by Carole Counihan and Penny Van Esterik, 67–79. New York: Routledge, 2013.

Hayles, N. Katherine. "The Cognitive Nonconscious: Enlarging the Mind of the Humanities." *Critical Inquiry* 42, no. 4 (2016): 783–808.

Heerey, Erin A., Dacher Keltner, and Lisa M. Capps. "Making Sense of Self-Conscious Emotion: Linking Theory of Mind and Emotion in Children with Autism." *Emotion* 3, no. 4 (2003): 394–400.

Hinderliter, Beth. "Citizen Brus Examines His Body: Actionism and Activism in Vienna, 1968." *October* 147 (2014): 78–94.

Höller, Carsten, and Rosemarie Trockel. "Introduction." *Antennae*, no. 12 (2010): 6–7; orig. publ. in *A House for Pigs and People*. Cologne: W. König, 1997.

Holmberg, Arthur. *The Theatre of Robert Wilson*. Cambridge: Cambridge University Press, 1996.

Howe, Michael J. A. *Fragments of Genius: The Strange Feats of Idiots Savants*. London: Routledge, 1989.

Hurley, Erin, and Sara Warner. "Special Section: 'Affect/Performance/Politics.'" *Journal of Dramatic Theory and Criticism* 26, no. 2 (2012): 99–107.

Jack, Jordynn. *Autism and Gender: From Refrigerator Mothers to Computer Geeks*. Champaign: University of Illinois Press, 2014.

Jarosi, Susan. "Traumatic Memory and the Continuum of History: Hermann Nitsch's Orgies Mysteries Theater." *Art History* 36, no. 4 (2013): 834–83.

Johnston, Kirsty. "Whose Awkward Moments? Affect, Disability, and Sex in *The Book of Judith*, *Time to Put My Socks On*, and *The Glass Box*." In *Theatres of Affect*, edited by Erin Hurley, 154–70. Toronto: Playwrights Canada Press, 2014.

Josa-Jones, Paula. "Common Body: The Dancer, the Horse." *Contact Quarterly* 36, no. 1 (2011): 13–19.

Kanner, Leo. "Autistic Disturbances of Affective Contact." *Nervous Child* 2 (1943): 217–50.

Kelleher, Joe. "Sentimental Education at the National Theatre." *PAJ: A Journal of Performance and Art* 27, no. 3 (2005): 45–54.

Keltner, Dacher, and John Haidt. "Approaching Awe, a Moral, Spiritual, and Aesthetic Emotion." *Cognition and Emotion* 17, no. 2 (2003): 297–314.

Kleb, William E. "*Curse of the Starving Class* and the Logic of Destruction." *Contemporary Theatre Review* 8, no. 4 (1998): 1–17.

Kolnai, Aurel. *On Disgust.* 1929. Edited by Barry Smith and Carolyn Korsmeyer. Chicago: Open Court, 2004.

Korsmeyer, Carolyn. *Savoring Disgust: The Foul and the Fair in Aesthetics.* New York: Oxford University Press, 2011.

Kubiak, Anthony. "Animism: Becoming-Performance, or Does This Text Speak to You?" *Performance Research* 17, no. 4 (2012): 52–60.

Kubiak, Anthony. "Cave Mentem: Disease and the Performance of Mind." *TDR* 59, no. 2 (2015): 114–28.

Kubiak, Anthony. "The Sacred Clade and the Rhizomatic Dis-Ease of History." *Modern Language Quarterly* 70, no. 1 (2009): 43–66.

Kuhn, John. "Getting Albee's Goat: 'Notes toward a Definition of Tragedy.'" *American Drama* 13, no. 2 (2004): 1–32.

Kuppers, Petra. *Disability and Contemporary Performance: Bodies on the Edge.* London: Routledge, 2003.

Kuppers, Petra. *Disability Culture and Community Performance: Find a Strange and Twisted Shape.* Houndmills, Basingstoke, Hampshire: Palgrave Macmillan, 2011.

Kuppers, Petra. "Outsider Histories, Insider Artists, Cross-Cultural Ensembles: Visiting with Disability Presences in Contemporary Art Environments." *TDR* 58, no. 2 (2014): 33–50.

Lefebvre, Henri. *The Production of Space.* 1974. Translated by Donald Nicholson-Smith. Malden, MA: Blackwell, 1991.

Lehmann, Hans-Thies. *Postdramatic Theatre.* Translated by Karen Jürs-Munby. London: Routledge, 2006.

Lewis, Michael. "Self-Conscious Emotions: Embarrassment, Pride, Shame, and Guilt." In *Handbook of Emotions*, edited by Michael Lewis, Jeannette M. Haviland-Jones, and Lisa Feldman Barrett, 742–56. New York: Guilford Press, 2008.

Linsley, Johanna. "Kira O'Reilly Playing in the Lab." *Contemporary Theatre Review* 25, no. 4 (2015): 518–33.

MacDonald, Helen. *H Is for Hawk.* New York: Grove Press, 2014.

Manning, Erin. *Always More Than One: Individuation's Dance.* Durham: Duke University Press, 2013.

Marjanić, Suzana. "The Zoostage as Another Ethical Misfiring: The Spectacle of the Animal Victim in the Name of Art." *Performance Research* 15, no. 2 (2010): 74–79.

Marra, Kim. "Massive Bodies in Mortal Performance: *War Horse* and the Staging of Anglo-American Equine Experience in Combat." In *Performing Animality: Animals in Performance Practices*, edited by Lourdes Orozco and Jennifer Parker-Starbuck, 117–34. Houndmills, Basingstoke, Hampshire: Palgrave Macmillan, 2015.

Marra, Kim. "Riding, Scarring, Knowing: A Queerly Embodied Performance Historiography." *Theatre Journal* 64, no. 4 (2012): 489–511.

Marranca, Bonnie, ed. *The Theatre of Images*. New York: Drama Book Specialists, 1977.

Massumi, Brian. *Parables for the Virtual: Movement, Affect, Sensation*. Durham: Duke University Press, 2002.

Mattfeld, Monica. "'Genus Porcus Sophisticus': The Learned Pig and the Theatrics of National Identity in Late Eighteenth-Century London." In *Performing Animality: Animals in Performance Practices*, edited by Lourdes Orozco and Jennifer Parker-Starbuck, 57–76. Houndmills, Basingstoke, Hampshire: Palgrave Macmillan, 2015.

Maurstad, Anita, Dona Davis, and Sarah Cowles. "Co-Being and Intra-Action in Horse-Human Relationships: A Multi-Species Ethnography of Be(com)ing Human and Be(com)ing Horse." *Social Anthropology* 21, no. 3 (2013): 322–35.

McCormack, Derek P. *Refrains for Moving Bodies: Experience and Experiment in Affective Spaces*. Durham: Duke University Press, 2014.

McDonagh, Patrick. *Idiocy: A Cultural History*. Liverpool: University of Liverpool Press, 2008. doi:10.5949/UPO9781846315367.

McGeer, Victoria. "Autistic Self-Awareness." *Philosophy, Psychiatry, & Psychology* 11, no. 3 (2004): 235–51.

McNally, Kieran. *Critical History of Schizophrenia*. New York: Palgrave Macmillan, 2016.

Miller, William Ian. *The Anatomy of Disgust*. Cambridge: Harvard University Press, 1997.

Mitchell, David T., and Sharon L. Snyder. *Narrative Prosthesis: Disability and the Dependencies of Discourse*. Ann Arbor: University of Michigan Press, 2000.

Mizelle, Brett. *Pig*. London: Reaktion Books, 2011.

Mukhopadhyay, Tito Rajarshi. *How Can I Talk if My Lips Don't Move? Inside My Autistic Mind*. 1st ed. New York: Arcade Publishing, 2008.

Muratova, Olga. "Dionysian Symphony of Distorted Reality: Elevator Repair Service's Eisegesis of *The Sound and the Fury*." *Contemporary Theatre Review* 19, no. 4 (2009): 448–60.

Murray, Stuart. *Autism*. New York: Routledge, 2012.

Murray, Stuart. "Autism and the Contemporary Sentimental: Fiction and the Narrative Fascination of the Present." *Literature and Medicine* 25, no. 1 (2006): 24–45.

Murray, Stuart. *Representing Autism: Culture, Narrative, Fascination*. Liverpool: Liverpool University Press, 2008.

Murray, Timothy. "Like a Prosthesis: Critical Performance à Digital Deleuze." In *Deleuze and Performance*, edited by Laura Cull, 203–20. Edinburgh: Edinburgh University Press, 2009.

Nadesan, Majia Holmer. *Constructing Autism: Unraveling the "Truth" and Understanding the Social*. London: Routledge, 2005.

Newton, Michael. *Savage Girls and Wild Boys: A History of Feral Children*. New York: Thomas Dunne Books/St. Martin's Press, 2003.

Ngai, Sianne. *Our Aesthetic Categories: Zany, Cute, Interesting*. Cambridge: Harvard University Press, 2012.

Novero, Cecilia. "Painful Painting and Brutal Ecstasy: The Material Actions of Günter Brus and Otto Muehl." *Seminar* 43, no. 4 (2007): 453–68.

Nussbaum, Martha Craven. *Upheavals of Thought: The Intelligence of Emotions*. Cambridge: Cambridge University Press, 2001.

O'Reilly, Kira. "Marsyas—Beside Myself." In *sk-interfaces*, edited by Jens Hauser, 96-101. Liverpool: Liverpool University Press, 2008.

Osteen, Mark, ed. *Autism and Representation*. New York: Routledge, 2008.

Orozco, Lourdes. *Theatre and Animals*. New York: Palgrave Macmillan, 2013.

Otto-Bernstein, Katharina. *Absolute Wilson: The Biography*. Munich: Prestel, 2006.

Parker-Starbuck, Jennifer. "Animal Ontologies and Media Representations: Robotics, Puppets, and the Real of *War Horse*." *Theatre Journal* 65, no. 3 (2013): 373–93.

Parker-Starbuck, Jennifer. "Chasing Its Tail: Sensorial Circulations of *One Pig*." *Antennae*, no. 27 (2013): 102–13.

Parker-Starbuck, Jennifer. *Cyborg Theatre: Corporeal/Technological Intersections in Multimedia Performance*. Houndmills, Basingstoke, Hampshire: Palgrave Macmillan, 2011.

Parker-Starbuck, Jennifer. "Pig Bodies and Vegetative States: Diagnosing the Symptoms of a Culture of Excess." *Women & Performance* 18, no. 2 (2008): 133–51.

Peterson, Michael. "The Animal Apparatus: From a Theory of Animal Acting to an Ethics of Animal Acts." *TDR* 51, no. 1 (2007): 33–48.

Phillips, Sarah. "The Pig in Medieval Iconography." In *Pigs and Humans: 10,000 Years of Interaction*, edited by Umberto Albarella, Keith Dobney, Anton Ervynck, and Peter Rowley-Conwy, 373–87. Oxford: Oxford University Press, 2007.

Preston, Stephanie D., and Frans B. M. de Waal. "Empathy: Its Ultimate and Proximate Bases." *Behavioral and Brain Sciences* 25 (2002): 1–72.

Prince, Dawn. "The Silence Between: An Autoethnographic Examination of the Language Prejudice and Its Impact on the Assessment of Autistic and Animal Intelligence." *Disability Studies Quarterly* 30, no. 1 (2010): http://dsq-sds.org/article/view/1055/1242

Prince-Hughes, Dawn. *Songs of the Gorilla Nation: My Journey through Autism*. New York: Harmony Books, 2004.

Prinz, Jesse J. *Gut Reactions: A Perceptual Theory of Emotion*. New York: Oxford University Press, 2004.

Probyn, Elspeth. *Blush: Faces of Shame*. Minneapolis: University of Minnesota Press, 2005.

Puchner, Martin. "Performing the Open: Actors, Animals, Philosophers." *TDR* 51, no. 1 (2007): 21–32.

Rabillard, Sheila. "Sam Shepard: Theatrical Power and American Dreams." *Modern Drama* 30, no. 1 (1987): 58–71.

Rae, Paul. "Xeno-." *Contemporary Theatre Review* 23, no. 1 (2013): 83–87.

Ridout, Nicholas. *Stage Fright, Animals, and Other Theatrical Problems*. Cambridge: Cambridge University Press, 2006.

Roach, Joseph. *Cities of the Dead: Circum-Atlantic Performance*. New York: Columbia University Press, 1996.

Robison, John Elder. *Look Me in the Eye: My Life with Asperger's*. New York: Crown Publishers, 2007.

Ross, Christine. *The Aesthetics of Disengagement: Contemporary Art and Depression*. Minneapolis: University of Minnesota Press, 2006.

Ross, Janice. "The Solo That Isn't a Solo: Ann Carlson's Dances with Animals." In *On Stage Alone: Soloists and the Modern Dance Canon*, edited by Claudia Gitelman and Barbara Palfy, 55–72. Gainesville: University Press of Florida, 2012.

Rothfels, Nigel. "Immersed with Animals." In *Representing Animals*, edited by Nigel Rothfels, 199–223. Bloomington: Indiana University Press, 2002.

Rozin, Paul, and April E. Fallon. "A Perspective on Disgust." *Psychological Review* 94, no. 1 (1987): 23–41.

Rozin, Paul, Jonathan Haidt, and Clark R. McCauley. "Disgust." In *Handbook of Emotions*, edited by Michael Lewis, Jeannette M. Haviland-Jones, and Lisa Feldman Barrett, 757–76. New York: Guilford Press, 2008.

Rozin, Paul, Jonathan Haidt, and Clark R. McCauley. "Disgust: The Body and Soul Emotion." In *Handbook of Cognition and Emotion*, edited by Tim Dalgleish and Michael J. Power, 429–45. Chichester: Wiley, NetLibrary, 1999.

Runswick-Cole, Katherine. "'Us' and 'Them': The Limits and Possibilities of a 'Politics of Neurodiversity' in Neoliberal Times." *Disability & Society* 29, no. 7 (2014): 1117–29.

Schechner, Richard. "Julie Taymor: From Jacques Lecoq to 'The Lion King': An Interview." *TDR* 43, no. 3 (1999): 36–55.

Schwartz, Peter Hammond. "Equestrian Imagery in European and American Political Thought: Toward an Understanding of Symbols as Political Texts." *Western Political Quarterly* 41, no. 4 (1988): 653–73.

Sedgwick, Eve Kosofsky. "Shame, Theatricality, and Queer Performativity: Henry James's *The Art of the Novel*." In *Gay Shame*, edited by David M. Halperin and Valerie Traub, 49–62. Chicago: University of Chicago Press, 2009.

Sedgwick, Eve Kosofsky, Adam Frank, and Irving E. Alexander. *Shame and Its Sisters: A Silvan Tomkins Reader*. Durham: Duke University Press, 1995.

Seshadri, Kalpana. *Humanimal: Race, Law, Language*. Minneapolis: University of Minnesota Press, 2011.

Shaughnessy, Nicola. "Imagining Otherwise: Autism, Neuroaesthetics and Contemporary Performance." *Interdisciplinary Science Reviews* 38, no. 4 (2013): 321–34.

Shukin, Nicole. *Animal Capital: Rendering Life in Biopolitical Times*. Minneapolis: University of Minnesota Press, 2009.

Shyer, Laurence. *Robert Wilson and His Collaborators*. New York: Theatre Communications Group, 1989.

Siebers, Tobin. *Disability Aesthetics*. Ann Arbor: University of Michigan Press, 2010.

Siebers, Tobin. *Disability Theory*. Ann Arbor: University of Michigan Press, 2008.

Siebers, Tobin. "Sex, Shame, and Disability Identity: With Reference to Mark O'Brien." In *Gay Shame*, edited by David M. Halperin and Valerie Traub, 201–16. Chicago: University of Chicago Press, 2009.

Silberman, Steven. *Neurotribes: The Legacy of Autism and the Future of Neurodiversity*. New York: Avery, 2015.

Simmer, Bill. "Robert Wilson and Therapy." *TDR* 20, no. 1 (1976): 99–110.

Siropoulos, Vagelis. "*Cats*, Postdramatic Blockbuster Aesthetics and the Triumph of the Megamusical." *Image & Narrative* 11, no. 3 (2010): 128-45.

Sirota, Karen Gainer. "Narratives of Distinction: Personal Life Narrative as a Technology of the Self in the Everyday Lives and Relational Worlds of Children with Autism." *Ethos* 38, no. 1 (2010): 93–115.

Snæbjörnsdottír/Wilson. "*Falling Asleep with a Pig* (Interview)." *Antennae*, no. 13 (2010): 38–48.

Solomon, Olga. "What a Dog Can Do: Children with Autism and Therapy Dogs in Social Interaction." *Ethos* 38, no. 1 (2010): 143–66.

Solomon, Olga, and Nancy Bagatell. "Introduction: Autism: Rethinking the Possibilities." *Ethos* 38, no. 1 (2010): 1–7.

Stallybrass, Peter, and Allon White. *The Politics and Poetics of Transgression*. Ithaca: Cornell University Press, 1986.

Sternfeld, Jessica. *The Megamusical*. Bloomington: Indiana University Press, 2006.

Strassler, Doug. "Building a Better Horse Puppet." *Show Business*, April/May 2011, 34.

Tait, Peta. "Confronting Corpses and Theatre Animals." In *Animal Death*, edited by Jay Johnston and Fiona Probyn-Rapsey, 67–84. Sydney: Sydney University Press, 2013.

Tammet, Daniel. *Born on a Blue Day: Inside the Extraordinary Mind of an Autistic Savant—a Memoir*. New York: Free Press, 2007.

Taylor, Sunaura. *Beasts of Burden: Animal and Disability Liberation*. New York: New Press, 2017.

Taylor, Sunaura. "Vegans, Freaks, and Animals: Toward a New Table Fellowship." *American Quarterly* 65, no. 3 (2013): 757–64.

Thompson, James. *Performance Affects: Applied Theatre and the End of Effect*. Houndmills, Basingstoke, Hampshire: Palgrave Macmillan, 2009.

Tomkins, Silvan, with the editorial assistance of Bertram P. Karon. *Affect, Imagery, Consciousness*. 1962. New York: Springer, 2008.

Treffert, Darold A. *Extraordinary People: Understanding "Idiot Savants"*. New York: Harper and Row, 1989.

Treffert, Darold A. "Savant Syndrome: Realities, Myths and Misconceptions." *Journal of Autism and Developmental Disorders* 44, no. 3 (2014): 564–71.

Trimingham, Melissa, and Nicola Shaughnessy. "Material Voices: Intermediality and Autism." *Research in Drama Education* 21, no. 3 (2016): 293–308.

Truchan-Tataryn, Maria. "Textual Abuse: Faulkner's Benjy." *Journal of Medical Humanities* 26, nos. 2–3 (2005): 159–72.

Umathum, Sandra, and Benjamin Wihstutz, eds. *Disabled Theater*. Zürich-Berlin: diaphanes, 2015.

Warner, Michael. "Pleasures and Dangers of Shame." In *Gay Shame*, edited by David M. Halperin and Valerie Traub, 283–96. Chicago: University of Chicago Press, 2009.

Welton, Martin. *Feeling Theatre*. Houndmills, Basingstoke, Hampshire: Palgrave Macmillan, 2012.

Wickstrom, Maurya. *Performing Consumers: Global Capital and Its Theatrical Seductions*. New York: Routledge, 2006.

Willey, Angela, Banu Subramaniam, Jennifer A. Hamilton, and Jane Couperus. "The Mating Life of Geeks: Love, Neuroscience, and the New Autistic Subject." *Signs* 40, no. 2 (2015): 369–91.

Williams, David. "The Right Horse, the Animal Eye—Bartabas and Théâtre Zingaro." *Performance Research* 5, no. 2 (2000): 29–40.

Wilson, Anne, and Peter Beresford. "Madness, Distress and Postmodernity: Putting the Record Straight." In *Disability/Postmodernity: Embodying Disability Theory*, edited by Mairian Corker and Tom Shakespeare, 143–58. London: Continuum, 2002.

Witham, Barry. "The Anger in *Equus*." *Modern Drama* 22, no. 1 (1979): 61–66.

Wolfe, Cary. "Before the Law: Animals in a Biopolitical Context." *Law, Culture and the Humanities* 6, no. 1 (2010): 8–23.

Wolfe, Cary. *What Is Posthumanism?* Minneapolis: University of Minnesota Press, 2009.

Woods, Alan. "'Bringing Together Man and Nature': The Theater of Julie Taymor." In *American Puppetry: Collections, History and Performance*, edited by Phyllis T. Dircks, 225–38. Jefferson, NC: McFarland and Co., 2004.

Yergeau, Melanie. "Clinically Significant Disturbance: On Theorists Who Theorize Theory of Mind." *Disability Studies Quarterly* 33, no. 4 (2013): http://dsq-sds.org/article/view/3876/405

Zallaa, Tiziana, et al. "Feelings of Regret and Disappointment in Adults with High-Functioning Autism." *Cortex* 58 (2014): 112–22.

# Index

Page numbers in italics indicate figures.